UNEQUAL BRITAIN AT WORK

Unequal Britain at Work

Edited by
ALAN FELSTEAD, DUNCAN GALLIE,
AND FRANCIS GREEN

OXFORD
UNIVERSITY PRESS

OXFORD

UNIVERSITY PRESS

Great Clarendon Street, Oxford, OX2 6DP,
United Kingdom

Oxford University Press is a department of the University of Oxford.
It furthers the University's objective of excellence in research, scholarship,
and education by publishing worldwide. Oxford is a registered trade mark of
Oxford University Press in the UK and in certain other countries

© Oxford University Press 2015

The moral rights of the authors have been asserted

First Edition published in 2015

Impression: 1

Published in the United States of America by Oxford University Press
198 Madison Avenue, New York, NY 10016, United States of America

British Library Cataloguing in Publication Data
Data available

Library of Congress Control Number: 2014957467

ISBN 978-0-19-871284-8

Printed and bound by
CPI Group (UK) Ltd, Croydon, CR0 4YY

Acknowledgements

Special thanks must go to thousands of anonymous survey respondents without whom it would not be possible to chart the pattern of *Unequal Britain at Work* over the past quarter of a century. We are also grateful to the Economic and Social Research Council (ESRC) Centre for Learning and Life Chances in Advanced Knowledge Economies and Societies (LLAKES) for providing the opportunity and funding for the authors of this book to meet in Oxford to discuss their findings. This book is part of the programme of LLAKES Theme 2: Learning, Work and the Economy. However, neither the ESRC nor the co-funders of the Skills and Employment Surveys detailed in the technical appendix bear any responsibility for the arguments advanced or the way in which the data have been interpreted in the chapters which follow. As always, the authors alone bear that responsibility.

Alan Felstead, Duncan Gallie, and Francis Green

Contents

List of Figures

List of Tables

Notes on Contributors

Ben Baumberg is Senior Lecturer in Sociology and Social Policy at the University of Kent and Co-Director of the University of Kent Q-Step Centre. His research focuses on the links between the workplace and the benefits system, and has a particular interest in the extent to which work intensification contributes to rising levels of incapacity.

David Blackaby is Professor of Economics at Swansea University. His main areas of research are labour markets, regional economics, and public policy with published papers in the *Economic Journal*, *Oxford Economic Papers*, and *Oxford Bulletin of Economics and Statistics*. He is a member of the NHS Pay Review Body, the Economics and Econometrics and Business and Management sub-panels for REF2014, and a fellow of the Learned Society of Wales.

Alex Bryson is Head of the Employment Group at the National Institute of Economic and Social Research. He is also a research fellow at the Institute for the Study of Labor (IZA), at Rutgers, and at the Centre for Economic Performance, London School of Economics. His research focuses on industrial relations, labour economics, and programme evaluation. He is on the editorial board of the *NIESR Economic Review* and was previously an editor of the *British Journal of Industrial Relations*.

Andy Charlwood is Professor of Human Resource Management and Organizational Behaviour at the School of Business and Economics, Loughborough University. He has previously held academic posts at the Universities of York, Warwick, Leeds, and Kent. His main research interests are on job quality, subjective well-being at work, and employee voice.

Alan Felstead is Research Professor at Cardiff School of Social Sciences, Cardiff University. He is also a visiting professor at the ESRC Centre for Learning and Life Chances in Knowledge Economies and Societies (LLAKES), UCL Institute of Education. He has published numerous books and articles on skills, training, and employment. Recent books include *Changing Places of Work* (Palgrave, 2005) and *Improving Working as Learning* (Routledge, 2009).

Duncan Gallie is Professor of Sociology, University of Oxford and Emeritus Fellow of Nuffield College, Oxford. His research has examined the changing nature of job quality both in Britain and Europe, the social consequences of unemployment, and attitudes to inequality. His most recent book is *Economic Crisis, Quality of Work, and Social Integration* (Oxford University Press,

2013). He has been Vice-President and Foreign Secretary of the British Academy.

Francis Green is Professor of Work and Education Economics at the ESRC Centre for Learning and Life Chances in Knowledge Economies and Societies (LLAKES), UCL Institute of Education. His research focuses on skills, training, work quality, and industrial relations issues. His most recent book is *Skills and Skilled Work: An Economic and Social Analysis* (Oxford University Press, 2013).

Hande Inanc is Policy Analyst at the Organisation for Economic Co-operation and Development (OECD) Statistics Directorate. Her research focuses on labour market insecurity and the life-course, job quality, labour market segmentation, occupational gender segregation, and employment-related well-being. Before joining the OECD she was a postdoctoral researcher at Nuffield College, University of Oxford, where she is currently an associate member.

Melanie Jones is Professor at Sheffield Management School, University of Sheffield. She is also a member of the ESRC research centre Wales Institute of Social and Economic Research, Data and Methods. Her research is in the area of empirical labour economics and particularly the relationship between health and work. Recent publications appear in journals including the *British Journal of Industrial Relations* and *Social Science and Medicine*.

Joanne Lindley is Reader in Economics at King's College London. She has published numerous government reports and peer reviewed articles. She specializes in the economics of education and inequality. Recent articles include 'The Gender Dimension of Technical Change and Task Inputs' (*Labour Economics*, 2012).

Clare Lyonette is Principal Research Fellow at the Institute for Employment Research, University of Warwick. She has published widely on women in the labour market and the quality of part-time work. Recent examples include 'Sharing the Load? Partners' Relative Earnings and the Domestic Division of Labour' (*Work, Employment and Society*, 2014) and '"Quality" Part-Time Work: A Review of the Evidence' (Government Equalities Office, 2010).

Gerry Makepeace is an Emeritus Professor of Economics at Cardiff Business School, Cardiff University. His research focuses on the comparison of labour market outcomes for different groups, most recently investigating public sector pay determination and applications of treatment models.

Nigel Meager is Director of the Institute for Employment Studies in the UK. He is a widely published labour economist whose research interests include changing patterns of work, the evaluation of labour market interventions, and international comparisons of employment policies.

Philip Murphy is Professor of Economics at Swansea University. He has held academic posts at the Universities of Manchester, East Anglia, and Aberdeen. His main research interests are in the area of labour economics and in particular on explaining differences in labour market outcomes between different groups of individuals. He has published in a wide range of economics journals including the *Economic Journal*, *Oxford Bulletin of Economics and Statistics*, and *Oxford Economic Papers*.

Tracey Warren is Professor of Sociology in the School of Sociology and Social Policy at the University of Nottingham. She has published numerous articles on the sociology of work time, gender, and class inequalities in Europe, and she co-authored the book *Work and Society: Sociological Approaches, Theories and Methods* (Routledge, 2008).

Victoria Wass is Reader at Cardiff Business School, Cardiff University. She recently led an ESRC-funded study on the impact of austerity on job design, working time, and well-being in the police service. Her main interest is in the impact and experience of disability in the workplace with recent publications in *Sociology* and *Work, Employment and Society*.

1

The Inequality of Job Quality

Francis Green, Alan Felstead, and Duncan Gallie

1.1. INTRODUCTION: 'GOOD JOBS', 'BAD JOBS', AND A QUARTER CENTURY OF POLITICAL AND ECONOMIC CHANGE

The idea of 'job quality' has attracted much attention in this quarter century of affluence and crisis. Crystallized in the 2000 resolution by the Lisbon Council of the European Union (EU) to target 'more and better jobs', and in successive similar invocations by the Organisation for Economic Co-operation and Development (OECD) to employment ministers, the governments of developed nations have been seeking the elixir of productivity rises through policies that simultaneously contribute to improving the employee's experience of work. In the wake of the recovery from the great recession of 2008, a concern with job quality has re-emerged among researchers, policy-advisers, and social statisticians in many countries.

This book is about the evolution of job quality over a quarter century in Britain, a modern liberal market economy. Its focus throughout is on how the quality varies among groups and sectors. In economics it is common to focus on wage gaps and dispersion, and there have been many studies linking inequality to technological and institutional change. Yet jobs also differ in other respects. As well as decent pay, a 'good job' offers the scope for development and for taking initiative and some control over one's tasks, the prospect of a reasonable work load, safe and pleasant working conditions, good social support from colleagues and superiors, opportunities for participation in organizational decision-making (whether direct or through the 'voice' of the union), and the flexibility to arrange working hours reasonably to balance one's work and non-work lives. 'Bad jobs' offer none or few of these.

Since there is much more to jobs than just the pay packet, and because other job features may partly or wholly compensate for unduly high or low pay, a more comprehensive examination of job differentiation—one that takes in other core aspects of job quality—is needed. Inequality is manifested through differentiation of job quality by socioeconomic group (gender and social class), by category of contractual relationship (employee/self-employed, part-time/full-time, and temporary/permanent), by sector of the economy (public/private), and by type of employment relation (union/non-union and whether using 'high involvement' management practices). These overlapping 'gaps' combine in a complex manner to yield the overall pattern of the inequality of job quality.

An egalitarian perspective on job quality would call, not for jobs to have equal requirements and material rewards, but for them to provide all workers over the life course with adequate opportunities for self-validation, for self-development, and for meeting their material needs. Where workers are denied such opportunities it is a loss to society as well as to workers themselves. Inequality in job quality is also an important element of social and economic inequality, and it has been argued in recent years that inequality is of concern, not only to those who value egalitarianism for its own sake, but also more widely because of a robust association between more equal and more success-ful societies (Wilkinson and Pickett, 2010). While the causal relationships between work, income inequality, and social cohesion are complex, the evi-dence is clear: poor working conditions are associated with lower levels of physical and mental health, with consequent economic and social costs (McKnight and Cowell, 2014; Nolan and Whelan, 2014).

To serve policy-makers, and those on all sides of industry who would wish to formulate strategies for change and improvement in both the level and distribution of job quality, there is a need to pose some relevant questions. We need to ask, for example, where the current distribution of job quality has come from and how it is changing. An accurate overall picture is required, since this is typically not provided in government statistics. And even if one often cannot confidently attribute causality it is relevant to ask, what have been the outcomes of the rise of neo-liberalism, the intensification of global com-petition, the progress of technology, and the onset of economic crisis? What difference have regulatory policies made, and do industrial relations still matter? How persistent are class inequalities and have they got worse? Is it better to be self-employed, and how much worse is it to be working on a temporary employment contract as opposed to an indefinite one? Do women (especially those working part-time) still get a bad deal at work, and have public sector workers really had the best jobs? How much of a difference does good management make to the experience of work?

Our period is framed by the Skills and Employment Survey (SES) data series (described below and in the Technical Appendix) of workers' reports about their jobs, begun in 1986 and culminating with the latest survey in 2012. During this time the make-up of the British workforce had steadily changed in several ways, two of which stand out: the workforce became less male-dominated and much better educated. Thus, the share of work hours performed by females rose from 32.2 per cent to 39.7 per cent; while the proportion of employed people having no qualifications at all dropped from 28.6 per cent to only 5.4 per cent. Both these changes may have affected the balance of workers' needs surrounding their jobs.

What were the external conditions in which their jobs were formed over the years? To set the scene for a quarter century of change in job quality, it is helpful to recall briefly the macroeconomic and political context in which workplace change has unfolded. The story begins in the midst of the era of Thatcherism, when the British economy was undergoing a process of profound restructuring and 'de-industrialisation' (Green, 1989). In just the brief interval from 1986 to 1992, manufacturing's share of employment in Britain fell from 28.7 per cent to 22.9 per cent, according to SES. With a deflationary macroeconomic stance that persisted until the late 1980s, unemployment was at or around 3 million from 1983 to 1987 inclusive, in 1984 peaking at nearly 12 per cent of the labour force, an extraordinarily high level by post-war standards. Given that manufacturing skills were often not so easily transferable to the growing service industries, much of this unemployment became structural and remained so for a considerable time. In an increasingly open economy, neo-liberal political values were in the ascendancy, driving a process of deregulation which extended into labour markets, including union decline (not least, the proscription of 'closed shops' after 1990) and the abolition in 1993 of all but one of the remaining wages councils which had provided residual protection against low pay in some industries. Union membership rates, which at their peak in 1980 were more than one in two (Booth, 1995), were in a steady decline throughout the 1980s and early 1990s. At the same time, the government fought a rearguard action against EU pressures for legislative protection of workers (Dickens and Hall, 2009). Privatization of the previously state-owned utilities and other industries then emerged gradually as perhaps the defining long-term strategy of Thatcherism, extending well into the period of Major's premiership. This change of ownership added to the flexibility with which managers were empowered to reform employment relations and lay behind some of the decline in collective bargaining (Brown et al., 2009).

The Blair 'New Labour' governments that followed in 1997 ushered in a period of re-regulation of the labour market, driven partly by EU directives and partly also by Labour's own ideological preference for legislating workers' rights to match their responsibilities. The new national minimum wage was introduced cautiously in 1999, not least because of the fears, backed by conventional economists, that this would cause employment loss. Yet, analyses from economists who recognized that labour markets could not be conceived in terms similar to spot markets for goods or for stocks and shares, showed that within limits a minimum wage would not be detrimental to employment

(Dickens et al., 1999). So it turned out, and later the Low Pay Commission, which had been charged with the task of monitoring the effects of the minimum wage and annually recommending changes, advised the government to raise the wage at a faster rate. The EU influence was heeded first through acceptance of the European Directive on Working Time, which came into legal force in 1998. The new law laid down that employees should not work for more than forty-eight hours a week (averaged over seventeen weeks), unless a (supposedly voluntary) opt-out was agreed by the employee. It also mandated a minimum of paid vacations with no opt-out possibility. There followed further EU-driven legislation to proscribe inequality of treatment between part-time and full-time workers (in 2001) or between those on fixed-term and those on indefinite contracts (in 2003). Eventually (in 2010) some protection was afforded to temporary agency workers. Employers with at least fifty workers were in addition obliged after 2005 to consult with their employees; however, this last intervention has been largely ineffective to date, probably as a result of its weak translation into British law (van Wanrooy et al., 2013, 60–3; see also Chapter 10). Meanwhile, independently of the EU, from 2003 employers had to formally consider employees' requests for flexible working arrangements, an obligation that was extended in 2007 and again in 2011 to a broader range of employees. And steps were taken through the 2010 Equalities Act to integrate and rationalize prior anti-discriminatory legislation while making some extensions to protected characteristics, for example surrounding age discrimination and sexual orientation.

Notably absent from this steady menu of re-regulation was any negation of the Conservative legislation which weakened trade union power. Nor was there any substantive attempt to re-ignite the manufacturing industry through a strategy for industry. The privatizations of Thatcher and Major were not repealed, the one main exception being in 2002 when Network Rail took over the responsibility for Britain's rail network. Indeed, if anything, through its private finance initiative programmes and its further contracting out of services, the Labour government extended further the sphere of the market. Targets and quasi-market incentives, along with sub-contracting requirements, became commonplace in many areas of public sector life, not least the National Health Service. And the long-term trend towards an ever more open economy continued. In no sense, then, did the New Labour years bring a reversal of the fundamental changes to labour and employment relations wrought in the Thatcher era.

The economic crisis that broke out from the financial sector in 2008, followed by the end of the era of Labour political rule in the May 2010 election, signalled a changed macroeconomic and a new political environment for British workplaces. Up to that point of crisis, the British economy had grown to become nearly 80 per cent richer (in terms of GDP per capita) than it had been in 1986; four years after the crisis broke it was still some 4.5

per cent below the pre-crisis peak. The impact on industry was mixed, with construction affected the most while energy utilities were largely unscathed. The large rise in unemployment, though somewhat less than predicted, was accompanied by the spread of insecurity, especially in the private sector at first. The resulting shift in the balance of power between employees and employers was hardly conducive to supporting processes of progressive change that might have favoured more consultation, more trust, and more worker commitment. The 'wage curve' (where greater unemployment reduces the rate of wage growth, even rendering it negative) was taking its toll, even among many higher-paid workers. Indeed, the strength of the relationship between unemployment and wages was already intensifying before the crisis set in (Gregg et al., 2014).

The effects of the crisis on jobs became potentially much broader when the new coalition government between the Conservatives and Liberal Democrats announced long-term plans to address the public sector deficit through a historic restructuring of the role of the state. Though the brunt of this offensive came through restrictions on government wage bills, especially in local government and other non-protected areas, new limitations to welfare and social security costs weakened the alternatives for all low-paid workers; this meant that the changing balance of power was likely to have been felt throughout the low-paid sectors of the economy. The public sector austerity and the feeble state of the economy were complemented by piecemeal acts of renewed deregulation of the labour market, such as the extension from one to two years of employment before fixed-term employees gained protection against unfair dismissal. The deregulation was not initially far-reaching, but the medium-term intention was reflected in the announced intention to make withdrawal from the European Working Time Directive a part of the negotiation for recommending Britain's continuing EU membership. All this was only counterbalanced to a small extent by planned further extensions to the rights to request flexible leave and to parental leave. Meanwhile reductions in health and safety inspectorates showed another intention to relax regulatory compliance control in practice. There was also a renewed enthusiasm for the state to withdraw from further spheres of economic life, exemplified by the sale of shares in Royal Mail following the Postal Services Act 2011, and by the contracting out of additional parts of the National Health Service—even though neo-liberal intentions had earlier had to be shelved with the decision to rescue the financial sector.

To this, most recent, deregulatory tendency should be added suggestive evidence that there had been increasing non-compliance with the national minimum wage since 2004, albeit from a low starting point, exacerbated by the recession (le Roux et al., 2013). Compliance is especially low among working illegal immigrants, of whom it is estimated that there were very approximately half a million in 2007, mainly in London (Gordon et al., 2009). A small minority of these will be trafficked, extremely vulnerable workers, deployed in the worst of British jobs.

It is against this ambivalent backdrop, then, that this book examines how job quality differs between groups and across time. We begin with a theoretical overview, before describing the main data series on which our new understandings are based.

1.2. THE EVOLUTION OF JOB QUALITY

'Job quality' is constituted by the features of jobs that on average contribute substantively to meeting people's needs from work. It is a set of characteristics rather than a single index, but there may remain some divergence of opinion over exactly which features are to be included and how sub-domains are weighted. A broadly acceptable set may be categorized under four headings: (1) wages and monetary rewards; (2) job prospects (including both career progression prospects and, in the opposite direction, insecurity); (3) intrinsic job quality (relevant features of the work itself, including the physical and social environment, the skill levels, discretion and variety of the tasks to be done, and the required work intensity); and (4) the quality of the working time (comprising how well the job is organized for meeting people's needs to balance work and domestic life). Rare is the study that can adequately capture all relevant features under these headings. Most research on job quality concentrates on specific aspects. Indeed, most studies are understandably focused on pay, which is not only of high importance for meeting living costs, but also carries a relatively easy metric for measurement. This book also tackles issues surrounding pay but takes a broader perspective on job quality, with a particular emphasis on elements of intrinsic job quality. A common theme of all chapters is their analyses of skills uses at work, task discretion, and work intensity.

Since people have varying needs often depending on their personal circumstances, including their stage in the life course, and since the satisfaction of those needs will also depend on the external environment, including the state of the labour market, perceptions of job quality will vary; nevertheless, adopting an objective conception of human needs from work allows the formation of an objective concept of job quality. For some purposes, however, it is also proper and useful to develop a somewhat broader concept, namely, the 'quality of employment', which includes relevant aspects of the external environment for work (Körner et al., 2011). Indeed, international organizations have been developing statistical frameworks to capture both job quality and wider contextual data. For this book, however, as for much of the recent literature, we focus on the concept of job quality defined as above.

This concept of job quality is objective because it is constituted by certain job features (whether or not self-reported by individuals), and not by subjective well-being (Green, 2006; Green and Mostafa, 2012). We hold that subjective interpretations of job quality, where the concept is identified with expressions of well-being or job satisfaction, are hard to defend (Brown et al., 2012). This conclusion does not proscribe the study of job-related well-being for itself, and it is valid to see job quality among the determining factors of job satisfaction, alongside norms and expectations.

One starting point for any discussion of job quality differentiation is the array of economic and social theory which emphasizes the differentiation of jobs by productivity and skill requirements and of workers by skill, and the sway of supply and demand forces. The supply of labour is determined by workers' needs, the demand for labour by their productivity in the job. The result of market forces is that better job quality is afforded to workers who are able to generate more value. Another starting point is theory that emphasizes the 'relative power resources' that different groups bring to the bargaining table, recognizing the importance of institutional factors, including collective bargaining, legal frameworks such as proscriptions on discrimination, regulatory conditions such as employment protection rights, and other non-competitive factors such as the cumulative segmentation of labour markets with restrictions on mobility.

These theories then yield a number of hypotheses about how job quality, and its variation between groups, might be expected to evolve. With economic development employees' material needs are more easily met and the balance shifts to meeting the needs for improved job quality along the other dimensions. It is typically found that working conditions are better in the more affluent countries (judged by GDP per head), even if there is a great deal of variation within those countries. Nevertheless, with the industrial structure shifting in more advanced economies towards the provision of services, the types of jobs available as the economy grows do not necessarily imply ever increasing job quality. Moreover, with increased female labour force participation and rises in education levels, the needs of employees are also changing, and these can modify the mix of job characteristics that make up job quality (emphasizing, for example, those aspects that contribute more to work–life balance).

It is also hypothesized that there will be changing inequalities, and in this the economics and power-resources theories are in broad agreement: both see a rise in inequality in the circumstances of recent decades. In the economic perspective technological change is predicted to engender increased demand for high-skilled workers, but may also lower the demand for medium-skilled workers relative to low-skilled workers, arising from automation of 'routine' (programmable) functions. When this technological imperative is added to other institutional and structural influences on employment demand, a polarization of jobs is predicted, with a relatively shrinking middle (Autor et al., 2003; Fernandez-Macias, 2012; Goos and Manning, 2007; Tahlin, 2013). Though not universal, where this polarization has occurred it has been because the jobs with intermediate pay were most intensive in programmable tasks. Differential automation also has implications for other aspects of job quality, but these depend on the relationship between routine tasks and these other aspects, which need not be the same as for pay. There may, for example, be a strong link between tasks being non-routine and workers being afforded greater discretion. If the displacement of routine functions leaves behind the jobs with more task discretion, it is possible to foresee a partial equalizing of task discretion between high-paid and low-paid jobs (Green et al., 2013; Kalleberg, 2011).

Job polarization, in turn, is held to bring about rising relative pay for the high skilled, but potentially a narrowing between the medium and low skilled, though these predictions can be counterbalanced by either supply side or institutional changes. The most significant supply-side factor is the changing relative supply of skilled labour: it is typically held that relative supply has struggled to keep up with skill-based demand, and that this has provided the fuel for rising wage inequality overall and rising gaps between socioeconomic groups (Machin, 2011). In this book and elsewhere increasing job quality gaps, from whatever cause, are also sometimes referred to as a 'polarization'. However, this meaning is different from the job polarization discussed above, constituted by a shrinking prevalence of middle-quality jobs.

Theory that stresses relative power resources (see Gallie, 2007b) also expects rising inequality associated with the rise of neo-liberalism, with associated anti-trade union laws and employer strategies, and a programme of deregulation of labour. As noted above, the re-regulations of the post-1997 era were but a partial counterbalance to the changes wrought during the period of Thatcherism, and barely dented the downward trend in trade union membership (see Chapter 7). The pressures of globalization are also expected to be reflected in the declining bargaining power of unions and of workers generally, limiting their ability to resist attempts by employers to extract more rents from the work arena. But the effects of those pressures are likely to vary between countries according to national government policies and regulatory regimes.

Even before the recent economic crisis, then, it could be expected that the gains from economic growth may not be reflected in improving job quality for all. With the Great Recession, however, came not only the spread of insecurity, but also a potential sea change in the power balance between employees and employers, a renegotiation of terms and a lowering of all aspects of job quality for those workers with the least resources.

If job quality were becoming generally more unequal since the 1980s, it would typically be the disadvantaged groups that experience the brunt of change; so an inegalitarian trend could be expected to be revealed also in rising gaps in job quality. The fact that Britain is characterized as a 'liberal market economy', with one of the lowest levels of employment protection and a declining union sector, adds to the expectation of rising gaps.

Nevertheless, there are also good reasons to expect that at least some job quality gaps will have been narrowing over time. Not least, the gender pay gap, once argued to have derived in part from a differential in job skill between men and women, might be expected to have eroded as women's educational achievements overtook those of men, and as discriminatory practices were gradually rooted out. Thus, across the Atlantic in the United States women have been 'swimming against the tide' of inequality (Blau and Kahn, 1997). Moreover, by virtue of being a member of the EU, British law became subject to EU directives, leading to the developing protections (noted above) that characterized the period from 1997. Regulatory progress over the long term also leads to improved protection against health and safety risks. Since it is normally the disadvantaged groups that experience such risks more intensively, such improvements both raise average job quality and lower its dispersion. Thus, it is quite possible that in some dimensions job quality could have become less unequal, and job quality gaps diminished.

Taken overall there are no decisive or overriding factors leading us to predict either that job quality gaps in all key dimensions will have risen over the period, or that they will have diminished. We therefore approach the empirical analyses in this book with complex expectations about how job quality gaps may have changed, open as they are to a contradictory set of pressures.

1.3. THE SKILLS AND EMPLOYMENT SURVEY SERIES

Finding out about job quality is problematic because it is a contested and often private arena. Many research studies have pursued qualitative approaches, using anthropological, psychological, or sociological methods. The approach followed here, which can be viewed as complementary to the qualitative literature, draws primarily on the SES series, a unique quantitative data set which extends from 1986 to 2012, with six surveys at intervals using nationally representative samples. The series provides a quarter-century window on the modern workplace as illuminated by workers' reports about their own jobs. The series began with the 'Social Change and Economic Life Initiative' carried out in 1986 and was followed by 'Employment in Britain' conducted in 1992. Then came the '1997 Skills Survey' which was repeated—with some new features—in 2001 and 2006. The 'Skills and Employment Survey 2012', the latest survey in the series, somewhat shifted the balance back towards coverage of employment issues. Although not originally designed as a series, a sub-set of identical items allows time comparisons to be made. For full details and sources, see the Technical Appendix.

The advantage of a quantitative approach is that we are able not only to examine nation-wide or group-wide trends, but to test whether hypotheses otherwise established for small well-defined groups or in case studies are valid when generalized to the population at large. The SES is unusual by international standards, because of its long historical perspective and its detailed coverage of both skills use and job quality themes; it provides a relatively full picture of the changing world of work through the eyes of the workers actually doing the work.[1] In the area of skills, it covers the uses of broad and generic skills in the workplace and (in recent years) a host of information about the intensity, cost, and experience of training. Many aspects of intrinsic job quality are covered, including task discretion, work effort, and other task characteristics related to quality, such as their variety or their repetitiveness. Indicators of extrinsic job quality include pay and hours, contract status, promotion opportunities, and job security. The SES also covers many aspects of motivation and job-related well-being.

Perhaps inevitably, no one survey series can adequately capture all aspects of job quality. For some aspects the span of time is restricted, and for others (notably job characteristics such as crèche availability, relevant for work–life balance) we have no data. To provide some context and fill gaps, the SES is occasionally supplemented in this book by evidence drawn from other series, including the Quarterly Labour Force Survey (QLFS) and the European Working Conditions Survey (EWCS).[2]

1.4. THE RELATIONSHIPS BETWEEN PAY AND OTHER TYPES OF JOB QUALITY

It might be advanced that, among the core aspects of job quality, pay is especially important, and moreover that the different dimensions of job quality are positively correlated with each other. Indeed, some argue that a single index of job quality may suffice to characterize jobs (Muñoz de Bustillo et al., 2011), a position that is contested elsewhere (Green et al., 2013). Others (typically economists) have eyes only for wages, in effect assuming that job quality is summed up as pay. The traditional constraint on studying non-wage

---

[1] Finland and Sweden both have long-running job quality surveys. Across Europe there is the five-yearly European Working Conditions Survey which dates from 1990 but has little information on skills use; South Korea now has a similar repeated survey.

[2] For details of these two surveys see, respectively, <http://discover.ukdataservice.ac.uk/ser ies/?sn=2000026> and <http://www.eurofound.europa.eu/working/surveys/>.

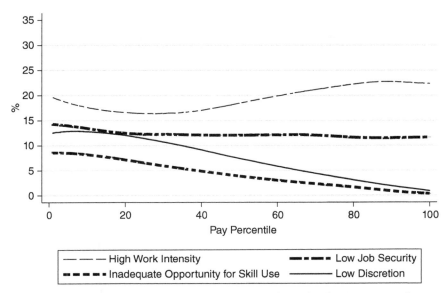

Figure 1.1. Percentage of Jobs with Low Non-Pay Job Quality by Pay Percentile

Notes: The lines show the smoothed value of each indicator of low job quality, following a locally weighted regression on pay percentile, sampling all those in employment in the UK aged twenty to sixty-five.
Low discretion: task discretion index less than 2 (on average less than 'a fair amount of influence' on choice, methods, pace, and quality standards of job tasks).
Inadequate opportunity to use skills: 'disagrees' or 'strongly disagrees' has enough opportunity to use own knowledge and skills.
Low job security: at least evens chance of losing job and becoming unemployed in next twelve months.
High work intensity: in top quintile of work effort index (average of seven standardized items that tap aspects of work intensity (Cronbach's alpha=0.70)).

Source: SES, 2006

job quality has been the measurement difficulties, which the SES attempts to address. We can use the SES to check if it is true that all elements of job quality are closely aligned with pay.[3]

Figure 1.1 illustrates how a simplification of job quality into a single measure based on pay would risk missing a lot. Ranking jobs by their hourly pay, it examines how the proportion with low job quality along four domains varies with position in the pay ranking.

If non-pay job quality was well aligned with pay, each domain of low job quality would slope down to zero at the top end of the pay spectrum. To illustrate, one measure of poor job quality is having an inadequate opportunity to use one's skills. We computed the proportion of respondents at each pay level who stated that they disagreed or strongly disagreed that they had 'enough opportunity to use their own knowledge and skills' in their job. This indicator is unambiguously

---

[3] 2006 is chosen for this check since this has the greatest sample size.

negatively related to pay—with hardly anyone at the top end of the pay distribution reporting a lack of opportunity to use their skills.

Another domain is task discretion, an important aspect of worker empowerment that is robustly associated with worker well-being. Here, the relationship with pay is less clear. We derived a task discretion index from four items reporting respondents' influence over the tasks they do, which ranged from 0 to 3. Low task discretion (measured by the proportion ranking under 2) is, on the whole, more common in low-paid jobs; however, the relationship is non-linear: jobs with low discretion are most prevalent at around the 15th to 20th percentile of the pay distribution. Moreover, even at the top end, there are many jobs will low discretion.

With other dimensions, the link with pay is yet lower or even negative. Thus, low job security (defined as having at least an evens chance of losing one's job and becoming unemployed in the next twelve months) is greatest at the bottom end of the pay distribution, but not by much: for the most part of the distribution, job security bears little relationship with pay. We obtained an index of work intensity using an average of seven standardised items that tap aspects of work intensity, and defined high work intensity, another dimension of low job quality widely recognized as detrimental to well-being, as being in the top quintile of this index. Figure 1.1 shows how it is worst at the top end of the pay distribution, consistent with a measure of compensating differentials, and best for jobs around the 20th to 30th pay percentile.

Even where the relationship with pay is positive, at the individual level the connection may be strong or weak. To examine this we computed the individual-level correlation coefficient between pay and each of the indicators of job quality. These were: 0.20 with the opportunity to use skills scale, 0.18 with task discretion, 0.03 with job insecurity, and 0.12 with the work effort index; in other words, high-pay jobs are high in some other dimensions but low in others, and anyway the connections, though statistically significant, are very loose.

Overall, the figure and correlation coefficients demonstrate that the characterization of higher-paid jobs as being higher on all aspects of job quality would be very misleading. Whether or not the compensating differentials derive from competitive equalizations between jobs, different aspects of job quality may indeed partially offset each other (see Chapter 8). There is, then, a strong case for studying multiple aspects of job quality beyond pay.

1.5. THE EVOLUTION OF AVERAGE JOB QUALITY IN BRITAIN

As a prelude to our enquiry into the evolving map of socioeconomic differentiation at work, it is useful to ask first about the *average* level of job quality:

what has happened over the roughly quarter century since the mid-1980s? We are able to answer this question in respect of most of the core aspects of job quality, several of which have been examined in detail for earlier periods in previous studies (e.g. Felstead et al., 2002, 2007; Gallie, 2005; Gallie et al., 2004; Green, 2001, 2006, 2011). Here, we update and overview progress over the whole period from 1986 to 2012. Figures 1.2 to 1.5 show that many aspects of job quality improved on average in Britain's work-places, as predicted by the rising affluence of the overall economy, at least until the onset of economic crisis; but there was also a deterioration in important respects.

Before the economic crisis average pay was increasing steadily in real terms from 1986 (see Figure 1.2), on average by 1.6 per cent per year, and by the late 2000s real earnings had risen to more than 40 per cent above their 1986 level—whether measured hourly or weekly. The progress was reversed, however, with the Great Recession and ensuing austerity budgets. By 2012, weekly wages had tumbled to the level of the early 2000s, this reversal being the largest since at least the 1920s and sharper than in all other major developed nations.

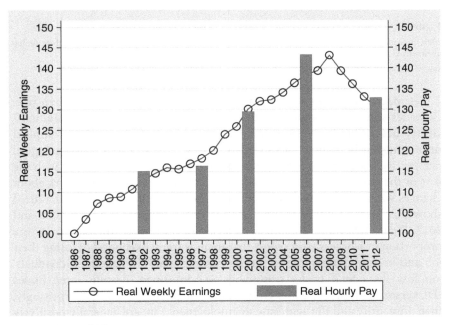

Figure 1.2. Real Wages

Notes: The RPI was used as the deflator, and the indices set to 1986 = 100.
'Real weekly earnings' is from the Monthly Wages and Salaries Survey and its predecessors; 'real hourly pay' refers to all in employment, including the earnings of the self-employed.

Source: SES and Office for National Statistics

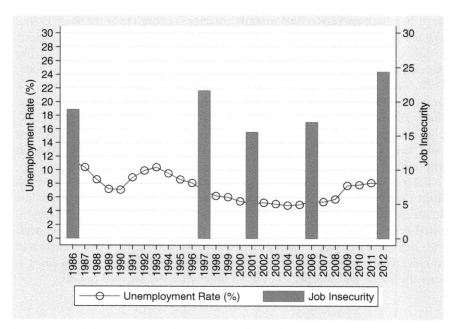

Figure 1.3. Job Insecurity and the Aggregate Unemployment Rate

Note: 'Job insecurity' is the percentage who report some likelihood of losing their job and becoming unemployed in the ensuing year.

Source: SES and Office for National Statistics

Yet macroeconomics reaches into the workplace in more ways than one. Consider security, another aspect of extrinsic job quality. Its opposite, insecurity, has deleterious effects on well-being that go beyond the implied uncertainty in household income (Nolan et al., 2000). From a psychological perspective insecurity is a stressor whose effects are associated partly with the fear of the psychic costs of job loss. Insecurity also encompasses fears about changes within the job (Greenhalgh and Rosenblatt, 1984). Gallie et al. (2013) show that fears of unfair treatment have risen strikingly between 2000 and 2012. Figure 1.3 shows the longer trend in job insecurity; the bars show the proportion of workers who report that there is some likelihood of losing their job and becoming unemployed in the ensuing year.[4] In general, individuals' job loss fears tend to be reasonably well-informed, despite some biases (Dickerson and Green, 2009; Green, 2009; Stephens, 2004). Unsurprisingly, then, insecurity and the aggregate unemployment rate are generally positively aligned: insecurity declined during the 1990s as unemployment fell, and both rose in the 2000s. Yet there have been deviations: earlier job insecurity

---

[4] Those answering 'very unlikely' have been classified as secure.

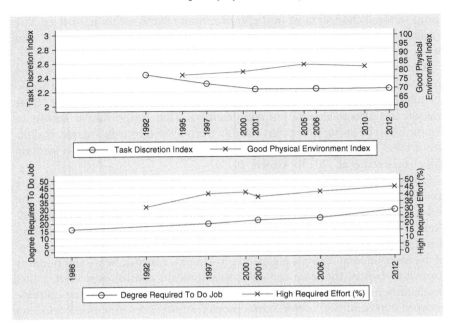

Figure 1.4. Intrinsic Job Quality

Notes: The good physical environment index counts the absence of nine hazardous/unhealthy working conditions (see Green et al., 2013). The task discretion index combines the responses to four items capturing worker influence over the tasks performed; see Gallie et al. (2004). High required effort is the percentage of jobs where respondents 'strongly agree' that their jobs require them to work very hard. Degree required to do job is the percentage of jobs where an applicant would need a Level 4 qualification to get the job and do it competently.

Source: SES and EWCS

was relatively low in 1986, considering that this was a time of record post-war unemployment; by contrast, job loss fears were somewhat high in 1997 despite lower and falling unemployment (Green et al., 2000).

Figure 1.4 shows trends in some core aspects of intrinsic job quality. Showing a significant improvement until 2005 was the state of the physical environment in which people work. The good physical environment index shown, which has a theoretical range from 0 to 100, displays the extent to which environmental hazards are absent from the workplace (where 100 would mean no hazards). In effect, the rising index tells us that there were fewer cases of people working in harsh or unsafe conditions. For example, in 1995, for 39.0 per cent of the British workforce the job involved 'tiring or painful positions' at least a quarter of the time, compared with only 30.8 per cent in 2010, according to the EWCS. It is reasonable to ask whether such changes are attributable to the rise of service industries and decline of traditional manufacturing, but in practice only a small part is due to such compositional change: most of the improvement came *within* industries. The combination of rising expectations, improved ergonomic knowledge and better regulation is likely to be behind this change.

Also improving is the skill level of jobs. To illustrate this we computed the proportion of jobs where a graduate-level qualification was required to do the job (where this level of qualification was cited as required, not only to get the job but also to do the job competently). That proportion is shown in Figure 1.4 to be rising slowly but steadily from 1986 onwards. Increased skills use is also manifested in other evidence such as the rising use of generic skills (Felstead et al., 2013b; Green, 2012).

However, these positive indications are counterbalanced by two unwelcome trends shown in Figure 1.4. During the 1990s there was a sharp decline in the index of task discretion, and through the subsequent period of 2001 to 2012 there is no sign of a reversal. Unfortunately, while individual task discretion was declining, it was not compensated by a growth of collective team control of decision-making. Despite a general growth of teamwork, semi-autonomous teamwork (where the team can exercise significant control over work tasks) declined between 1992 and 2006 (Gallie et al., 2012). Despite some increase between 2006 and 2012, semi-autonomous teamwork remained well below its level in 1992 (Inanc et al., 2013).

A second negative development was with respect to work intensity. For a long-run perspective we report 'High Required Effort'—the proportion reporting strong agreement with the question 'My job requires that I work very hard' (the composite index of work effort used above is not available for as many waves of the survey). There was a marked intensification of work effort in the early 1990s. Thereafter, while work effort levelled off (as in many European countries) from the second half of the 1990s to the early 2000s, it rose again over the 2006–2012 period.

There has been an improvement in the average quality of working time, where the latter is defined in relation to the need for a good work–life balance. The deleterious effects of long-hours working provided a health and safety rationale for the European Working Time Directive, leading to the regulation of working hours in Britain from October 1998, putting limits on working more than forty-eight hours a week unless employees opted out. In fact average weekly hours, which had remained relatively stable for most of the Thatcher era, began to resume their slow historical decline in the mid-1990s (Green, 2011). This decline was reflected in a fall after 1997 in the proportion of workers putting in more than forty-five hours a week, shown in Figure 1.5. Time quality also improved slowly in other respects. There was, for example, less Sunday working—the number who never worked on Sundays rose from 59.6 per cent in 1995 to 64.9 per cent in 2010; night-time working also declined—the monthly average fell from 2.14 to 1.95 night shifts, though evening working (for at least two hours) rose from an average of 3.9 to 4.4

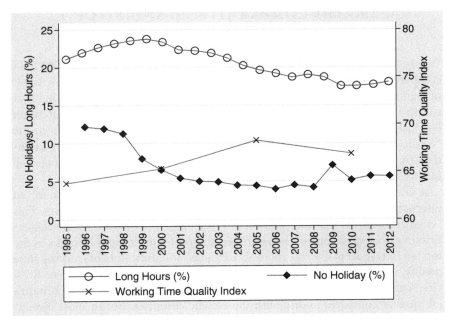

Figure 1.5. The Quality of Working Time

Notes: Long hours and holidays apply to employees. The working time quality index for Europe combines indicators of working hours and of night-time, evening, Saturday, and Sunday working; see Green and Mostafa (2012).

Source: QLFS and EWCS

evenings a month. Most of these changes occurred in the late 1990s and early 2000s. The 'working time quality' index shown in Figure 1.5 integrates several aspects of the length and scheduling of work hours in a single measure which has in principle a range of 0 to 100 (Green et al., 2013). The graph of this index sums up the improvements that occurred in the 2000s compared with the 1990s. Finally, thanks to the European Working Time Directive, which mandated paid holidays for all workers, the proportion of workers receiving no paid holidays was cut by two thirds between 1996 and 2006 to only 4.0 per cent, only to edge up a little in response to the crisis—the residual being at least in part down to non-compliance.

In sum, compared with the situation a quarter century earlier in the era of high Thatcherism, average job quality in Britain improved in several ways—pay, the physical environment, the skill level, and the quality of working time—but it deteriorated in respect of work intensity and job control. The onset of global economic crisis began to reverse the progress on pay and, at least in the short term, heightened insecurities.

1.6. THE COMPARATIVE STANDING OF
JOB QUALITY IN BRITAIN

Where did these trends leave the average British workplace in 2012, in comparison with other nations? It is sometimes held that, with its low levels of regulation, job quality might be expected to be lower in Britain than in other countries where most workers are better protected, or where more attention has historically been paid to job quality by social partners (especially in the Nordic region). Nevertheless, Britain remains one of the more affluent countries in Europe and so could be expected to have a reasonable average job quality.

A comparison has become possible with the development of harmonized international data sets covering the whole economy or particular sectors. This evidence confirms that the position of the average British job broadly reflects Britain's position as one of the wealthier economies in Europe—it ranks in the top ten in respect of average monthly earnings, and indicators of working time quality, intrinsic job quality, and job prospects (e.g. Gallie, 2003; Green, 2013; Green and Mostafa, 2012; Holman, 2013a, 2013b; Olsen et al., 2010). Britain's job quality compares poorly with the Nordic countries, but in most dimensions is close to the corporatist countries, and substantially above that in southern and Eastern European countries. In terms of job insecurity, the fact that the perceptions of insecurity in Britain are low relative to those recorded in many European countries (besides the Nordic countries) is entirely understandable where those other countries have higher rates of unemployment (Green, 2009).

Focusing on working time quality, Britain has among the longest weekly hours for men working full time, but for all workers together Britain's hours are around the European average. Britain's average workplace scores well for its hours flexibility—as indicated by the ease (greater than the European average) with which workers can take time off to take care of personal or family matters. Before the economic crisis 'work–family conflict', as registered in tensions, appears to have been somewhat higher in the UK than in many northern European countries (Chung, 2011; see also Beham and Drobnič, 2011; Prag et al., 2011); yet between 2004 and 2010 there was only a very modest rise in work–family conflict, compared with much more serious rises in five other countries (Germany, Czech Republic, Greece, Portugal, and Spain) (McGinnity and Russell, 2013).

One respect in which the British workplace is especially badly placed, however, is job control. Several studies have consistently shown the superior levels of task discretion afforded in workplaces in the Nordic countries (e.g. Gallie, 2003). While some have shown task discretion in Britain to be similar to northern European countries (other than the Nordic region) and above those of Eastern Europe (Gallie and Zhou, 2013), some recent evidence ranks the level of task discretion in England and Northern Ireland as 17th among twenty-two OECD countries (OECD, 2013a, 145).

If *average* job quality in Britain's workplaces is on the whole unremarkable in an international comparative perspective, regrettably lagging behind the Nordic countries but otherwise largely reflecting its comparative level of development, what marks Britain out is its inequality of pay, the greatest in Europe and close to that in the United States (Green, 2013). Similarly, the proportion of low-wage jobs in Britain is especially high in comparison with similarly developed northern European countries (Mason et al., 2008). Yet, perhaps surprisingly, Britain's inequality in respect of other aspects of job quality is not exceptional, according to evidence from the European Working Conditions Survey. Britain is generally less equal than the Nordic countries and the Netherlands in most non-wage aspects of job quality, but does not stand out in comparison with other large European economies; inequality in non-wage job quality is generally more severe in Greece, Portugal, and Spain (Green et al., 2013).

1.7. JOB QUALITY GAPS

This last observation takes us to the heart of our subject matter: the manifold patterns of differentiation of job quality in multiple domains across sectors and among socioeconomic groups in Britain. The point of this book is to trace and analyse these evolving patterns.

A good deal is already known about the differentiations of job quality in the domain of wages. In respect of gender, for example, the predominant expectation has been that a combination of rising female education levels and progressive anti-discriminatory law will have led to a diminishing gender wage gap, despite the persistence of gendered jobs and family roles. So, indeed, it has turned out, with the male–female wage gap for those in their early thirties roughly halving between those born around 1950 and those born around 1970 (Manning and Swaffield, 2008); as Lindley shows in Chapter 3, the gender wage gap conditional on education continued to fall for workers aged over thirty-five between 1997 and 2010, though it was still substantial at around 15 per cent. This narrowing of the gender pay gap contrasts with rising overall pay inequality, both for the whole workforce and among the sexes separately. Indeed Britain's unenviable distinction on pay inequality is the consummation of a thirty-five-year trend of rising inequality (Machin, 2011). Until the mid-1990s inequality rose rapidly across the population; from then on there was little change in the lower half of the pay distribution but a continuing, if slower, rise at the top part of the distribution, with remarkable pay rises for those at the very top (Lindley and Machin, 2013; Machin, 2011).

Concerning other domains, we know that there have also been some changes in the *overall* dispersion of non-pay aspects of job quality, albeit less dramatic than those surrounding pay. Evidence based on the European Working Conditions Survey indicates that, since 1995, job quality in Britain has become a little more unequal in two intrinsic dimensions—work intensity and combined skills use/task discretion—but less unequal in others—good physical environment and working time quality (Green et al., 2013). There is also a little piecemeal evidence of changing job quality gaps. It is found, for example, that differential access to training, once in men's favour, has evolved over time so that by the 2000s training opportunities at work were more prevalent among women than men (Jones et al., 2007). Overall, however, rather little is known about how job quality in general is differentiated between sectors and groups, or about how this differentiation has evolved.

Succeeding chapters in this book have been designed to fill this lacuna in our knowledge of British jobs. While a common emphasis is on key non-wage aspects of job quality, in particular skills utilization, task discretion and work effort, in some cases attention is paid also to wages, building on an existing literature where the wage gap may have figured prominently, in order to reveal an integrated and up-to-date picture about how jobs differ.

The story begins with the differentiation of job quality according to social class (Chapter 2), and proceeds to an analysis of gender and job quality (Chapter 3). There follows a trio of chapters (4 to 6) which examine job quality differentiation according to the type of contractual arrangement between employer and employee; these look at the part-time/full-time divide, the distinctions between jobs with 'permanent' and temporary job contracts, and the contrasts between the jobs of the self-employed and of employees. Chapters 7 and 8 then investigate institutional factors, including the union/non-union job quality gap and the private sector/public sector gap. Chapter 9 focuses on a prominent typology of the form of management, by examining the differences between companies according to whether they have adopted 'high-involvement' management practices.[5]

Chapter 10 concludes, not just with a summary of findings, but with a change of tone by us, the editors. We leave behind the dispassionate mission of previous chapters and return to the essential connection between job quality and well-being. If, as the evidence shows, the design of jobs and the creation of

---

[5] Other gaps of considerable interest concern those between regions/nations of the UK (especially the 'North–South' axis) and those between ethnic groups. Unfortunately, fine-grained geographical analysis is not possible, while differentiation between several ethnic minority groups is also precluded by sample sizes. However, where regional samples have been boosted some regional analysis is possible (e.g. Felstead, 2009).

high job quality matter greatly for the well-being of British workers, what are the potential policy interventions and instruments that could be brought to bear to improve job quality, especially for those in bad jobs so that gaps can be narrowed? This question will be posed in full awareness of the constraints surrounding workplace interventions in a neo-liberal market economy, both challenging those constraints and working between them. We argue that there is potential scope for job quality improvements if proper attention is given to this objective, both by governments and by other social partners; we suggest that it is not appropriate to adopt an outright pessimistic perspective, where it is judged that bad jobs are inevitable and must be tolerated and that any interventions are detrimental to employers' flexibility and to workers' prospects of employment. Rather, we draw on existing approaches both in Britain and elsewhere to consider potential productive interventions that might, indeed, make a difference in the workplace.

2

Class Inequality at Work: Trends to Polarization?

Duncan Gallie

2.1. INTRODUCTION

Extensive class inequalities have been shown to be not only damaging for the personal well-being of the disadvantaged but corrosive of the quality of relationships and of institutional trust within the broader society (Gallie, 1983; Wilkinson and Pickett, 2010). A good deal of research has pointed to sharply widening inequalities of income in the UK since the 1980s. But we know much less about changes in other aspects of work quality. Has increased class polarization between those at the top and the bottom of the class structure in terms of income been reinforced by greater inequality in other aspects of work, or has a trend to class convergence in the intrinsic quality of work partially offset income polarization? There has been considerable theoretical speculation on these issues, but a notable lack of empirical examination using data that capture developments over a significant span of time.

2.1.1. Theories in Conflict

The classic scenario of class polarization, developed by researchers working in the neo-Marxian tradition, focused on a growing divergence in job quality between those in higher and those in lower or working-class positions, in particular with respect to pay, skill, job control, and work intensity (Braverman, 1974; Friedmann, 1946).[1] Capitalist development was thought to be associated with a progressive simplification of work tasks in the lower

---

[1] This differs from the concept of polarization as a 'hollowing out' of the class structure used in some recent literature.

reaches of the class structure, increasingly tight monitoring of work perform-ance, and an intensification of work effort. The deskilling of work allowed employers to drive down pay rates and hence labour costs. This scenario was initially developed with respect to the changes in the work conditions of manual employees with the introduction of Taylorist techniques of manage-ment and the spread of mass-production technologies exemplified by the assembly line. In the 1970s the argument was extended into a wider 'proletar-ianization' thesis which postulated a more general trend to the deterioration of working conditions, that included lower-class white-collar workers, in par-ticular clerical employees and technicians (Braverman,1974; Crompton and Jones, 1984).

From the 1990s, the emphasis on the growth of class inequalities at work shifted from a primary concern with the changing nature of the work process to an emphasis on inequalities in job security. The significance of class differentials in job insecurity had been highlighted already both by labour market segmentation theory and by class schema that emphasized the contrast between 'service' and 'labour contracts' (Goldthorpe, 2000). The new devel-opment was the view that there was a trend towards rising insecurity in lower class positions (Rosenberg, 1989), as result of a drive by employers towards greater numerical flexibility in the face of increased product market volatility. This resulted in a growing reliance on non-standard forms of employment, in particular short-term temporary contracts, to facilitate quick reductions of the workforce in times of economic difficulty. The trend was towards casualiza-tion or even the growth of a 'precariat', whereby, for those in the lowest occupational classes, stable employment careers would disappear and be replaced by alternating spells of work on short-term contracts and unemploy-ment (Standing, 2011).

The class polarization thesis has been heavily contested over many decades by arguments coming from quite diverse perspectives. The earliest questioned the assumptions of theories of polarization about the implications of devel-opments in technology. While accepting that earlier phases of industrializa-tion tended to reduce skills and discretion at work in the lower or working classes, this was seen as a relatively temporary phase in industrial develop-ment. The emergence of more advanced technologies tended to reverse the trend towards deskilling and lead instead to a generalized process of the upskilling of manual work (Blauner 1964; Kerr et al., 1960). Although early arguments focused on a relatively restricted sector of continuous-process production, very similar accounts were to emerge later when the spread of micro-processors led to much more extensive automation of industry (Piore and Sabel, 1984). Even studies of the car industry, which often had been cited as the exemplar case of tendencies to deskilling, began to emphasize the emergence of a new production model that required higher levels of manual worker skill (Kern and Schumann, 1987, 1992).

A second argument pointing to class convergence rather than polarization was developed later by an influential strand of managerial theory, which came under the diverse names of 'high-involvement' or 'high-performance' management (Beer et al. 1984; Lawler, 1986; Lawler et al. 1995; Walton, 1985). This suggested that, with greater global competition, product quality would become increasingly important to business success. This requires not just more effort by employers, but a higher level of employee performance. It was argued that it could only be achieved by gaining employee commitment, through increasing employee autonomy and discretion at work. This would necessarily erode the distinctiveness of traditional class differences and make manual jobs more similar to white-collar occupations.

A third scenario that depicted class convergence came from a very different direction. It was seen as resulting less from an improvement in the conditions of employment of those in lower class positions than from a deterioration of the quality of work of those in higher classes. An influential statement of this position was Edwards' (1979) account of the development of systems of control of work performance. The critical development was the introduction of new systems of 'bureaucratic control'—involving control through organizational rules and procedures of individual appraisal—to intensify the work effort of the increasing numbers of managerial, administrative, and technical specialists. Its implementation implied the erosion of the high level of autonomy that had traditionally characterized the work of those in higher class positions. While Edwards' work was largely focused on developments in the private sector of industry, some of its key themes were to be found as principles informing the 'new public sector management' programmes that gained popularity in the 1990s. These promoted the introduction of targets, monitoring, and appraisals to improve both effort and work quality in the public services (see also Chapter 8).

It is notable that the convergence arguments have focused primarily on the non-financial aspects of job quality. There has been little contestation of the view that there has been growing polarization with respect to pay. This is scarcely surprising given the overwhelming evidence of a marked growth in overall pay inequality since the 1980s, which is likely to be reflected in class differentials. The central challenge of the convergence theorists (as of theorists of compensating differentials) is whether or not growing class polarization in pay has been to some degree offset by convergence with respect to the intrinsic aspects of work and job insecurity.

2.1.2. Problems of Empirical Assessment

There are a number of issues that need to be addressed in moving to an empirical assessment of these different arguments. The first is the operationalization of the concept of class in large-scale data sets. Class is usually conceived in terms of an employment relationship involving inherent conflicts of interest between employers and employees. It therefore needs to take account of position with respect to the power structure of the organization and the extent to which work roles service the structure of control. An influential discussion of the concept by Goldthorpe (2000) links this to differences in the nature of contracts. At one extreme, professional, administrative, and managerial staff have a 'service contract' that is designed to develop their loyalty and bind them to the organization in the longer term, while, at the other, low-skilled manual workers have a 'labour contract' based upon short-term reward for discrete amounts of labour. Other categories of employee are involved in employment contracts that involve different mixes of service and labour contract principles.

The principal sociological categorization of classes derived from these principles (the Erikson-Goldthorpe-Portocarcero class classification) was the starting point for the development by the Office of National Statistics of the National Statistics Socio-Economic Classification (NS-SEC), which has been extensively validated in terms of its empirical capacity to differentiate employees in terms of various dimensions of employment relationships (Rose and Pevalin, 2003). It takes as the central dimension of class the extent to which employment contracts are based on a longer-term 'service' form of contract or a shorter-term 'labour' contract form. We have taken NS-SEC, then, as the indicator of class, aggregating the main categories into six classes of employees: higher managers and professionals; lower managers and professionals; intermediate occupations; lower supervisory and technical; semi-routine; and routine. Given the quite diverse usages of the concept of 'routine' in the literature, for clarity we term the last of these categories routine low skilled (cf. Chapter 3).

A further question is the nature of the relevant comparisons. The concepts of 'higher' and 'lower' or 'working-class' segments of the class structure, deployed in much of the general theoretical literature, are rather vague with respect to particular types of employee. It is clearly important, given the emphasis on contractual distinctions in the class literature, to examine whether or not there has been polarization between higher managers and professionals, on the one hand, and those in routine low-skilled occupations on the other. But it also should be noted that much of the earlier empirical discussion of changes in the quality of work at the lower end of the class structure focuses on employees who are normally classified as operatives or semi-routine employees. This is true, for instance, both of writers who have emphasized increasing managerial control through technical means such as the assembly line and of theorists who have pointed to the way jobs are being improved by the introduction of new technologies. We will focus, then, on polarization with respect to *both* routine low-skilled and semi-routine work.

Finally, it is important to recognize that there is a literature that suggests that class effects may be moderated by other factors such as sex and ownership. Given occupational gender segregation, and the possibility that employers treat male and female employees in rather different ways, broad class bands may span jobs that differ considerably depending on the sex of the employee. Similarly, as class concepts are rooted in a theory of dynamics of ownership, it is important to see whether the extent of polarization is similar or differs between the private and public sectors. Employer strategies in the private sector are likely to be responses to competitive market pressures, while those in the public sector are responses to governments' provision of budget resources, spending priorities, policies about service delivery, and beliefs about effective systems of performance control. While in the immediate post-war period, the public sector is generally thought to have encouraged progressive employment policies (indeed to have provided a model of a good employment relationship), it is important to examine whether such practices have survived in a period of more severe budgetary constraint.

As we do not have a consistent detailed indicator of ownership for the full period of our surveys, we take as a proxy the distinction between public service industries (public administration, education, and health) and a subset of other industries. For the years for which we have detailed ownership data, approximately 77 per cent of employees in the public service industries were in the public sector and 90 per cent or more of employees in the extractive, transformative, distributive, and producer service sectors were in the private sector. We exclude, however, the extractive industries in constructing a 'predominantly private' sector, given the greater importance of state-owned mining in the earlier period. By way of shorthand, we refer to these respectively as the public and private 'industry sectors'.

With respect to the empirical analysis, we begin by examining the trends in the class structure over the period covered by our surveys and then turn to the issue of changes in class differentials in the aspects of job quality that are the central concern of this book—pay, the level of skills, the discretion or control that employees can exercise at work, and the level of work intensity. Given the debates in the literature, we turn finally to the issue of differentials in job insecurity. To test whether there had been significant change in class differentials between periods, we have conducted regression analyses which included class/year interactions for all years. These are based on logistic regressions for binary variables and OLS regressions for all other variables. Because of the availability of data, the earliest period in our data series differs depending upon the particular aspect of job quality under discussion, but it is either 1986 or 1992. To simplify presentation, we present in the tables only the interaction coefficients for the comparison between the earliest and latest period in each table, which give a picture of the extent of change over the period as a whole.

2.2. TRENDS IN CLASS STRUCTURE

There is reasonably consistent evidence from studies that have defined occupational classes in terms of relative pay that, at least in Britain, occupations which earlier had intermediate levels of pay experienced particularly notable reductions in their relative size over time (Goos and Manning, 2007; Oesch, 2013). There was strong growth of more highly-paid occupations, but also some growth in the low-paid. Was the same pattern evident for classes defined in terms of employment relationships?

It can be seen in Table 2.1 that part of the picture is similar to that given by the literature using pay as the key criterion for class. There was a considerable expansion of the higher class categories, with a seven percentage point rise between 1986 and 2012 in the proportion in higher managerial and professional occupations and an eleven percentage point rise in lower managers and professionals. But developments in the central reaches of the class structure are varied. There was no change in the proportion of those in 'intermediate' occupations taking the overall period between the mid-1980s on the one hand and 2012 on the other, although there has been a relatively small decline since the peak in 2001. There has been, however, a very marked decline in the proportion of employees in lower supervisory and technical work. Taken together, the share of these two classes has declined from 35 per cent in 1986 to 29 per cent in 2012. Most important, it should be noted that there is no evidence of an expansion of the lowest class—that of routine low-skilled workers—in contrast to studies that define classes in terms of pay; rather its share of the workforce has declined by two percentage points over the two and a half decades.

Table 2.1. Changes in Class Structure, 1986–2012 (Percentage of Employees by NS-SEC)

	1986	1992	1997	2001	2006	2012	% Change 1986–2012
Higher managers and profs	7.6	9.1	11.0	13.7	15.0	14.6	+7.0
Lower managers and profs	20.8	30.2	29.9	28.6	30.9	32.1	+11.3
Intermediate occupations	12.3	12.2	12.3	14.0	12.8	12.2	−0.1
Lower super and technical	22.6	18.0	16.3	14.6	14.4	13.7	−8.9
Semi-routine	23.9	17.1	19.6	16.8	15.2	16.5	−7.5
Routine/low skilled	12.7	13.6	10.9	12.3	11.7	10.9	−1.8
N	3491	3336	2155	3943	5542	2448	

2.3. CLASS AND PAY

The one issue around which there is relative consensus in the literature is that there has been a sharp increase in pay differentials since the 1980s and this could be expected to be reflected in increasing inequalities in pay across the class structure.

Table 2.2 shows the pattern in our data with respect to gross hourly pay adjusted to 2012 prices. The coefficients (all of which are statistically significant) give the relative pay differential by class for each year estimated by a regression analysis that takes the pay of higher managers and professionals as the point of reference. It can be seen that already in 1986 there was a sharp class gradient. But the relative disadvantage of all classes with respect to professionals and managers strengthened progressively with each successive year until 2006. The final column captures the overall increase in the differential between 1986 and 2012. This growing divergence between the top and bottom of the class hierarchy represents a classic picture of class polarization. But it is also clear that there was a growth of pay inequality right across the class structure.

Did the pattern differ substantially between male and female employees or between people who worked in the private or public sectors? Table 2.3 shows the overall change in differentials between 1986 and 2012 (the equivalent of the last column of Table 2.2) for the two categories of employee. It can be seen that the general pattern of increasing pay inequality between classes was true for both men and women separately and for employees both in the private and public sectors. But there were differences in the extent to which pay differentials increased. The rise in class pay inequality was more marked for men than for women and it was considerably greater in the private than in the public industry sector.

Table 2.2. Class Pay Relativities by Year (Gross Hourly Earnings at 2014 Prices)

NS-SEC	1986	1992	1997	2001	2006	2012	Interaction coefficient 2012
Higher mgr-prof	ref	ref	ref	ref	ref	ref	ref
Lower mgr-prof	−1.926	−2.071	−3.443	−9.339	−9.495	−8.156	−6.230***
Intermediate	−6.734	−6.184	−7.746	−13.621	−15.195	−11.739	−5.005***
Lower sup-tech	−5.409	−5.658	−7.558	−13.786	−14.705	−12.732	−7.323***
Semi-routine	−7.423	−7.689	−9.909	−16.487	−17.416	−14.982	−7.559***
Routine/low skilled	−7.126	−7.517	−10.891	−16.561	−17.236	−15.310	−8.184***
N	3072	2660	1962	3645	4899	2101	

Note: *** = sig at 1 per cent level. The interaction coefficient 2012 is relative to 1986.

Table 2.3. Overall Change in Class Pay Differentials, 1986 to 2012, by Sex and Industry Sector

NS-SEC	Men	Women	Private	Public
Higher mgr-prof	ref	ref	ref	ref
Lower mgr-prof	−8.680	−4.133	−8.429	−2.005
Intermediate	−6.109	−4.970	−7.695	−0.661
Lower sup-tech	−8.338	−6.447	−9.812	−2.273
Semi-routine	−9.752	−6.685	−10.910	−1.518
Routine/low skilled	−9.935	−6.615	−11.333	−2.385

Note: Gross hourly earnings. All coefficients are significant at the 1 per cent level.

2.4. CLASS AND SKILL

The Skills and Employment Surveys (SES) started from the assumption that job skill as 'substantive complexity' is best proxied by the learning time necessary to be able to do the job. At least three distinct types of knowledge acquisition have to be taken into account: general education, vocationally specific training, and knowledge acquired on the job. The surveys provide three questions designed to tap these different types of learning requirements.

The first, indicating the general education needed, asked: 'If they were applying today, what qualifications, if any, would someone need to get the type of job you have now?' The highest qualification given was allocated to one of six broad qualification categories: no qualifications, poor lower secondary, good lower secondary, upper secondary, non-degree higher education, and degree-level higher education.

The second, focusing on vocational training, asked people the duration of the training they had received since completing full-time education for their current type of work. There were seven response options, running from 'less than one week' to 'two years and over'. The third measure, tapping initial on-the-job learning, asked 'How long did it take for you after you first started doing this type of job to learn to do it well?', giving the same duration categories as in the previous measure.

Summary indices were constructed for each measure by scoring the responses for the levels of required qualifications (a five-point score) and for the duration categories for the length of training and on-the-job learning times (seven-point scores). A factor analysis showed that there was a single underlying dimension to these three measures.[2] To simplify the presentation, we take the factor score as our measure of overall job skill level.

---

[2] The factor had an eigenvalue of 1.84 and accounted for 61 per cent of the variance.

Table 2.4. Mean Overall Job Skill Scores

NS-SEC	1986	1992	1997	2001	2006	2012	Interaction coefficient 2012
Higher mgr-prof	2.26	2.20	2.43	2.24	2.27	2.24	ref
Lower mgr-prof	1.99	1.99	2.08	2.05	2.10	2.01	0.049
Intermediate	1.18	1.21	1.42	1.30	1.40	1.42	0.262***
Lower sup-tech	1.49	1.42	1.65	1.60	1.49	1.47	0.006
Semi-routine	0.68	0.68	0.74	0.78	0.84	0.89	0.226***
Routine/low skilled	0.68	0.68	0.58	0.62	0.67	0.51	−0.150
All employees	1.31	1.41	1.54	1.52	1.59	1.56	
	3273	3087	2110	3824	5376	2297	

Note: *** = sig at 1 per cent level. The interaction coefficient 2012 is relative to 1986.

As was noted in Chapter 1, there has been a continuous upward shift in the qualifications required for jobs for all employees across the years of the surveys. However, as can be seen in Table 2.4, there was much less change *between* classes. There was evidence of a relative rise in job skills among those in intermediate and in semi-routine class positions (as is shown by the final column which gives the statistical significance of the interaction terms between class and year when comparing 2012 with 1986). But, overall, the notable finding is the high level of stability of pattern across the period. There was no evidence of polarization. Further analyses showed that this was the case for both men and women.

But, while the overall picture is one of stability in class differentials, further analysis revealed some evidence of polarization in the private industry sector. Taking the period as a whole, the position of routine low-skilled employees in the private sector had become significantly worse relative to higher professionals and managers. This divergence took place primarily in the period 2006 to 2012, suggesting it may have reflected employer responses to the economic crisis. In contrast, in the public services sector, there was no change in the relative position of routine low-skilled employees over the period as a whole. Moreover, there was a significant and progressive improvement in the relative skill level of semi-routine employees.

2.5. CLASS AND DIRECT PARTICIPATION

Scenarios of change in employment relations in recent decades have focused on two principal aspects of direct participation: task discretion (or the direct control that employees can exercise over their day-to-day work tasks) and organizational participation (the ability to exercise voice over wider organizational issues). Neo-Marxian theorists have particularly emphasized tendencies to polarization in task discretion, whereas some theories of the 'knowledge-economy' would imply a degree of class convergence in both forms of participation as lower-level employees are increasingly involved in decision-making in the 'learning organization'.

2.5.1. Task Discretion

Taking first task discretion, a measure is derived from four questions, posed initially in 1992, asking people how much influence they personally had over how hard they worked; deciding what tasks they did; deciding how to do the tasks, and the quality standards to which they worked. For each item there was a four-point response scale, ranging from a great deal of influence to no influence at all. A summary index was created by averaging across the four items.

Taking the overall period there was a marked decline of individual task discretion between 1992 and 2012. This occurred principally between 1992 and 2001 and then levelled off. As can be seen in Table 2.5, the decline between 1992 and 2001 affected all social classes, as did the subsequent period of stability between 2001 and 2006. But in the final period, there was some class convergence: there was a continued decline in task discretion among higher managers and professionals and lower supervisors and technicians, stability among lower managers and professionals and intermediary workers, and a rise in task discretion among semi-routine and routine low-skilled employees.

The fact that the pattern of change across the overall period was so widespread among employees in different classes meant that class differentials were little affected. For employees in most classes, there was no significant change between the differential relative to higher managers and professionals in 2012 compared to 1992. It was only semi-routine workers that saw a significant improvement in their relative position. This was entirely attributable to the pattern in the private industry sector: although there was a decline

Table 2.5. Task Discretion, 1992–2012 (Mean Scores)

NS-SEC7	1992	1997	2001	2006	2012	Interaction coefficient 2012
Higher mgr-prof	2.59	2.55	2.38	2.40	2.30	ref
Lower mgr-prof	2.65	2.48	2.37	2.34	2.34	−0.021
Intermediate	2.38	2.22	2.12	2.11	2.10	0.009
Lower sup-tech	2.48	2.32	2.28	2.28	2.20	0.008
Semi-routine	2.17	1.95	1.89	1.87	2.03	0.146**
Routine/low skilled	2.19	1.94	1.86	1.80	1.84	−0.061
All employees	2.44	2.27	2.18	2.18	2.18	
	3276	2148	3938	5530	2439	

Note: ** = sig at 5 per cent level. The interaction coefficient 2012 is relative to 1986.

over time in the task discretion of semi-routine workers, their relative position improved because the decline in task discretion among professionals and managers was even sharper.

2.5.2. Organizational Participation

Public discussion about participation has focused to a greater extent on potential changes in organizational participation than on employee control over their immediate work tasks. This is reflected in the popularization of new managerial theories of 'employee involvement', the advocacy of ideas of 'partnership' by Labour in the years following its return to power in 1997 and the implementation in 2005 of the new European Union (EU) Directive on employees' rights for information and consultation.

The Skills and Employment Surveys have included since 1992 two types of question relating to organizational participation. The first asks whether there are meetings between management and employees in which employees can express their views about what is happening in the organization. The second seeks to capture the degree of influence employees have over decisions affecting work organization. It asks: 'Suppose that there was going to be some decision made at your place of work that changed the way you do your job. Do you think that you personally would have any say in the decision about the change or not?' Those who replied affirmatively were then asked whether they would have a 'great deal', 'quite a lot', or 'just a little say'. A measure of participative influence was created with a score ranging from 0 for those who had no say at all to 3 for those who had 'a great deal of say'.

A comparison of the pattern across the years (Table 2.6) confirms the picture given by other sources, in particular the Workplace Employment Relations Survey (Kersley et al., 2006; vanWanrooy et al., 2013; Willman et al., 2009), that recent decades have seen a substantial expansion of direct

Table 2.6. Percentage of Employees with Consultative Meetings by Class, 1992–2012

NS-SEC7	1992	1997	2001	2006	2012	Interaction coefficient 2012
Higher mgr-prof	80.1	81.8	80.5	82.8	85.7	ref
Lower mgr-prof	75.6	79.8	78.4	81.5	83.8	0.106
Intermediate	59.7	67.0	63.8	68.9	67.4	−0.075
Lower sup-tech	60.5	63.5	60.6	66.7	67.1	−0.128
Semi-routine	49.2	61.5	55.4	63.0	68.9	0.417*
Routine/low skilled	41.9	34.9	38.0	46.0	43.2	−0.356
All employees	62.7	67.1	65.2	71.1	72.9	
	3319	2139	3922	5491	2400	

Note: * = sig at 10 per cent level. The interaction coefficient 2012 is relative to 1992.

consultation over organizational issues. Whereas, in 1992, 63 per cent of employees reported that there were meetings in their workplace where they could express their views about organizational issues, the proportion had risen to 73 per cent by 2012. The introduction of the Information and Consultation of Employees Regulations between 2005 and 2008 might have been expected to accelerate the trend. But there was no evidence that this was the case: there was only a very slight increase between 2006 and 2012. This possibly reflected the relatively weak way in which the EU Directive was transposed into UK law (see Chapter 10).

Did the extension of consultation mean that it became more evenly spread across employees in different class positions? Taking the pattern in 1992, there was clearly a very sharp class hierarchy: 80 per cent of higher managers and professionals had a channel for expressing their views on organizational issues, but this was the case for only 42 per cent of routine low-skilled employees. Comparing class differentials over the whole period, the most notable finding is again their very high level of stability. Even after the implementation of the new regulations only a minority of routine employees had a channel for expressing their views, less than half the proportion of those in the highest class position. It was only in the case of semi-routine workers that there was an indication of improvement relative to higher managers and professionals and this was only at a borderline level of statistical significance (p = <0.10).

Possibly the effect of an increased emphasis on employees' rights to participation would be more evident in the effective influence it gave them than in the prevalence of formal procedures. The 'Information and Consultation' regulations placed a particular emphasis on influence over changes in work organization. But it is notable that for employees as a whole, there was in fact no change at all in the average participative influence score between 1992 and 2012 (Table 2.7). An initial rise in involvement between 1992 and 2001 was sharply reversed in the subsequent period. While the degree of organizational participation of all classes declined after 2001, the extent to which this was the

Table 2.7. Employee Influence over Decisions about Work Organization (Mean Scores)

NS-SEC7	1992	2001	2006	2012	Interaction coefficient 2012
Higher mgr-prof	1.53	1.66	1.43	1.30	ref
Lower mgr-prof	1.35	1.39	1.24	1.09	−0.021
Intermediate	0.77	1.06	0.88	0.80	0.275***
Lower sup-tech	1.08	1.13	1.10	0.91	0.071
Semi-routine	0.69	0.83	0.68	0.71	0.259***
Routine/low skilled	0.56	0.77	0.70	0.65	0.327***
All employees	0.95	1.17	1.05	0.95	
	3295	3931	5514	2430	

Note: *** = sig at 1 per cent level. The interaction coefficient 2012 is relative to 1992.

case varied by class. Both higher and lower professionals and managers had a
particularly sharp reduction in influence over organizational decisions after
2001. In contrast, semi-routine and routine low-skilled employees had a
below-average decline in the same period, resulting in an improvement in
their position relative to higher managers and professionals.

There was then a narrowing of the class gap in organizational participation over the period. But this was primarily attributable to the sharp
decline in the involvement of professionals and managers, rather than to
the spread of new management involvement practices to those in lower
class positions.

There was an important difference in the experience of changing organizational participation of men and women. The relative increase in effective
influence for semi-routine and routine low-skilled employees was only significant for men. This was paralleled by a difference between the predominantly public and private industry sectors. In the public service industry group,
there were no significant changes in class differentials with respect to influence, whereas in the private sector there was a narrowing of the gap for all
classes relative to higher managers and professionals.

As can be seen in Table 2.8, both sex and sector appear to have had an effect
on participative influence. In the public service industry sector, there were no
changes in class differentials for men, and there was even a negative change for
female lower professionals and managers, lower supervisors and technicians,
and semi-routine employees. In the private industry sector, there was a
significant improvement for women only among intermediary and semi-
routine employees. For men, however, there was an improvement for intermediary, lower supervisory and technical, semi-routine, and routine low-
skilled employees. In short, convergence in class differentials in organizational
participation appears to have been primarily in the private sector industries
and particularly involved men in those industries.

Table 2.8. Interaction Coefficients for Year 2012 (relative to 1992) for Influence over
Decisions about Work Organization by Sex and Industry Sector

	Predominantly private		Predominantly public	
	Male	Female	Male	Female
Higher mgr-prof	ref	ref	ref	Ref
Lower mgr-prof	0.231	0.312	−0.137	−0.675***
Intermediate	0.506**	0.520**	−0.085	−0.311
Lower sup-tech	0.325**	0.150	0.101	−0.507 **
Semi-routine	0.418***	0.436*	0.195	−0.398 *
Routine/low skilled	0.609***	0.399	0.181	−0.316

Note: *** = sig at 1 per cent level; ** = sig at 5 per cent level; * = sig at 10 per cent level.

2.6. CLASS AND WORK INTENSITY

Views about changes in class differentials have perhaps been most contradictory with respect to work intensity. Whereas labour process analysis emphasized work intensification among those in lower class positions, more recent analyses have underlined the increased pressure on managers and professionals, due to new demands for accountability and new forms of performance control.

Is there evidence of the shift that Edwards (1979) predicted, away from direct supervision, towards forms of bureaucratic control that would have particularly strong implications for those in higher class positions? The Skills and Employment Surveys have regularly included a question about the importance of different factors in determining how hard people work. The evidence across the period 1992 to 2012 provides only partial support for Edwards' thesis. Bureaucratic control, as reflected in the role of reports and appraisals in determining effort, did indeed rise in importance, from 15 per cent of the workforce in 1986 to 31 per cent in 2012. But direct supervisory control expanded rather than contracted: only 27 per cent of employees reported that supervisors were important in determining how hard they worked in 1986, whereas the proportion had risen to 43 per cent by 2012.

Moreover, as can be seen in Table 2.9, the growth of supervisory control was far from being limited to those in lower class positions—indeed it was substantially greater among both higher and lower professionals and managers than among either routine low-skilled or semi-routine employees. At the same time, the increase of control by reports and appraisals was also greatest among higher managers and professionals (+17.8 percentage points). The tightening of organizational control of work effort was then more strongly focused on higher occupational classes than on lower.

Table 2.9. Determinants of Work Effort: Percentage Supervisors and Percentage Reports and Appraisals

NS-SEC7	1986	Supervisor		Reports and appraisals		
		1992	2012	1986	1992	2012
Higher mgr-prof	24.3	44.0	44.3	22.9	41.4	40.9
Lower mgr-prof	24.0	36.6	45.2	24.3	38.8	39.7
Intermediate	30.9	39.9	44.1	17.7	25.6	29.8
Lower sup-tech	29.2	36.1	49.6	14.1	21.9	29.8
Semi-routine	25.2	32.8	38.9	8.5	13.7	22.8
Routine/low skilled	25.0	37.1	36.5	4.5	8.4	6.0
All employees	26.6	37.0	43.3	14.8	26.8	30.9
N	3492	3337	2449	3490	3335	2448

Were such changes reflected in people's experiences of the pressures in their work? The surveys included a range of potential variables for measuring work intensity. As we are concerned with change over the longer term, we focus only on those indicators that were asked in 1992 and provide information across a number of the surveys. There are five items for which we have data in 1992, 2001, 2006, and 2012. Three take the form of a statement in relation to which people were asked to evaluate their own work, while the other two are direct questions. The wording of the five items was as follows:

- 'I work under a great deal of tension.' (Strongly agree, agree, disagree, strongly disagree)
- 'My job requires that I work very hard.' (Strongly agree, agree, disagree, strongly disagree)
- 'I often have to work extra time, over and above the formal hours of my job, to get through the work or help out.' (Very true, true, somewhat true, not at all true)
- How much effort do you put into your job beyond what is required? (A lot, some, only a little, none)
- How often does your work involve working at very high speed? (All the time, almost all the time, around three quarters of the time, around half the time, around a quarter of the time, almost never, never).

Work intensity is multi-faceted but the items nonetheless have a scale alpha of 0.66. A scale, with a range from 1 to 4.6, was constructed by averaging the five items (aggregating the two highest and the two lowest response categories of the 'high speed' item to give it a more similar scaling to the others).

Taking the period as a whole, there was a significant increase in work intensity. But the extent to which this occurred varied considerably by class (Table 2.10). It is notable that, even in 1992, work intensity was greatest among managers and professionals on the one hand and lower supervisors and technicians on the other. It was lowest among those in the semi-routine

Table 2.10. Class and Work Intensity (Mean Scores), 1992–2012

NS-SEC7	1992	2001	2006	2012	Interaction coefficient 2012
Higher mgr-prof	2.82	3.18	3.17	3.20	ref
Lower mgr-prof	3.00	3.24	3.24	3.24	−0.144***
Intermediate	2.74	2.98	2.89	2.95	−0.172***
Lower sup-tech	2.87	2.99	3.01	3.14	−0.109*
Semi-routine	2.60	2.86	2.84	2.93	−0.057
Routine/low skilled	2.68	2.80	2.77	2.87	−0.196***
All employees	2.82	3.04	3.04	3.09	
N	3268	3927	5520	2425	

Note: *** = sig at 1 per cent level; * = sig at 10 per cent level. The interaction coefficient 2012 is relative to 1992.

and routine low-skilled classes. Over the period as a whole it increased for all classes. But two very different classes experienced the sharpest rise in work intensity: higher professionals and managers and employees in semi-routine work. The work intensity of higher professionals and managers therefore rose significantly relative to routine low-skilled employees, but not relative to semi-routine workers. This pattern was similar for male and female employees.

Overall work intensity scores were similar in the predominantly public and private industry sectors until 2001, but then diverged between 2001 and 2012 with a greater increase in work intensity in the public services sector (+0.38 as against +0.22). Moreover, the increase in work intensity for higher professionals and managers relative to routine low-skilled employees was considerably greater in the public service industries than in the predominantly private industries. It was only in the public services that there was significant growth of the differential between the top and bottom of the hierarchy.

2.7. JOB INSECURITY

There also have been very diverse arguments about trends in class differentials with respect to job security. Some have stressed the role of employer flexibility policies in heightening insecurity for those in lower class positions, while others have argued that there has been a relative deterioration in the job security of those in higher class positions.

The most consistent indicator in the surveys is a question set that first asks 'Do you think there is any chance at all of you losing your job and becoming unemployed in the next twelve months?' and then asks those who thought that there was a chance to rate the likelihood of this happening on a five-point response set. By combining the responses to the two questions, we have constructed a measure of job insecurity that runs from 0 for those who thought there was 'no chance' of losing their job to 5 for those who thought it was 'very likely'. The measure was first asked in 1986 and subsequently in all surveys from 1997.

In Table 2.11, it can be seen that job insecurity varied substantially over the period, falling from 1997 to 2001, then rising steeply between 2006 and 2012—indeed, reaching by 2012 the highest point registered in any of the surveys of the series, including 1986 when unemployment was substantially higher. This broad pattern is consistent with the well-established finding that job insecurity is related (albeit sometimes with a lag in time) to the economic cycle.

Taking the pattern of class differences in 1986 it can be seen that job insecurity was lowest for professionals and managers and for intermediate

Table 2.11. Class and Job Insecurity (Mean Scores), 1986–1996

NS-SEC7	1986	1997	2001	2006	2012	Interaction coefficient 2012
Higher mgr-prof	0.62	0.83	0.54	0.64	0.89	ref
Lower mgr-prof	0.44	0.67	0.53	0.50	0.70	−0.020
Intermediate	0.58	0.58	0.40	0.67	0.86	0.001
Lower sup-tech	0.73	0.74	0.55	0.46	0.81	−0.195
Semi-routine	0.82	0.69	0.59	0.61	0.62	−0.480***
Routine/Low skilled	1.01	0.83	0.68	0.65	0.89	−0.402***
All employees	0.70	0.71	0.54	0.57	0.77	
	3289	2116	3858	5452	2288	

Note: *** = sig at 1 per cent level.

employees and highest for semi-routine and above all routine low-skilled employees. But the level of insecurity changed in a very different way for different classes over the period. It is notable that job insecurity was higher in 2012 than it had been in 1986 for managers and professionals, for intermediary employees and for lower supervisors and technicians—but it was lower for semi-routine and routine low-skilled employees. The pattern of change over time for professionals and managers appears to have been rather different from that of other categories of employee: insecurity rose between 1986 and 1997, whereas it fell or was stable for other classes; it also rose between 2001 and 2006, whereas for other classes (apart from intermediary employees) it was either stable or continued to decline. In general, changes in job insecurity among professionals and managers appear to have been less closely linked to the economic cycle than was generally the case.

The result of these divergent trends was that class differentials in insecurity had significantly changed by 2012 compared to 1986, in the direction of a substantial convergence between the highest and lowest classes. Separate analyses by sex indicate a similar direction of change for both men and women.

The notable divergence was once more to be found in the experiences of employees in the predominantly public and private industry sectors. Change in class differentials was much less marked in the private industry group, with only some evidence of an improvement in the position of semi-routine employees (at a p = <0.10 level of significance). In the public sector the coefficients for change were much stronger and highly significant, in part reflecting a much sharper decline in the security of managers and professionals. Indeed, the traditional class hierarchy with respect to job insecurity, in which employees in higher classes were relatively secure and those in lower classes bore the main burden of insecurity, had effectively disappeared in the public sector (Table 2.12).

Table 2.12. Class Interactions for Year 2012, contrasted with 1986, for Job Insecurity in Private and Public Industry Sectors

	Private industry	Public services
Higher mgr-prof	ref	ref
Lower mgr-prof	0.004	−0.428**
Intermediate	0.290	−0.502**
Lower sup-tech	−0.009	−0.556*
Semi-routine	−0.348*	−0.828***
Routine/low skilled	−0.081	−1.843***

Note: *** = sig at 1 per cent level; ** = sig at 5 per cent level; * = sig at 10 per cent level.

2.8. CONCLUSION

There have been sharply contrasting long-term scenarios of the changing nature of class inequalities in advanced industrial societies—with some predicting increasing class polarization and others class convergence in the quality of work and employment conditions. This chapter has sought to assess these arguments using the exceptionally rich over time data of the Skills and Employment Surveys, which make it possible to examine not only the financial but also the non-financial aspects of job quality.

The evidence clearly confirms that there was indeed a marked polarization of pay that grew stronger right across the period from 1986 to 1992. This was reflected not only in the growing differential between higher managers and professionals on the one hand and routine low-skilled employees on the other, but in increasing differentials for all classes relative to professionals and managers. This raises the issue of whether the growth of class inequalities in pay was paralleled by increasing inequalities or by compensatory improvements in other non-financial aspects of job quality.

Taking the *overall* pattern of class differentials with respect to non-financial job quality, the notable feature of the data is the very high level of stability of class inequalities across the decades. Evidence for significant change is relatively rare. There was no general trend towards either polarization or convergence across the period. This was the case for both male and female employees.

This overall pattern conceals, however, rather more change *within* particular industry sectors. There were notable differences between the public service and private industry sectors in the way class differentials changed over the period. This suggests that, at least for recent past decades, class analysis needs to take account of the differing nature of ownership and accountability structures, rather than assume a common market-driven dynamic across the economy. Further, in assessing these trends, it is important to draw a distinction between two sectors of the working class—those in semi-routine or semi-skilled work on the one hand and those in routine low-skilled work on the other. Although often treated in a homogeneous way in theoretical arguments about changes in class inequality at work, their fortunes have in practice developed in rather different ways across the period.

In the private sector, there was evidence of skill polarization, with a decline in the relative skill position of routine low-skilled employees. In the public services in contrast there was no significant change in skill differentials between these classes. Instead there was evidence of convergence, with rising job skill requirements among public sector semi-routine employees, leading to a measure of class convergence.

It is often assumed that skill level determines other aspects of job quality, in particular employees' involvement in decision-making in the workplace, but in practice the patterns of change were quite distinct. In the public sector, there was no overall change of class differentials with respect to decision-making, despite the rising skill levels of semi-routine employees. In the private sector, although there was polarization of skills, there was convergence in class positions with respect to employee participation. Among routine low-skilled employees there was some relative improvement in involvement in wider organizational consultation. For semi-routine employees there was relative improvement with respect to both individual task discretion and wider organizational participation. However, it is important to note that this did not come about primarily through the processes most frequently evoked by theorists of convergence, namely the spread of employee involvement policies to lower levels of the class structure. Rather, it was principally due to a marked deterioration of the position of those in higher professional and managerial work. In the case of individual task discretion, involvement in decisions declined for those in lower class positions, but the decline was even greater among professionals and managers. With respect to wider organizational participation, there was indeed some improvement in the involvement of both semi-routine and routine low-skilled employees, possibly encouraged by the EU regulations on employee consultation, but the decline in involvement of those in higher class positions made an even greater contribution to convergence.

There was class divergence over the period with respect to work intensity—to the detriment of those in higher class positions. But this was not class polarization in the sense of increasing advantage to those in higher classes. It reflected the fact that, although work intensity increased for all classes, it increased more sharply for those in higher professional and managerial positions than for employees in routine low-skilled work. Moreover, this divergence was only significant in the public services sector. Class differentials with respect to semi-routine work remained unchanged, since work intensity also rose particularly strongly for this category.

Finally, there was class convergence with respect to job insecurity, but again only in the public services sector. This again primarily reflected a particularly sharp increase in job insecurity among managers and professionals in public services.

Despite the stability of class differentials within the workforce as a whole, a closer examination within industry sectors reveals then evidence of both class polarization and class convergence with respect to specific non-financial dimensions of job quality. There was polarization with respect to job skill levels in the private industry sector. In contrast, there was class convergence with regard to involvement in decision-making in the private sector and to job insecurity in the public sector.

But, in the cases of convergence, this was not due primarily to an improvement in the situation of those lower class positions, despite the importance attached in much of the literature to the spread of more inclusive management policies. Rather, it consisted of 'downward class convergence' resulting from managerial policies that led to a deterioration in the non-pay job quality of higher professionals and managers—reduced involvement in decision-making in the private sector, and higher job insecurity in the public services sector. The principal driver of changes in class inequalities in the quality of work over the last two and a half decades has been employer policies towards higher managers and professionals: they markedly improved their relative position with respect to pay, but this was at the cost of a deterioration in the non-financial aspects of the quality of their jobs.

3

Gender Differences in Job Quality

Joanne Lindley

3.1. INTRODUCTION

Research on the job quality gap between men and women has been mainly focused on wages. The gender wage differential has been falling in Britain and this decline has been attributed to changes in the education and labour market participation of women (Harkness, 1996). The differential has been found to be low at the point of labour market entry, but to increase substantially as workers age (Manning and Swaffield, 2008). There is also some evidence of other gender gaps in job quality, notably surrounding work effort, with women often reporting higher levels of required work effort than men (Gorman and Kmec, 2007). These gaps are found in the context of overall work intensification across all British jobs, declines in task discretion, and an asymmetric polarization of the British jobs structure in which high-skilled jobs have expanded the most while middle-ranking jobs have been in relative decline (Gallie et al. 2004; Goos and Manning, 2007; Green, 2006). One principal aim of this chapter is to investigate the differences in job quality in the domains of work effort and task discretion, and how they have changed up to 2012; at the same time, the chapter examines how the gender pay gap over the life course has been evolving.

A key part of the story of job quality differentiation lies in the occupational distribution of men and women, which turns out to be important for explaining some of the changes in job quality. Therefore, the chapter investigates to what extent changes in the occupational distribution of men and women are linked to the process of job polarization. The basic technological explanation for job polarization is that the falling price of information technology has led to the displacement of routine labour (that is, intensive in more easily programmed tasks) by technology capital. As routine tasks tended to be performed in jobs situated in the middle of the pay distribution, economies with access to information technology have witnessed decreasing employment shares in the middle of the earnings distribution. For a survey of this literature see Acemoglu and Autor (2011). Goos and Manning (2007) found simultaneous growth in low-quality ('lousy') and high-quality ('lovely') jobs between 1979 and 1999, with jobs disappearing from the middle of the job quality distribution and the high-quality jobs growing the fastest. Their paper has stimulated much discussion of the 'shrinking middle'. Employment growth at the bottom of the job quality distribution has mainly occurred in the service sector. Examples of such jobs are cleaners, child care workers, hairdressers, and restaurant workers. Given that these service sector jobs are traditionally undertaken by women, the aim here is to investigate to what extent (if any) the occupational distributions of men and women have converged and whether this is associated with gender differences in job polarization.

The next section provides a discussion of why gender differences in job quality are likely to persist. Section 3.3 documents the evolution of gender differences in pay, work intensity, and task discretion over time, but also presents changes in potential underlying drivers, like qualifications and skills, as well as changes in the occupational distribution of men and women. Following this, section 3.4 investigates to what extent changes in these drivers can explain the fall in the gender pay gap and changes in gender differences in work intensity. In section 3.5 we look for evidence of female occupational upgrading, and in section 3.6 we investigate job polarization separately for women and men. The final section concludes.

3.2. WHY MIGHT GENDER DIFFERENCES IN PAY AND JOB QUALITY EXIST?

The fall in the UK gender pay gap has traditionally been attributed to the increase in the educational attainment of women (Harkness, 1996). However, more recent evidence shows that women have caught up with men in terms of their average educational qualifications. For example, Lindley and Machin (2012) reported that the proportion of UK male and female graduates had reached parity by 2011. This might lead us to question whether the fall in the gender pay gap might slow down and eventually stop altogether.

Yet there are other human capital differences between men and women that explain wages and might be more persistent. For example, there is evidence that degree subjects differ between men and women. Machin and Puhani (2003) document gender differences in subject of degree and show that these explain a significant portion of the gender pay gap amongst UK college graduates. In addition, there is evidence that the occupational choices of men and women differ. According to Manning and Swaffield (2008), women were more likely to enter into clerical and secretarial jobs, as well as personal and protective service occupations, and less likely to enter into craft and elementary occupations, relative to men in 1991. These initial occupational differences explain a significant proportion of the gender pay gap. This suggests that gender pay differences might persist as a consequence of women continuing to choose subjects and occupations that lead them into more traditionally female roles. According to the standard human capital model, women will choose subjects and thus occupations that equate the marginal costs and benefits of education. Since women spend less time in the labour market as a consequence of childrearing, their benefits from human capital investments are relatively lower and consequently they will be less likely to invest in high-cost subjects (and thus enter into the highest-paid occupations), on average. For the same reasons, women will also be less attached to the labour market (which implies they will be more likely to accept low-skilled, part-time, and temporary jobs, see Chapters 4 and 5). So as long as women continue to take time out of the labour market for childrearing we can expect some persistence in occupational segregation and consequently the occupational gender pay gap will remain.

In terms of gender differences over the life course, a recent study by Manning and Swaffield (2008) showed that the wages of women grow significantly more slowly than those of men, even after taking into consideration differences in human capital, occupations, and career breaks from childrearing. This differential growth is partially explained by differences in the subsequent acquisition of human capital and labour market experience, as well as job shopping and differences in the psychological determinants of wages. Yet a large proportion still remained unexplained. This suggests that within-occupational gender differences might also persist, even after conditioning on differences in human capital and occupational choices. Such unexplained differences have traditionally been attributed to discrimination, which can arise purely as a statistical artefact based on asymmetric information amongst employers on the future childbearing plans of women, see Phelps (1972).

Of course, there may also be important gender differences in other non-pay aspects of job quality which have changed over time. Differences in the occupational distribution of men and women could again explain differences in job quality, but if female wages grow more slowly than those of men within occupations, then perhaps women are compensated through lower work intensity. Contrariwise, work intensity might be relatively higher for women as a consequence of women having less flexibility in the labour market based on imperfect competition (or monopsony) explanations, see Manning (2005). In fact, research by Gorman and Kmec (2007) supports this hypothesis, since they show that in 1997 and 2001 UK women reported higher levels of working very hard vis-à-vis their male counterparts. Moreover, the gender differences they observed could not be completely explained by differences in job characteristics, family commitments, or individual characteristics, and consequently the authors attribute the residual to employers imposing stricter employment standards on women than they do on men. If these low-quality jobs are also low paid, we might expect the gender work intensity differential to fall over time in the same way as the gender pay differential has fallen.

Finally, changes in the occupational distribution of men and women could partially explain why jobs have polarized into low-quality (lousy) and high-quality (lovely) jobs. Goos and Manning (2007) undertook a counterfactual exercise to demonstrate that changes in the gender and age composition of the UK labour force can only partially explain the growth in lousy jobs between 1979 and 1999, whilst educational upgrading can completely explain the growth in lovely jobs. In this chapter we therefore revisit these issues by focusing more specifically on the role of changes in the occupational differences between men and women.

3.3. GENDER DIFFERENCES IN PAY, WORK INTENSITY, AND HUMAN CAPITAL

In this section we document gender differences in pay and work intensity over time using the Skills Employment Surveys (SES) for workers aged between twenty and sixty. For pay we use hourly earnings, which are inflated to 2012 prices using the Retail Prices Index. Pooling the 1997, 2001, 2006, and 2012 SES provides data on 8,523 men and 8,497 women overall, but this falls to 6,484 and 4,181 workers, respectively, when we restrict the sample to full-time workers with earnings information.[1] We focus on full-time pay in order to avoid making comparisons between men and women part timers, since the former are a very small group and the latter are relatively less attached to the labour market.

To measure gender differences in work intensity three self-reported variables are used. The first captures general work intensity. This is a binary variable equal to one for those who strongly agree that their job requires that they work very hard. The second two capture whether workers' jobs require them to work at high speed or to tight deadlines. Again these are binary variables equal to one for those who reported working under these conditions more than three quarters of the time. To capture task discretion we use the task discretion index as described in the Technical Appendix. The task discretion index is the mean score for four individual task discretion questions capturing how much influence the worker has on deciding (a) how hard he/she works, (b) what tasks he/she performs, (c) how the tasks are carried out, and (d) the quality standards to which he/she works. These each take values between 0 and 3, with 3 indicating the highest level of discretion enjoyed.

---

[1] Sample weights are used throughout the analysis to ensure that the sample is nationally representative according to the standard socioeconomic categories as checked by comparison with the Quarterly Labour Force Survey. See the Technical Appendix.

Table 3.1 shows average gross hourly pay, the proportion of workers reporting high work intensity, and average task discretion by gender over time. We start in 1997 because this allows us to also use the Quality Labour Force Survey (QLFS) for the same period later on, though some of the work intensity variables were only collected from 2001 onwards. The first row shows that the mean gross hourly pay of males was £9.17 in 2012 compared to £8.24 for women, and that this difference is statistically significant at the 5 per cent level. The average change over time for men was only 97p, whilst for women it was £1.40, though the changes were not statistically different for men and women.

Women report lower levels of task discretion than men in 2001 and 2006, although the gender differential is statistically insignificant in 1997 and 2012. Overall, task discretion has fallen over time which supports the findings of Green (2008), though more so for men relative to women, suggesting gender convergence. Again, this could be a consequence of female occupational desegregation since task discretion is higher amongst skilled workers.

More women than men reported working very hard, which supports the findings of Gorman and Kmec (2007), who find the same for 2001. Working at high speed and to tight deadlines are both facets of working hard, yet more women reported working at high speed (42.5 per cent compared to 37.3 for men) and less said they are working to tight deadlines (60.5 for men compared to 54.1 for women) in 2012. By just focusing on working hard, Gorman and Kmec (2007) miss fundamental gender differences in these work intensity measures. In terms of changes over time, the proportions of women reporting that their job requires them to work very hard and work to tight deadlines have both increased over time, though only the increase in working to tight deadlines is significantly greater than that for men.

The gender differences in pay, work intensity, and task discretion observed so far could be a consequence of gender differences in qualifications and skills. Consequently, Table 3.2 compares the highest qualifications and skill use of men and women. Qualifications are measured using highest National Vocational Qualification (NVQ), where Level 4/5 contains graduates. The skill use variables are derived from a whole range of questions asking respondents how important various tasks are in their job. These are combined using factor analysis in Green (2012) to provide a number of skill-use variables, but only numeracy, literacy, problem solving, and professional communication are used here.[2] Again following Green (2012), computer use complexity is also included to look for differences in technological skills.[3]

---

[2] The task questions are based on the question 'how important is each task in performing your job?' The potential answers are 1 'Not at all important', 2 'Not very important', 3 'Fairly important', 4 'Very important', 5 'Essential'. Green (2012) uses thirty-two job tasks to generate eight specific measures of tasks by averaging the scores of the component tasks. Table 3.A1 in the Appendix to this chapter provides detailed descriptions of the task measures used.

[3] Computer use complexity consists of four categories: 'none', 'simple', 'moderate', and 'complex' use. Individuals are asked which of these four measures best describes the use of

Table 3.1. The Evolution of Earnings and Work Intensity by Gender

	Men					Women					
	1997	2001	2006	2012	2012–1997	1997	2001	2006	2012	2012–1997	Difference in the Difference
Mean full-time gross hourly pay^A	8.21	10.02	10.51	9.17	0.967** (0.316)	6.88$^{\$\$}$	7.71$^{\$\$}$	8.80$^{\$\$}$	8.24$^{\$\$}$	1.359** (0.315)	0.391 (0.446)
Proportion who strongly agree that job requires working very hard	38.58	37.04	39.21	41.52	2.939 (2.203)	43.03$^{\$\$}$	41.17$^{\$\$}$	45.24$^{\$\$}$	49.55$^{\$\$}$	6.516** (2.279)	3.578 (3.170)
Mean task discretion index	2.34	2.26	2.27	2.22	-0.111** (0.029)	2.29	2.21$^{\$\$}$	2.21$^{\$\$}$	2.27	-0.018 (0.302)	0.093** (0.042)
Proportion almost all the time Job requires working at very high speed	–	35.38	34.72	37.29	1.914 (1.998)	–	41.98$^{\$\$}$	41.03$^{\$\$}$	42.51$^{\$\$}$	0.524 (1.989)	-1.390 (2.820)
Proportion almost all the time Job requires working to tight deadlines	–	57.71	57.80	60.52	2.811 (2.011)	–	46.07$^{\$\$}$	50.72$^{\$\$}$	54.12$^{\$\$}$	8.044** (1.996)	5.233* (2.833)
N	1274	2187	3699	1363		1149	2052	3711	1585		

Notes: Using the SES for workers aged twenty–sixty. ^{A} sample sizes for full-time workers with earnings are 1,073, 1,878, 2,551, 982 for men and 610, 1,110, 1,671, 790 for women. B sample sizes for full-time workers are 1,239, 2,133, 2,628, 1,283 for men and 1,111, 2,006, 3,663, 1,480 for women. All estimates are weighted using person weights. Standard errors are in parentheses. Where $^{\$\$}$ ($^{\$}$) denotes statistically significant from men at the 5 (10) per cent level, whilst ** (*) denotes statistically significant at the 5 (10) per cent level for changes over time and differences in changes over time.

Table 3.2. Mean Qualifications and Skill Utilization by Gender

	Men					Women					Difference in the Difference
	1997	2001	2006	2012	1997–2012	1997	2001	2006	2012	1997–2012	
Highest qualification level:											
NVQ Level 4/5	28.43	33.99	36.88	42.32	13.89** (2.17)	24.37$$	31.09	38.01	44.00	19.63** (2.13)	5.74* (3.04)
NVQ Level 3	20.59	27.18	26.07	24.14	3.54* (1.87)	15.00$$	18.95$$	20.98$$	20.57$$	5.56** (1.75)	2.02 (1.26)
NVQ Level 2	25.43	16.88	15.65	16.24	−9.19** (1.80)	32.91$$	26.91$$	23.33$$	22.09$$	−10.82** (1.99)	−1.63 (2.69)
NVQ Level 1	8.59	9.88	10.48	11.20	2.61* (1.40)	8.13	8.91	8.91$	8.01$$	−0.12 (1.32)	−2.74 (1.92)
No qualifications	16.96	12.06	10.92	6.11	−10.85** (1.38)	19.59	14.15$	8.77$$	5.34	−14.25** (1.41)	−3.40* (1.98)
Skill utilization:											
Numeracy	1.98	2.13	2.10	2.16	0.172** (0.059)	1.58$$	1.68$$	1.74$$	1.79$$	0.207** (0.059)	0.035 (0.083)
Literacy	2.41	2.54	2.59	2.53	0.118** (0.051)	2.36	2.48	2.64	2.67$$	0.310** (0.055)	0.193** (0.075)
Problem solving	2.87	2.96	2.97	2.91	0.045 (0.045)	2.57$$	2.63$$	2.71$$	2.64$$	0.063 (0.048)	0.018 (0.066)
Professional Communication	2.12	2.19	2.26	2.30	0.186** (0.043)	1.99$$	2.11$$	2.28	2.30	0.305** (0.045)	0.119* (0.062)
Computer use complexity	1.39	1.63	1.73	1.85	0.448** (0.056)	1.23$$	1.43$$	1.59$$	1.69$$	0.462** (0.047)	0.014 (0.073)
N	1274	2187	3699	1363		1149	2052	3711	1585		

Notes: Using the SES for workers aged twenty–sixty. All estimates are weighted using person weights. Standard errors are in parentheses. Where $$ ($) denotes statistically significant from men at the 5 (10) per cent level, whilst ** (*) denotes statistically significant at the 5 (10) per cent level for changes over time and differences in changes over time.

Overall, Table 3.2 shows that the education levels of men and women have increased differentially over time to the extent that the gender gap in the proportion of graduates has completely closed. Across the rest of the educational distribution, the proportion of NVQ Level 2 workers is higher for women, whilst the proportion of women with NVQ Level 1 or less is lower than for men. Thus, there are more men at the bottom of the educational distribution and no more of them at the top. These findings support those of Lindley and Machin (2012), who find similar patterns using the QLFS over a similar time period. In terms of skills used in the job, men report higher levels of numeracy, problem solving, and computer use complexity, with the gaps remaining fairly constant over time. Women have higher levels of literacy use (but only since 2012) and in 2012 there was no gender difference in professional communication skills. So despite the worsening position of men in terms of their relative educational attainment, men still reported using higher levels of numeracy, problem solving, and computer use complexity in their jobs in 2012.

These task differences suggest that there remains a significant difference in the jobs that men and women do. To examine this question Table 3.3 compares the one-digit occupational distribution by gender using the 1997 and 2012 SES. Overall this shows that although the occupational distribution of men and women differs, women have upgraded their occupations over time. Men are more likely to be managers and senior officials or employed in skilled trades or process, plant, and machine jobs. Women are more likely to be in administrative and secretarial, personal services, and sales and customer service jobs. The proportion of women in elementary occupations has fallen by 4.3 per cent and this is statistically different from that of men by 6.1 per cent. Also, the proportion of women in professional occupations has incresed by 2.9 per cent, compared to a fall of 0.5 per cent for men, which is statistically larger by 3.4 per cent. This suggests that there might be gender differences in job polarization patterns, given that previous research shows that job growth has mainly occurred in the low-paid service sector and for high-paid managers and professionals, see Goos and Manning (2007).

3.4. EXPLAINING GENDER DIFFERENCES IN PAY AND WORK INTENSITY

In this section we estimate regression equations to explain the gender differentials observed for 2012 in Table 3.1. These are for log hourly wages, working very

---

computers or computerized equipment in their jobs. Simple computer use consists of straightforward use (e.g. printing out an invoice in a shop), whereas moderate computer use is, for example, word processing/spreadsheets or email. Complex computer use involves analysis or design, statistical analysis, and programming.

Joanne Lindley

Table 3.3. Gender Differences in the Occupational Distribution of Workers

	Men			Women			
	1997	2012	Change	1997	2012	Change	Diff-in-diff
One-digit SOC:							
Managers and senior officials	17.06	19.79	2.731 (1.758)	9.68$^{\$\$}$	12.58$^{\$\$}$	2.903* (1.580)	0.173 (2.363)
Professional occupations	13.61	13.14	−0.462 (1.549)	10.50$^{\$\$}$	13.45	2.951** (1.481)	3.413 (2.143)
Associate prof and technical	12.08	16.04	3.956* (1.564)	11.56	18.91$^{\$}$	7.346** (1.598)	3.390 (2.235)
Adminstrative and secretarial	7.79	4.85	−2.933* (1.112)	20.65$^{\$\$}$	14.79$^{\$\$}$	−5.863** (1.703)	−2.929 (2.034)
Skilled trades	21.45	18.55	−2.895 (1.771)	2.81$^{\$\$}$	2.30$^{\$\$}$	−0.508 (0.655)	2.387 (1.887)
Personal service occupations	1.77	2.25	0.485 (0.569)	10.46$^{\$\$}$	14.45$^{\$\$}$	3.989** (1.382)	3.505** (1.505)
Sales and customer service	3.38	3.87	0.489 (0.978)	14.01$^{\$\$}$	9.99$^{\$\$}$	−4.103** (1.498)	−4.502** (1.789)
Process, plant, and machine	14.26	11.13	−3.123* (1.430)	4.49$^{\$\$}$	2.01$^{\$\$}$	−2.482** (0.853)	0.641 (1.665)
Elementary occupations	8.62	10.37	1.754 (1.420)	15.84$^{\$\$}$	11.52	−4.323** (1.618)	−6.077** (2.153)
N	1274	1363		1149	1585		

Notes: Using the SES for workers aged twenty–sixty. All estimates are weighted using person weights. Standard errors are in parentheses. Where $^{\$\$}$ ($^{\$}$) denotes statistically significant from men at the 5 (10) per cent level, whilst ** (*) denotes statistically significant at the 5 (10) per cent level for changes over time and differences in changes over time.

hard, task direction, working at very high speed, and working to tight deadlines. We start with the raw differentials and then sequentially include the potential determinants discussed in Tables 3.2 and 3.3, as well as the respondents' age. We start by controlling for age and highest educational qualifications, we then add skill use intensity, and finally we additionally control for three-digit occupation.

The top three rows in Table 3.4 are observed between 1997 and 2012, whilst the bottom two are observed only between 2001 and 2012. The first and second columns in Table 3.4 show that female pay was 0.075 log points (7.8 per cent) lower than male pay on average in 2012 compared to 0.165 log points (17.9 per cent) lower in 1997.[4] So that's a fall of 10 per cent, which is statistically significant. For work intensity, the proportion of women reporting working very hard and at very high speed was 8 and 4.5 per cent higher, respectively, than for men in 2012. The proportion of women reporting

---

[4] Since wages are in natural logs percentages are calculated from $e^{0.165} - 1 = 0.179$ for 1997 and $e^{0.075} - 1 = 0.078$ for 2012.

Table 3.4. Gender Differentials for Earnings and Work Intensity, 1997–2001 and 2012

	Raw differential		Controlling for age and HNVQ		Controlling for age, HNVQ, and skill utilization		Controlling for age, HNVQ, skill utilization and three-digit occupation		
	1997	2012	1997	2012	1997	2012	1997	2012	2012–1997
Full-time log gross hourly pay	−0.165** (0.027)	−0.075** (0. 029)	−0.157** (0.023)	−0.107** (0.026)	−0.174** (0.021)	−0.103** (0.025)	−0.138** (0.025)	−0.072** (0.026)	0.066* (0.036)
Working very hard	0.045** (0.022)	0.080** (0.023)	0.051** (0.022)	0.078** (0.023)	0.060** (0.022)	0.083** (0.023)	0.071** (0.027)	0.052** (0.026)	−0.019 (0.037)
Task discretion	−0.047 (0.030)	0.045 (0.030)	−0.035 (0.030)	0.035 (0.030)	0.010 (0.030)	0.075** (0.031)	0.021 (0.036)	0.100** (0.035)	0.079 (0.050)
	2001	2012	2001	2012	2001	2012	2001	2012	2012–2001
Working at very high speed	0.066** (0.017)	0.052** (0.023)	0.066** (0.017)	0.059** (0.022)	0.087** (0.017)	0.075** (0.024)	0.068** (0.021)	0.071** (0.028)	0.003 (0.035)
Working to tight deadlines	−0.116** (0.017)	−0.064** (0.023)	−0.112** (0.017)	−0.065** (0.023)	−0.076** (0.017)	−0.045* (0.023)	−0.023 (0.021)	0.013 (0.027)	0.035 (0.033)

Notes: Using the SES for workers aged twenty–sixty. All estimates are weighted using person weights. Wages are measured in natural logs, so the coefficients refer to log point changes. Standard errors in parentheses, where **(*) denotes statistically significant from men at the 5 (10) per cent level. Conditioning on eight age dummies, four HNVQ dummies, three skill use variables (numeracy, literacy, professional communication, and problem solving), computer use complexity, and three-digit occupation.

working to tight deadlines was 6.4 per cent lower than for men in 2012. The raw gender differential for task discretion is statistically insignificant.

The third and fourth columns in Table 3.4 show that controlling for highest qualification makes little difference to most of the raw gender differentials we observe, with hourly pay in 2012 being the exception. Controlling for highest NVQ increases the gender pay differential in 2012 from 0.075 to 0.107 log points, which suggests that gender differences in age and qualifications were working in favour of men rather than women, although the differential falls back to 0.72 once we condition on occupation in the final column.

Additionally, controlling for skill utilization (in column 6) reduces the 2012 conditional gender differential for hourly pay, working long hours, and working to tight deadlines. These are all outcomes where the gender differential is negative (since women earn less than men and also report lower levels of work intensity). In contrast, controlling for skill use increases the 2012 gender differential for working very hard and working at high speed (where women report higher levels of work intensity). The task discretion differential is also now statistically significant, suggesting that women have more discretion over their tasks than similarly educated and skilled men.

The penultimate column shows that the 'within' occupation gender pay differential is 0.072 log points. Therefore the 'between' occupation is 0.031 log points (3.1 per cent).[5] This implies that roughly 31 per cent of the 2012 conditional gender pay differential (0.031 of the 0.103) can be explained by differences in occupations. All of the working to tight deadlines gender differential is 'between' occupations. Conversely, the gender differential for working at high speed and for task discretion remains largely unchanged after controlling for occupations, which suggests that when more women report working at high speed (or report higher levels of task discretion) it is mainly within occupations. However, when more men report working to tight deadlines it is mainly between occupations. Controlling for one-digit industry makes little difference to these results. The working very hard gender differential is also largely within occupations. In terms of changes over time in the within-occupation job quality gaps, only the pay gap has closed over the period. The within-occupational gender differences in work intensity appear entrenched since they remained constant over time.

3.5. GENDER DIFFERENCES IN WITHIN-OCCUPATIONAL PAY AND WORK INTENSITY OVER THE LIFE COURSE

Table 3.4 showed that 70 per cent of the gender pay differential remained after conditioning on occupations in 2012. Moreover, when women report higher

---

[5] Since 0.103 − 0.072 = 0.031.

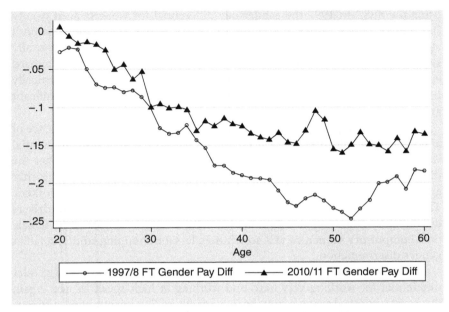

Figure 3.1. The Conditional Gender Log Hourly Pay Differential by Age, 1997–1998 and 2010–2011

Notes: Using the QLFS 1997–1998 and 2010–2011 for full-time workers aged between twenty and sixty.

work intensity (through the requirement to work very hard or at high speed) this is also largely within occupations. We therefore investigate the evolution within occupations over the life course of the gender pay gap and the gender differential for working hard and at high speed. Manning and Swaffield (2008) used panel data to explain changes in the gender pay gap in early career. They found no evidence of a gender pay gap at the point of labour market entry and attributed the gap to differential growth (they find this to be around 25 per cent after ten years). We therefore look for similar earnings and work-intensity patterns across different age cohorts.

Figure 3.1 plots the conditional gender pay gap by age using the 1997–1998 and 2010–2011 QLFS for a sample of full-time workers aged between twenty and sixty. The gender pay gap here conditions on highest qualifications and three-digit occupation. The data in Figure 3.1 are smoothed using a moving average filter and overall show differential growth which is much flatter after around age thirty-five for the more recent data. The unsmoothed conditional gender pay differential (standard error) across all workers is −0.17 (0.004) in 1997 and −0.12 (0.006) in 2010; these estimates are slightly larger than those found using the SES.[6] In 1997 the gender pay differential for workers aged twenty (born in 1977) is statistically insignificant at −0.05 (0.034). It remains so until age twenty-three, when the differential (standard error) becomes statistically significant at −0.06 (0.019). In 2010 the gender pay differential (standard error) for workers aged twenty (born in 1990) is positive but also statistically insignificant at 0.10 (0.087), and becomes negative and statistically significant at age twenty-seven when it is −0.07 (0.032).

Clearly this supports Manning and Swaffield's findings with no evidence of a significant gender pay gap on labour market entry, but with differential wage growth for men and women. However, we also demonstrate that the differential has fallen over time. In 2010–2011 the gap stopped growing after age thirty-five, whereas in 1997–1998 it continued to grow for older workers. This of course could be a consequence of changes in any of the drivers discussed by Manning and Swaffield (2008), including increases in female post-compulsory human capital acquisition, less job shopping, and/or a fall in gender discrimination.[7]

In Figure 3.2 we pool the 1997–2012 SES to plot the conditional gender differential for working very hard and working at high speed by age. Again these are smoothed using a moving average filter. The unsmoothed differentials (standard errors) across the full sample are 0.08 (0.012) and 0.07 (0.011), respectively. The prima-facie evidence from Figure 3.2 indicates that the gender work intensity gap is fairly similar, regardless of whether working very hard or working at high speed are used, with some evidence of long-term differential growth. However, the unsmoothed gender gap (standard error) at age twenty is 0.12 (0.080) for working very hard, which is statistically significant, whereas the gender gap (standard error) for working at high speed is 0.08 (0.071), which does not become statistically significant until age thirty-three when it is 0.17 (0.071). So, like the gender pay gap there is no evidence of a gender differential at the point of labour market entry for working at high speed, but this is not the case for working very hard which is consistently higher for women relative to men across all ages. Again, this differential growth in both pay and job quality (as measured by working at high speed) is indicative of greater labour market inflexibility from family-related commitments and childbearing.

So far Table 3.4 has shown us that 70 per cent of the 0.10 log points (10 per cent) gender pay differential in 2012 was within occupations, although in Figure 3.1 we saw that this is mainly a consequence of differential wage

---

[6] Conditioning on highest qualifications and three-digit occupation (but not skill use) provides a gender pay differential (standard error) of −0.15 (0.026) and −0.08 (0.027) using the 1997 and 2012 skills surveys.

[7] In the absence of panel data that would provide sufficient sample sizes, we cannot further investigate the potential drivers of this differential wage growth here.

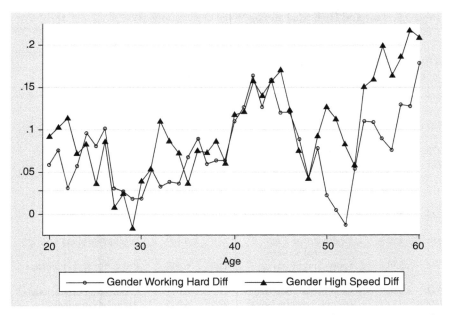

Figure 3.2. The Conditional Gender Differential for Proportions of Jobs Requiring Working Hard and at High Speed, by Age, 1997–2012

Notes: Using the SES 1997–2012 for workers aged between twenty and sixty.

growth. But Table 3.4 also showed that 30 per cent of this gender pay gap can be explained by differences in occupations, whilst Table 3.3 showed occupational desegregation for women. Therefore, in the next section we look for evidence of female occupational upgrading.

3.6. GENDER DIFFERENCES IN JOB POLARIZATION

The focus of this section now returns to the gender differences in occupations that were observed in Table 3.3. Here we investigate the extent to which jobs have polarized differently for men and women. If women have upgraded their occupations whilst men have downgraded theirs, then we might expect the increase in employment at the top of the job quality distribution to only be for women and the increase at the bottom (in low-wage service jobs) to only be for men. Following the existing literature on job polarization, the approach is to rank occupations in terms of their job quality in 1997 and then investigate whether the highest- and lowest-quality jobs have grown differently for men and women. We therefore use the QLFS to rank seventy-one three-digit occupations in terms of their median wage in 1997.

Table 3.5. Low and High Median Log Wage Occupations, 1997

SOC code	Median log wage	Bottom quintile (lowest pay)	SOC code	Median log wage	Top quintile (highest pay)
922	4.174	Elementary personal services	221	6.273	Health professionals
923	4.234	Elementary cleaning	351	6.230	Transport associate professionals
925	4.256	Elementary sales	113	6.184	Functional managers
711	4.344	Sales assistants and retail cashiers	111/2	6.136	Corporate/production managers
612	4.357	Childcare and rel personal services	213	6.136	ICT professionals
622	4.443	Hairdressers and related	242	6.136	Business and stat professionals
611	4.913	Healthcare and rel personal services	241	6.109	Legal professionals
344	5.011	Sports and fitness occupations	117	6.047	Protective service officers
543	5.075	Food preparation trades	212	6.047	Engineering professionals
623/9	5.112	Housekeeping/personal services	243	6.045	Architects, planners/ surveyors
613	5.147	Animal care services	211	6.035	Science professionals
414/5	5.153	Admin occupations (coms and general)	231	6.016	Teaching professionals
913	5.153	Elementary process plant occupations	331	6.001	Protective service occupations
911	5.193	Elementary agricultural occupations			
421	5.220	Secretarial and related occupations			

Notes: Using the 1997 QLFS for seventy-one consistently defined three-digit occupations.

The top and bottom 20 per cent paid occupations in 1997 are presented in Table 3.5. These support the findings of Goos and Manning (2007), since the highest-paid (lovely) jobs were mainly professionals and managers, whilst the lowest-paid (lousy) jobs were mainly low-paid service jobs. In order to look for evidence of job polarization that differs by gender we use worker level data from the 1997 and 2010 QLFS to compare subsequent changes in employment shares.[8] Table 3.6 shows that for men there is clear evidence of job polariza-

---

[8] We use the QLFS 1997 to 2010 because the standard occupational codes switch from SOC2000 to SOC2007 in the first quarter of 2011. Given that occupations are coded according to SOC90 between 1997 and 2001, we concord the SOC90 to SOC2000 in our 1997–2001 data but to also concord to SOC2007 would significantly reduce the number of occupations.

Table 3.6. Changes in the Highest- and Lowest-Paid Occupations by Gender

	Men			Women			
	1997	2010	Change	1997	2010	Change	Diff-in-diff
Top-paid 20th	26.31	28.59	2.281**	14.26$	19.28$	5.019**	2.738**
percentile in 1997			(0.204)			(0.177)	(0.167)
Middle-paid 60th	63.00	58.29	−4.714**	39.91$	40.40$	0.488**	5.202**
percentile in 1997			(0.223)			(0.230)	(0.321)
Lowest-paid 20th	10.69	13.12	2.432**	45.84$	40.33$	−5.507**	−7.939**
percentile in 1997			(0.152)			(0.232)	(0.277)
N	121,639	86,290		108,103	83,563		

Notes: Using the QLFS for workers aged twenty–sixty. All estimates are weighted using person weights. Where $ denotes statistically significant from men at the 5 per cent level. Standard errors are in parentheses where ** (*) denotes statistically significant at the 5(10) per cent level.

tion.[9] The proportion of men in the top quintile (in the lovely jobs) in 1997 was 26.3 per cent and this increased to 28.6 per cent in 2010, whilst the proportion of men in the lowest quintile (the lousy jobs) grew from 10.7 per cent to 13.1 per cent. For women, there is much larger job growth in the highest-paid jobs since the proportion significantly increases by 5 per cent (from 14.3 to 19.3 per cent) but the proportion of women in the lowest-paid jobs fell significantly by 5.5 per cent, which suggests occupational upgrading. One important observation is that women were over-represented in the low-paid jobs compared to men (45.8 per cent of women compared to only 10.7 per cent of men) in 1997, whilst there were relatively more men in the highest-paid jobs than women (26.3 per cent of men compared to 14.3 per cent of women).

To look more closely at occupational segregation by gender as well as changes over time, we use the SES self-reported question 'what is the ratio of men or women doing your kind of work in your workplace?' Table 3.7 disaggregates workers and their responses to this question according to whether their occupation was in the top or bottom quintile of the occupational pay distribution in 1997, or in the middle three quintiles. The upper panel shows that in 1997 36.4 per cent of workers in the highest paid jobs reported their jobs were mainly being done by men, with 32.9 per cent of workers reporting a fairly equal gender mix. The final column shows that for this

---

[9] In Table 3.A2 in the Appendix to this chapter we do not find that jobs have polarized in the traditional sense of the word since employment shares have increased for the top quintile of paid jobs by 3.42 per cent, but employment in the middle and bottom quintile paid jobs have both fallen by 2.547 and 0.876 per cent, respectively. However, the fall at the bottom (0.876) is less than that in the middle (2.547), which suggests a U shape. Also, the approach used here does not take into account that some occupations were smaller in 1997 and thus had the capacity to grow by more. We have weighted our estimates here by individual person weights and not using weights for occupational size.

Table 3.7. Changes in Gender Segregation for the Highest- and Lowest-Paid Jobs, 1997–2012

	1997	2001	2006	2012	2012–1997
Top-paid 20th percentile in 1997					
Exclusively by men	17.17	20.07	10.94	10.08	−7.09** (2.12)
Mainly by men	36.35	29.21	26.70	25.45	−10.90** (2.88)
A fairly equal mix	32.86	31.10	37.93	43.13	10.27** (3.07)
Mainly women	12.06	13.59	20.15	17.48	5.42** (2.27)
Exclusively by women	1.57	6.03	4.28	3.86	2.29** (1.06)
N	454	955	1572	595	
Middle-paid 60th percentile in 1997					
Exclusively by men	26.13	28.10	23.65	22.18	−3.95** (1.61)
Mainly by men	28.34	22.66	24.01	25.37	−2.97* (1.67)
A fairly equal mix	26.25	24.46	29.72	30.70	4.45** (1.71)
Mainly women	14.00	16.74	16.11	15.85	1.86 (1.35)
Exclusively by women	5.28	8.05	5.51	5.90	0.62 (0.87)
N	1283	2134	3749	1540	
Lowest-paid 20th percentile in 1997					
Exclusively by men	5.50	7.03	5.82	5.50	0
Mainly by men	8.53	9.15	9.67	9.53	0.99 (1.48)
A fairly equal mix	26.54	26.18	31.21	42.23	15.68** (2.42)
Mainly women	42.50	33.99	37.05	28.19	−14.31** (2.43)
Exclusively by women	16.93	23.65	16.25	14.56	−2.37** (1.87)
N	706	1150	2089	813	

Notes: Using the SES for workers aged twenty–sixty. All estimates are weighted using person weights. ** (*) denotes statistically significant at the 5 (10) per cent level.

group of workers there has been substantial gender convergence, with 43.1 per cent reporting a fairly equal gender mix in 2012, providing an increase of 10.3 per cent. At the bottom end of the job quality distribution, the increase in the proportion of workers reporting a fairly equal gender mix was even higher at 15.7 per cent. These jobs are mainly being done by women but again there is clear evidence of gender convergence. What is different from the lovely jobs is that there was a fall in the proportion of jobs undertaken mainly by women (14.3) and a rise in those being done by both men and women (15.7). But there has been no change in the proportion mainly undertaken by men. In the middle-ranked jobs the increase in the jobs with a fairly equal mix of men and women has increased by much less (4.5 per cent) and there has been a fall in the number of workers reporting their jobs are mainly and exclusively undertaken by men (−3 and −4), whilst there is no change in the proportion mainly or exclusively undertaken by women.

Overall, the results in this section support those found by Goos and Manning (2007) since the increase in lovely jobs has largely been for women. However, this section also importantly demonstrates that men have increased their share of employment in low-paid jobs that were undertaken both by men and women and lost their exclusively male jobs from the top and middle of the pay distribution. Conversely, women have gained from occupational upgrading because the share of mixed gender jobs has increased at the top of the pay distribution but also the share of female-dominated jobs has increased as well, whilst the share of low-paid jobs done by women has at the same time fallen. In short, women have gained from occupational upgrading, whilst men have lost out from job polarization. Women still lose out from slower unexplained average wage growth within occupations, but this disadvantage has also fallen over time.

3.7. CONCLUSION

In line with the expectation that, with slowly declining gender discrimination, the job quality gap between men and women could be expected to narrow over time, the relative economic situation of British working women has indeed been improving over time. The gender pay gap has fallen from 14.8 per cent in 1997 to 7.5 per cent in 2012, after conditioning on age, highest qualifications, skill use, and differences explained by occupations.[10] Contrariwise, the non-pay gender gaps in inequality are more entrenched and do not appear to significantly change over time. Looking over the life course, as in 1997, there was no evidence of a conditional gender pay gap at age twenty in 2010. The pay gap emerges and expands in the first decade or so as a consequence of differential pay growth, but unlike in 1997 the gap in 2010 levels off after age thirty-five.

Overall, there were no significant gender differences in task discretion in 1997 or 2012 but within skill utilization groups and occupations, women reported higher levels of task discretion in 2012. The estimate of the change over time was positive but not statistically significant. Similarly for work intensity, as measured by two indicators, the requirement to work hard, and to work at high speed, there is little evidence of gender convergence. For both these measures, women continue to experience greater work intensity. Nevertheless, it has to be cautioned that the work effort measures are not unanimous in finding harder work for women: in respect of working to tight deadlines, another commonly used indicator of work effort, men are found to have higher work intensity than women, and continued to do so throughout our period.

---

[10] This is calculated from $e^{0.138} - 1 = 0.148$ for 1997 and $e^{0.072} - 1 = 0.075$ for 2012 from Table 3.4.

In accounting for these job-quality gaps in pay and work intensity, occupations and occupational segregation appears to matter. Women have improved their employment levels in higher-paid professional jobs and reduced their employment in low-paid service sector jobs. These changes are associated with occupational upgrading between 1997 and 2012. Across the spectrum of jobs, there has been a rise in the share of jobs that are seen as equally for men or women. In the top quintile of the pay spectrum, the proportion of jobs done exclusively by men has declined. Meanwhile, in the bottom quintile the share of jobs done exclusively by women has fallen. Men have thus lost out from female occupational upgrading since men have increased their share of employment in low-paid jobs. When it comes to job polarization, then, since 1997 this has indeed been the reality for men: the middle-quality jobs have continued to decline, while both top jobs and low-quality jobs have expanded. For women, however, the changing employment structure has favoured the expansion of high-skilled jobs exclusively.

APPENDIX

Table 3.A1. The Composition of the Specific Task Measures from the SES

Task	Variables and description from the UK Skills Surveys
Literacy:	Reading written information, e.g. forms, notices, or signs
	Reading short documents, e.g. letters or memos
	Reading long documents, e.g. long reports, manuals, etc.
	Writing material such as forms, notices, or signs
	Writing short documents, e.g. letters or memos
	Writing long documents with correct spelling/grammar
Numeracy:	Adding, subtracting, multiplying, or dividing numbers
	Calculations using decimals, percentages, or fractions
	More advanced mathematical or statistical procedures
Professional communication:	Instructing, training, or teaching people
	Persuading or influencing others
	Making speeches or presentations
	Planning the activities of others
	Listening carefully to colleagues
Problem solving:	Spotting problems or faults
	Working out the cause of problems or faults
	Thinking of solutions to problems
	Analysing complex problems in depth
Computer use complexity:	Importance of computer use and complexity of computer use:
	Not at all = 0
	Straightforward use = 1
	Moderate use = 2
	Complex use = 3
	Advanced use = 4

Notes: Based on the factor analysis conducted in Green (2012).

Table 3.A2. Job Polarization: Employment Changes in the Highest- and Lowest-Paid Occupations

	1997	2010	Change
Top-paid 20th percentile in 1997	20.79	24.21	3.423** (0.138)
Middle-paid 60th percentile in 1997	52.43	49.89	−2.547** (0.164)
Lowest-paid 20th percentile in 1997	26.78	25.90	−0.876** (0.144)
N	229,742	169,853	

Notes: Using the QLFS for workers aged twenty–sixty. All estimates are weighted using person weights. Standard errors are in parentheses. Where ** (*) denotes statistically significant at the 5 (10) per cent level.

4

The Quality of Part-Time Work

Tracey Warren and Clare Lyonette

4.1. INTRODUCTION

In this chapter, we explore trends over time in the quality of part-time (PT) jobs in comparison with full-time (FT) jobs in Britain. PT working is a key feature of the everyday working lives of millions of workers in Britain, but extensive research has shown that PT jobs in Britain are of substantially lower quality than FT ones. PT workers are more heavily concentrated in less-skilled occupations that provide them with poorer working conditions than their FT counterparts. In this chapter we interrogate this dominant familiar depiction of the quality of PT work in Britain by assessing changes over time. We ask whether there was a reduction, expansion, or stability in the PT/FT gap in job quality up to 2012, with a particular focus on the impact of the economic crisis which began in 2008–2009.

For many decades, PT work in Britain has been criticized for its low quality. It has been associated with poorer access to development opportunities than FT work (e.g. Connolly and Gregory, 2008a), leading to lower career advancement in the longer term (Hoque and Kirkpatrick, 2003). PT work has also been consistently shown to pay less than similar FT work (Connolly and Gregory, 2008b; Warren, 2003). In spite of these inequalities between FT and PT jobs, working PT is a common strategy used by many women across Britain. Women with caring responsibilities have dominated the PT labour market for half a century and, since 1986, a constant substantial minority of women workers (around 40 per cent) have worked PT, with higher figures for women with dependent children (Figure 4.1a). There has been growth over time in the proportions of men working PT, from 2 per cent to 9 per cent of male workers between 1986 and 2012, but women still accounted for the majority (79 per cent) of the PT workforce in 2012 (Figure 4.1b).

Dominant theoretical explanations for this heavy concentration of women in PT jobs were traditionally split into two broad camps: one emphasizing

a. Level of part-time 1 working amongst workers

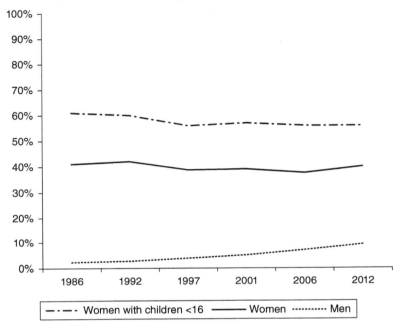

b. Proportion of workers who are

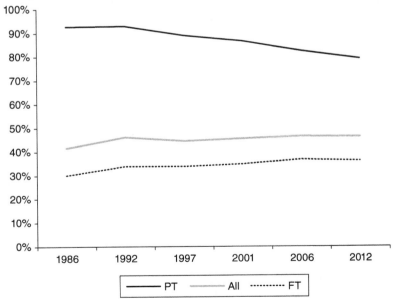

Figure 4.1. Part-Time Working

Notes: PT = <30 hours a week.

Source: SES

supply and the other the demand forces that shape the labour market. Theories stressing supply factors have included the neo-classical human capital-based explanations of Mincer and Polacheck (1974), for example, the 'new home economics' of Becker (1985), and the 'preference theory' of Hakim (2000). All have been discredited for their fundamental assumption that PT employment for women is a natural development and/or a free and rational choice, with counterarguments that structural constraints have a greater impact on women's decisions to work PT (e.g. Beechey and Perkins, 1987; Ginn et al., 1996; McRae, 2003; Procter and Padfield, 1999). Demand theories of PT employment focus instead on who creates PT jobs and why, and this 'why' element altered over time as the economy changed from boom to recession. So whilst an early demand-based explanation lay in employers' attempts to fill labour gaps in times of post-war economic expansion (Beechey and Perkins, 1987), times of economic crisis led to a theoretical focus on PT employment as providing a cheaper, more efficient workforce in processes of economic restructuring. Theorists thus stressed the role that PT work can play in increasing workplace flexibility: in employer initiatives to extend opening hours and to utilize cheaper and more readily replaceable employees (Applebaum, 1992; Atkinson, 1987).

We have returned to this older and rather simplified split between supply vs. demand theories of PT employment here because those early supply accounts assumed that, in a rational labour market, PT jobs differed from FT jobs only in their hours (Tam, 1997). In contrast, demand-led theories began to see PT and FT jobs as potentially occupying qualitatively different labour market positions, with PT jobs being of much lower quality than FT. The demand-based explanations of PT employment were influenced by such writers as Doeringer and Piore (1971) and Barron and Norris (1976) and their elaboration of theories of 'primary' and 'secondary' labour markets. A primary labour market sector is characterized by high wages, job security, unionized firms, and good promotional prospects whilst a secondary sector has low wages, reduced job opportunities, and low security. The two labour markets were seen to be so separate that movement from the secondary to the primary market was difficult, if not impossible. Atkinson (1987) later proposed 'core' and 'peripheral' labour markets, the former dominated by FT employees on a career track and the periphery by part timers and those on short-term contracts. Women workers, and female part timers in particular, were seen to be over-concentrated, and even trapped, in the secondary and peripheral markets.

These early labour market theories were very influential in explaining the expansion of PT employment, but they have been criticized (Pollert, 1991). A key limitation is that they approached the PT workforce as a homogenous group, disregarding variation amongst part timers by sex or by hours worked. Their usefulness in explaining the female dominance of PT employment is a well-recognized problem, with influential writers pointing to the fact that the theorists took the sexual division of labour as given, assuming women were more suited to working PT than men (Beechey, 1978). Variation in job quality within the PT category was also a key omission: a far more complex picture emerges when the PT/FT dichotomy is disaggregated (Fagan and Rubery, 1996; Warren and Walters, 1998).

An important factor generally thought to underlie women's dominance of the PT labour market is their caring responsibilities. Women with such commitments are more likely than other women (and men) to work PT in Britain, and this picture has remained constant over many years. The more children a female employee has, the more likely she is to work PT, rather than FT (Lyonette et al., 2010). Although childcare costs have been subsidized for working parents on lower incomes since the late 1990s, when the New Labour government introduced a range of measures to reduce child poverty by enabling low-income mothers to go out to work, UK families still spend more on childcare than any other Organisation for Economic Co-operation and Development (OECD) country (OECD, 2010). Unable to cover the expense of full-time formal care, lower-paid women with pre-school children have been forced to rely heavily upon grandparents and other relatives to provide informal childcare while they work PT hours to contribute to the household income (Crompton and Lyonette, 2010; Warren et al., 2010).

Women in higher occupational groups have been more likely to work FT, however. For example, research using Labour Force Survey data from 2008 demonstrated that 60 per cent of mothers working PT were employed in only four occupational areas: 'elementary administration and service', 'sales and customer service', 'caring personal service', and 'administrative' jobs (Durbin and Tomlinson, 2010; Tomlinson et al., 2009). At the same time, only 3 per cent of mothers working PT were corporate managers (Tomlinson et al., 2009). Indeed, the majority of women working PT in more senior roles had managed to negotiate a reduction in hours after working FT, rather than being hired as a PT employee (Tilly, 1996; Tomlinson, 2006). The lack of 'good' PT jobs available has meant that many professional women in demanding FT jobs end up crowding into lower-level PT jobs after having children (Grant et al., 2005), working below their skills and capabilities (Darton and Hurrell, 2005; Women and Work Commission, 2006). These low-quality PT jobs can then 'trap' the women who take them into long-term inferior labour market positions with serious ramifications for lifetime earnings and economic well-being (Connolly and Gregory, 2008a; Warren, 2001, 2004, 2008).

The above depiction of PT work in Britain is a very familiar one, emerging from large-scale surveys and in-depth studies across multiple disciplines over many years (e.g. Burchell et al., 1997; Gallie et al., 1998, 2004; Walters, 2005). Here we add to the body of research on the quality of PT jobs by responding to the criticisms of early labour market theorists who treated PT workers as a homogeneous group. Accordingly, we examine not only the differences in quality between FT and PT jobs, but also explore the differences in quality between part timers who work shorter and longer hours.

There have been more recent developments that may have led to the improvement of part-time work. For example, pressures from Europe have been leading to significant changes to regulations protecting PT workers' rights in the workplace, such as the Part-Time Workers (Prevention of Less Favourable Treatment) Regulations in 2000. In addition, the Labour government under Tony Blair pushed further forward with policies to create more and better PT posts as part of European-wide gender equality campaigns (e.g. Department for Communities and Local Government, 2006). Due to long-term problems with recruitment and retention in certain sectors and occupations, and the need for greater diversity within workforces, there has been some optimism from researchers that recognition by employers of a business case for increasing flexible working arrangements would lead to more 'quality' PT jobs (e.g. Edwards and Robinson, 2004).

As a result of more family-friendly working arrangements, it was hypothesized that employees would reciprocate with greater commitment and loyalty (Cegarra-Leiva et al., 2012). Moreover, institutional theory suggests that organizations also adapt to societal values, responding to pressures to maintain their legitimacy (DiMaggio and Powell, 1983). For example, in certain sectors and in particular occupations, such as accountancy, companies have been increasingly promoting themselves as family-friendly in order to attract and retain good employees (Cooper et al., 2001) and also to appeal to clients. Research undertaken by PricewaterhouseCoopers found that work–life balance, rather than income, was the main factor in choice of employer for almost half of new graduates worldwide (cited in Edwards and Wajcman, 2005). Taking all of these factors into account, one may assume that the gap between the quality of FT and PT jobs was likely to decrease. Indeed, before the onset in 2008 of recession, evidence suggested that the PT/FT gap was beginning to narrow (Gallie and Zhou, 2011).

Finally, the recession and the economic crisis in Britain makes it essential to return to the fundamental question of the quality of PT jobs. On the one hand, new opportunities for quality PT jobs might have been created. In contrast to previous recessions, many employers were vigorously pursuing strategies to retain staff for as long as possible, in order to best position themselves for an economic upturn. Introducing more flexible and reduced hours can help reduce costs while retaining staff. At the same time, employers were seen to be providing greater flexibility for their employees. The economic crisis could therefore act as a facilitator for those employees wishing to reduce their hours or work more flexibly over the longer term. As a result, the traditional preferences by employers and managers for constantly visible and present workers may be challenged (Lewis and Rapoport, 2009).

On the other hand, while some employers might have been more amenable to increasing PT work for a wider range of employees, labour force statistics suggested a more negative picture of the quality of PT jobs since the recession. While there was a substantial expansion of PT working soon after 2008, and most especially for men (Grimshaw and Rafferty, 2013; ONS, 2012b), this growth in PT working did not spread across all occupations but was more heavily skewed towards lower-level jobs. Furthermore, many of the new part timers were so-called 'involuntary' PT workers who took a PT job because they were unable to find suitable FT work (Bell and Blanchflower, 2011, 2013; Felstead, 2011). We are particularly interested in the implications of these labour market changes for the evolution and distribution of the quality of PT jobs in Britain.

In this chapter, we explore the quality of PT jobs in comparison with FT jobs over time in Britain, drawing and building upon previous work in the area (e.g. Felstead and Gallie, 2004; Felstead et al., 2000; Gallie and Zhou, 2011). We also add to the growing body of research into the quality of PT jobs by making comparisons between shorter- and longer-hours PT jobs, as described in the next section.

4.2. DATA CONSIDERATIONS

There are numerous ways to differentiate PT from FT workers. For consistency across the Skills and Employment Survey (SES) datasets, our definition of PT work is set at less than thirty hours a week. The quality of PT jobs is known to vary by hours worked (Anxo et al., 2007; Warren and Walters, 1998) and accordingly we also disaggregate the PT band into 1–19 and 20–29 weekly hours. In the following sections, we include data over time for female PT and FT workers, as well as some comparative 2006–2012 data for men working PT and FT, in spite of the small numbers of male part-timers overall. Using the new dataset to examine the quality of PT jobs, we are able to examine a broader range of job characteristics than the traditional emphasis on pay differences, while simultaneously disaggregating PT workers into short- and longer-hours workers and including data on male part-timers that span the period of the economic crisis.

4.3. PART-TIME JOBS IN THE
OCCUPATIONAL STRUCTURE

It has been demonstrated in many previous studies that PT jobs are more readily available in lower-level occupations (e.g. Anxo et al., 2007; Durbin and

Tomlinson, 2010; Thornley, 2007; Tomlinson et al., 2009; Warren, 2001). As a result, many women—including the highly qualified—crowd into these lower-level jobs, especially during the key child-rearing years, and often remain trapped, unable to get back onto the career ladder (e.g. Connolly and Gregory, 2008a; Grant et al., 2005). However, there has been an increase over time in the number of higher-level PT jobs in Britain (Gallie and Zhou, 2011). In 2012, almost a third (31 per cent) of female part-timers in the SES were in higher-level non-manual jobs (associate professional/technical, managerial, professional), compared with only 13 per cent in 1986. Nevertheless, there was still a much higher proportion of FT women than PT women in these jobs (55 per cent in 2012, up from 26 per cent in 1986).

When we disaggregate the PT band into shorter and longer hours, the percentage of female part timers working longer weeks (20–29 hours) increased over time, rising from 40 per cent in 1986 to 52 per cent in 2012 (53 per cent for male part-timers in 2012). The longer-hours PT workers were more likely to work in higher-level occupations than other part timers in each year analysed, suggesting that longer PT hours work represented a middle ground in terms of job quality for women, falling midway between FT and short PT jobs. By 2012, over a third (36 per cent) of those women working between 20 and 29 hours per week were in higher level non-manual jobs, compared with a fifth (22 per cent) of shorter-hours part-timers (Figure 4.2). Shorter-hours female part timers in 2012 (working one–nineteen hours per week) were the women most likely to work at the bottom of the occupational hierarchy in sales work, as operatives and in elementary jobs (48 per cent compared with 24 per cent of those women working 20–29 hours a week). Over half (51 per cent) of male part-timers in 2012 were also concentrated in low-level occupations, a substantial increase after 2006 (39 per cent) (see Figure 4.2).

Over-concentrated in lower-level jobs, female part-timers were also the group most likely to be working predominantly with other women. Occupational segregation is commonly described as the concentration of men and women in different kinds of jobs (horizontal segregation) and/or in different grades or levels (vertical segregation). Research has shown that as more women enter the labour market, they are frequently recruited into jobs defined as 'female jobs' (e.g. Gonäs and Karlsson, 2006). As noted earlier, sectors with a high rate of PT employment also tend to be the most feminized and have high proportions of lower-paid jobs (Thornley, 2007). Respondents in the SES survey were asked to consider the ratio of men to women within their workplace doing their type of job. Across all years, female part-timers (short- and longer-hours part-timers, so we do not disaggregate them here) were the workers most likely to work predominantly with other women (57 per cent in 2012), but the PT/FT gap amongst women had narrowed over time (Figure 4.3).

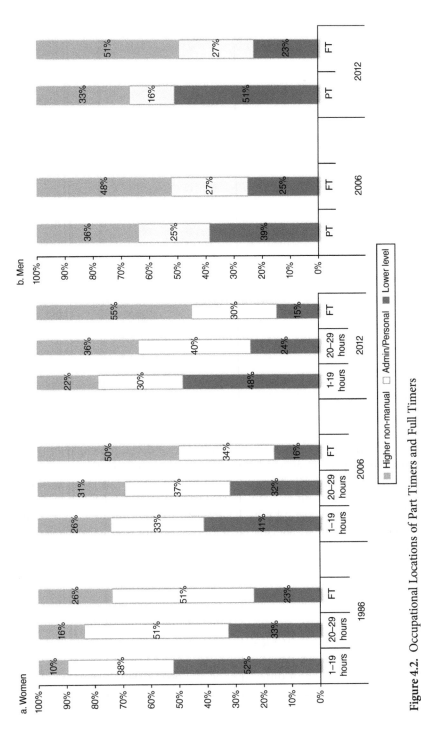

a. Women

b. Men

Figure 4.2. Occupational Locations of Part Timers and Full Timers

Notes: Higher non-manual = managers/professionals/assoc prof. Admin/personal = admin and secretarial/skilled trades/personal services. Lower = sales/operatives/elementary.

Source: SES

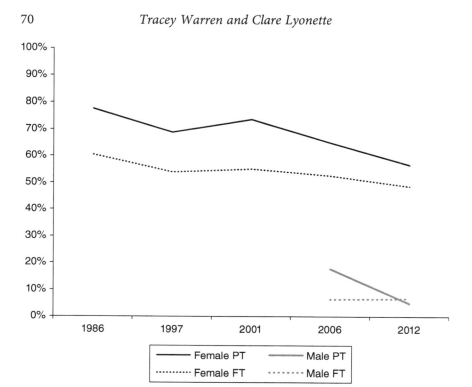

Figure 4.3. Ratio of Men to Women Doing the Job in the Workplace: Proportion Working Mainly/Almost Exclusively with Women
Source: SES

To sum up this section: there were some positive developments over time, with more female part timers working in more senior level positions, although women working longer PT hours were more likely to be working in these higher-level jobs than women with shorter PT hours. A PT/FT gap in occupation level still persisted up to 2012, however: women in lower-level occupations remained far more likely to work PT than other women workers. Not only were almost half of female part timers working in lower-level jobs, the majority were still concentrated in workplaces where their jobs were done mainly by women.

4.4. PART-TIME WAGES

Reflecting the persistence of differences in the occupational locations of PT compared with FT workers, above, a PT/FT wage gap amongst women also persisted over time, to the detriment of part-timers. Exploring gross hourly wages, in 2012 the raw PT/FT wage gap stood at 17 per cent (Figure 4.4a), the same level as in 1986. Much of this gap can be explained by women's levels of education: so when, in 2012, education level was entered into a wage regression, working PT or FT was no longer statistically significant. We discuss education more in the next section. Figure 4.4a also shows that the PT/FT wage gap was lowest amongst female graduates (Level 4 + NVQ) and widest for women with NVQ levels 1–3. The post-recessionary expansion in the number of men working PT was associated with a drop in male part-timers' hourly wages, relative to male full timers. In 2006, the part timers had held an hourly wage advantage, but by 2012 the PT/FT wage gap amongst men stood at 10 per cent, and remained statistically significant (at 1 per cent) after controlling for level of education held. As with women, the PT/FT wage gap was at its narrowest (6 per cent) amongst male graduates.

The wide PT/FT wage gap amongst women was applicable to women working short and longer PT weeks (hence data not shown), but there was wide wage diversity amongst the part timers by occupation. We compared women's hourly gross wages using the male FT mean as a benchmark each year. We calculated a wage gap by dividing wage by the male FT mean (for each year), identifying gaps as positive when women's wages were higher than the male mean (Figure 4.4). Women in higher-level non-manual jobs, both PT and FT, fared better per hour than male full-timers. Indeed, female part-timers in these jobs did even better than their full-time counterparts. The most wage-disadvantaged women each year, however, were part-timers in lower-level jobs, over half of whom (54 per cent) had a level of education at NVQ 2 or less (GCSE or less).

4.5. PART-TIME SKILLS AND TRAINING

Occupations and wages are commonly used to compare the quality of PT and FT jobs. As we have seen above, they usefully demonstrate the persistence of a substantial PT/FT gap in job quality in Britain, but also point to diversity amongst female part timers that the PT/FT dichotomy disguises. The SES data allow us to explore other indicators of the quality of PT jobs to better consider the evolution and distribution of the quality of PT jobs in Britain over time, moving beyond the traditional focus only on occupation and pay.

Earlier analysis of skill levels using SES data debated whether all groups of workers were benefiting equally from a general upskilling of jobs (Felstead et al., 2000; Gallie et al., 1998; Horrell, 1994). By 1997, whilst women full timers were found to be converging on men in terms of the qualifications needed to get their jobs, the learning time to carry them out and the training period associated with the work (Felstead et al., 2000, 725), 'pockets of

a. PT/FT wage gap amonst women, by level of education held, 2012

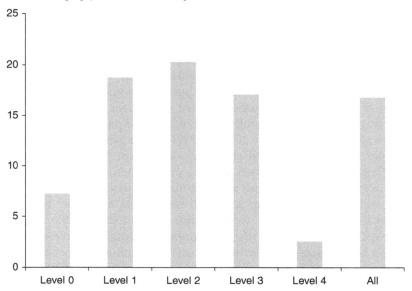

b. Women's gross hourly wages relative to the male FT hourly mean each year 1

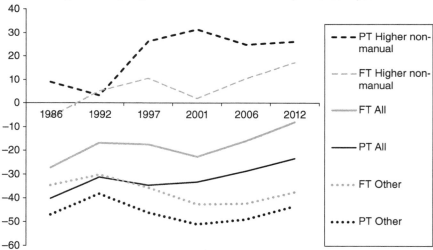

Figure 4.4. Wage Gaps

Notes: ((Women hourly gross wage/male FT hourly gross mean)*100) – 100. Male means: 1986 £4.4; 1992 £7.1; 1997 £8.2; 2001 £10.9; 2006 £13.2; 2012 £14.1.
PT/FT gap = 100 – [(PT/FT)*100].

Source: SES

cumulative disadvantage remain, especially among PT and other "non-standard" workers'. Drawing upon the 2001 survey, Felstead and Gallie (2004) also concluded that PT jobs, on average, still required lower qualification levels and shorter amounts of training from workers.

Our results look beyond 2001 and they affirm a general increase over time in the educational levels required for the jobs done by respondents. Moreover, this overall increase persisted beyond the recession and into 2012. The mean score for required educational level for women's jobs rose from 1.38 in 1986 to 2.36 in 2012 (Table 4.1). A substantial and statistically significant PT/FT gap, however, persisted across all the years. It was still as wide as 22 per cent in 2012, although this was a large drop from the 51 per cent of 1986. Comparing the two groups of part-timers, in each year, longer-hours female part-timers reported higher levels of required education than other women working PT (in 2012 the scores were 2.30 and 1.72, respectively, statistically significant at 1 per cent), though still lower than female full-timers. The jobs of male part-timers demanded the lowest educational levels in both 2006 and 2012, and hence the PT/FT gap was larger still amongst men (29 per cent in 2012).

The increase in level of education required for the job portrays a positive picture of the upskilling of work over time, with women faring better than men, and a narrowing of the PT/FT gap amongst women up to 2012. However, SES data, like other sources, also show a general increase in the levels of education held over time. What were the implications of this for whether the education levels that were held by workers matched, exceeded, or were less than the qualifications required for the job being done? Here we are drawing upon influential debates over the proportions of female part-timers who are 'working below potential'. In 1986, around a third of women workers were working below their potential in that they had achieved a higher level of education than was needed for the work that they were currently doing (37 per cent of PT compared with 29 per cent of FT, statistically significant at 1 per cent). This educational mismatch grew after 1992 for women, but fell from 2006. In 2012, still fully 41 per cent of PT (49 per cent for shorter-hours part-timers) and a third of female full-timers were underemployed in terms of their levels of education. The mismatch for male part-timers was even higher and rising after the recession so that, in 2012, over half (54 per cent) of men working PT had higher levels of education than their job required. This may support the argument that these men are taking short-term PT jobs as a stop-gap measure through the worst of the recession and may revert to better FT jobs once the labour market fully recovers.

We then considered a) how long respondents felt that it had taken them to learn to do their job well, and b) the length of training received for the type of work being carried out. The scores on the learning and training indexes give more support to the overall picture of general improvements over time, persistent statistically significant PT/FT gaps, longer-hours PT jobs as a

Table 4.1. Skill Requirements for Job

	Women						Men	
	1986	1992	1997	2001	2006	2012	2006	2012
1. Education level required for current job: mean score[1]								
PT	0.85	1.16	1.25	1.41	1.70	2.02	1.61	1.66
FT	1.75	2.14	2.15	2.27	2.38	2.59	2.15	2.34
PT 1–19 hours	0.69	0.95	1.11	1.19	1.49	1.72		
PT 20–29 hours	1.08	1.37	1.43	1.64	1.88	2.30		
All	1.38	1.73	1.80	1.94	2.12	2.36	2.11	2.28
Gaps (%)								
PT/FT[4]	51.4***	45.8	41.9***	37.9***	28.6***	22.0***	25.1***	29.1***
Short PT/Long PT[5]	36.1***	30.7***	22.4**	27.4**	20.7***	25.2***		
2. Education level held is higher than education level required for the job (%)								
PT	36.8	32.2	36.1	43.3	47.0	41.0	50.4	54.0
FT	29.3	25.1	30.2	33.2	35.1	32.1	37.8	36.1
PT 1–19 hours	42.9	36.2	37.9	45.6	51.3	48.9		
PT 20–29 hours	28.0	27.7	34.0	41.5	42.8	35.2		
All	32.4	28.1	32.4	37.1	39.6	35.8	38.7	37.8
3. Learning time to do the job well: mean score[2]								
PT			3.34	3.48	3.81	3.77	3.56	2.97
FT			4.50	4.47	4.55	4.45	5.00	4.78
PT 1–19 hours			3.05	3.15	3.54	3.22		
PT 20–29 hours			3.70	3.84	4.04	4.30		
All			4.05	4.08	4.27	4.20	4.90	4.62
Gaps (%)								
PT/FT[4]			25.8***	22.2***	16.3***	15.3***	28.8***	37.9***
Short PT/Long PT[5]			17.6**	17.9***	12.4***	25.1***		
4. Length of training had for the type of work being done:[3] mean score								
PT	0.77	1.21	1.72	1.70	2.31	1.94	1.85	0.95
FT	1.87	2.30	2.72	2.46	2.88	2.55	2.57	2.41
PT 1–19 hours	0.63	1.03	1.53	1.27	1.99	1.51		
PT 20–29 hours	0.98	1.41	1.91	2.10	2.60	2.34		
All	1.42	1.84	2.34	2.16	2.66	2.31	2.52	2.27
Gaps (%)								
PT/FT[4]	58.8***	47.4***	36.8***	30.9***	19.8***	23.9***	28.0***	60.6***
Short PT/Long PT[5]	35.7*	26.9**	19.9	39.5***	23.5***	35.5***		

Notes: [1]Educational level range 0–4 (0 = no qualifications). [2] Learning time range 1–7: 1 = <one week; 2= <one month; 3 = 1–<three months; 4 = 3–<six months; 5 = 6–<twelve months; 6 = 1–<two years; 7 = two+ years. [3]Training time range 1–6: 1 = <one month; 2 = <three months; 3 = 3–<six months; 4 = 6–<twelve months; 5 = 1–<two years; 6 = two+ years. [4]PT/FT gap = 100 – [(PT score/FT score)*100]. [5]Short PT/Long PT gap = 100– [(Short PT score/Long PT score)*100].

Difference between the two categories (PT vs. FT. Short PT vs. Long PT): level of significance: *** = 1 per cent, ** = 5 per cent; * = 10 per cent.

Source: SES

middle ground between FT and shorter PT jobs, and high levels of disadvantage for the small group of men working PT. The PT/FT gap for learning times amongst women narrowed over time, but the gap for training, though narrowing until 2006, had widened a little by 2012. Unlike the case with level of education, there is also some evidence here to suggest a drop in job quality after the recession: between 2006 and 2012 almost all groups of workers saw falls in the time taken to learn to do the job well and the length of the training needed for their job.

4.6. PART-TIME WORK INTENSITY AND DISCRETION

Not only have we been able to examine skills and training as key indicators of job quality, the SES datasets also allow us to analyse differences between PT and FT workers in the levels of work intensity and discretion.

Many working PT find that they have too much to do in a short space of time, especially those in more senior-level occupations, where PT workers already tend to work longer hours than those in lower-level PT occupations (e.g. Smithson et al., 2004). Evidence after the recession that began in 2008 showed that many companies cut their workforces and that the number of employees working PT hours grew, raising concerns that the same amount of work was being done with reduced staffing and hence work intensity was increasing. Studies using this data series have shown how 'hard work' grew after 2006, following a decade when there had been little change (Felstead et al., 2013b; Gallie, 2005; Green, 2006). How did part-timers compare with full-timers?

We report on an overall measure of work intensity: whether respondents strongly agreed that their jobs required them to work 'very hard' (Figure 4.5). Across all years, female full-timers stood out amongst the workers, female and male, followed by women working longer PT hours, further supporting our argument that the latter group occupies a middle ground in job quality amongst women workers. There was also a creep upwards over time in hard working for most groups (Figure 4.5a). Within the work–time groups, it was largely those with the highest levels of education who were most likely to be working very hard, but female full-timers still retained the lead within each educational grouping. In 2012, fully 61 per cent of female graduates working FT (NVQ Level 4+) reported working very hard (compared with 46 per cent of equally qualified male full timers; Figure 4.5b). In spite of the better quality of female FT than PT jobs in terms of skills, training, and learning required for the job, FT women seem to pay for this advantage by having to work harder than women working PT, or than men working either FT or PT.

Level of work intensity links us to long-standing questions around workers' discretion over what they do in the workplace. There is a well-known variation

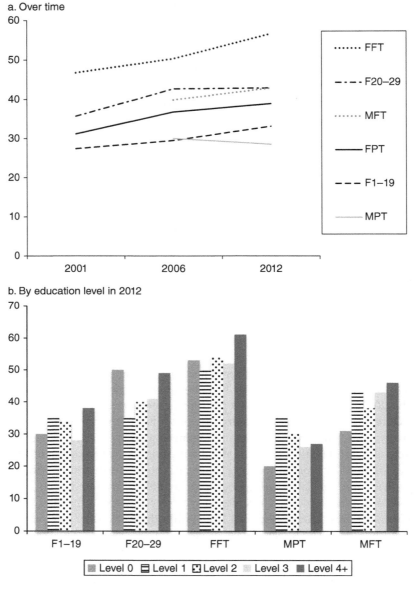

Figure 4.5. Work Intensity: Percentage who Strongly Agree that Their Job Requires that They Work 'Very Hard'

Notes: FT: full timers; 20–29: twenty–twenty-nine weekly hours; 1–19: one-nineteen weekly hours; F: women; M: men.
Education level: NVQ Levels 0, 1, 2, 3, and 4+

Source: SES

in workers' self-control of their own work. Certain jobs remain very 'Taylorist', in which various aspects of work, including how hard workers work, are rigidly controlled and monitored closely (whether by employers, managers, customers, or machines). Far more autonomy is commonly available at higher levels of the occupational hierarchy (Edwards, 1979). The PT/FT split has been firmly implicated here (Fagan, 2001).

We report mean scores on an overall task discretion index that amalgamates workers' discretion in four areas: how hard they work, what tasks they do, how they do those tasks, and the quality standards to which they work (Table 4.2). The index ranges from 0 to 3, with 3 the highest level of discretion. The discretion levels reported by women working PT were lower than for full-timers (and statistically significant) up until 2006, after which the PT/FT gap virtually disappeared. Longer-hours PT women again occupied a middle ground, but the difference between the PT groups was neither large nor statistically significant.

Women workers, in PT and FT jobs, saw their overall discretion fall in the 1990s, but discretion levels rose again in the following decade, including after the recession. Discretion levels rose for male part timers too, but those reported by male full-timers fell just a little from 2006 to 2012, thus narrowing the male PT/FT gap (it was no longer statistically significant by 2012). The groups of male full-timers who saw the largest of these drops in discretion levels were in administrative and secretarial jobs (though only 5 per cent of male full timers were in this occupational category in 2012), and operatives (11 per cent).

Table 4.2. Task Discretion

	Women					Men	
	1992	1997	2001	2006	2012	2006	2012
Mean score[1]							
PT	2.40	2.16	2.10	2.13	2.26	2.07	2.16
FT	2.48	2.37	2.28	2.26	2.28	2.28	2.23
PT 1–19 hours	2.36	2.18	2.05	2.10	2.22		
PT 20–29 hours	2.44	2.14	2.14	2.14	2.25		
All	2.45	2.29	2.21	2.21	2.27	2.27	2.22
Gaps (%)							
PT/FT[4]	3.4**	8.7***	8.0***	5.8***	0.9	9.0***	3.2
Short PT/Long PT[5]	3.2	−1.8	4.2*	1.7	1.3		

Notes: [1]Overall discretion scale 0–3 (3 = Highest level of discretion). [2]PT/FT gap = 100 − [(PT core/FT score)*100].

Difference between the two categories (PT vs. FT. Short PT vs. Long PT): level of significance: *** = 1 per cent, ** = 5 per cent; * = 10 per cent.

Source: SES

In spite of the many positive changes in the quality of work over time, there was a reversal, or at best a stalling, in terms of task discretion in the 1990s. By 2012, however, there were signs of improvement, particularly for women and part-timers.

4.7. SUBJECTIVE EVALUATIONS

This chapter has focused on objective measures of job quality, reflecting Green's (2006) emphasis on the importance of the features of a job when measuring its quality. We end, however, by examining subjective measures: orientations to work and job satisfaction. These have been core topics in research into women's working lives and in particular into the heavy concentration of women with caring responsibilities working in PT jobs in Britain.

Part-timers' levels of satisfaction with their jobs have stimulated one of the most contentious debates in the study of women's working lives in Britain. Over-concentrated in objectively lower-quality jobs than full-timers, women working PT have nevertheless expressed satisfaction with many aspects of their jobs. Given the juxtaposition of lower-quality jobs and these higher levels of job satisfaction, in 1991 Hakim infamously asked whether women working PT should accordingly be termed 'grateful slaves'. Yet other research since then has questioned this idea of a female PT worker whose work orientation is such that she places a low priority on paid work, has chosen to work PT hours in a less demanding job, cares less about the quality of that job, and so is more easily job satisfied. Some argue that the greater responsibility placed upon women for caring and domestic tasks limits their choices (e.g. Ginn et al., 1996) and restricts their 'agency freedom' as far as their employment decisions are concerned (Lewis and Giullari, 2005). While many women say they like to work PT (Gash et al., 2012; Scott and Dex, 2009) and PT working women have tended to report lower work–life conflict (Crompton and Lyonette, 2007) and higher life satisfaction (Gash et al., 2012) than female full-timers, any such evaluations by women in PT work are likely to be highly influenced by the availability (or lack) of any viable alternatives. In fact, other studies have shown that female PT workers are those most likely to be dissatisfied with their variety of work and their ability to learn new things (European Commission, 1998), and also with terms of pay and job prospects, particularly those women working in lower-skilled PT jobs (Taylor, 2002; Walters, 2005).

We considered whether women who worked PT in the SES stood out from female full timers in their work orientations and job satisfaction. Respondents were asked if they would continue to work if they did not need to for financial reasons. There were increases in women's work commitment over time, for both FT and PT workers. For example, in 1986, 64 per cent of FT and 58 per cent of PT women said they would continue to work. By 2012, the figures had risen to 71 per cent and 69 per cent, respectively. The narrowing of an already small gap in work commitment between female PT and FT workers calls into question the notion of 'home-centred' female part-timers and work-committed female full-timers.

What were the patterns of satisfaction amongst PT and FT workers? In the SES, workers were asked about their satisfaction with various aspects of work, including the job itself, the hours, promotion prospects, relationship with their boss, and opportunities to use initiative and pay. Women working PT were not markedly different in the ranking of their assessments from those working FT (Table 4.3). In 2006 and 2012, the friendliness of the people was rated highly by both groups, whilst chances for promotion and fringe benefits scored poorly. In both years, female part-timers were far more satisfied than full timers with their hours worked and the amount of work, as many other studies have shown, whilst full-timers scored higher than women working PT in using their abilities and prospects for promotion. These relationships were largely stable between 2006 and 2012, though levels of satisfaction on most items had fallen a little. In 2012, the shorter-hours-PT women workers were more satisfied than women working longer PT with some aspects of their job (including job security, pay, their managers, and the friendliness of the people), but they were the least satisfied women when it came to fringe benefits. By 2012, a significant gap in satisfaction with job security had appeared between these two groups of women. By 2012, male part-timers were less likely to be satisfied than male full-timers on every item in Table 4.3.

4.8. CONCLUSION

In returning to early labour market theory focusing on supply- and demand-led explanations of PT employment, and the differentiation between primary and secondary, or core and peripheral labour markets, we nevertheless argue that a more nuanced picture emerges once the category of PT workers is disaggregated by sex and hours worked. In this chapter, we have been able to provide an analysis of trends over time in the quality of PT jobs, up to and including the recession that began in 2008, while also demonstrating women's continuing dominance of PT work and differences between shorter-hours- and longer-hours PT women workers. We were also able to include data on the small number of PT male workers since the recession. In so doing, a picture emerged of both stability and change over time in the quality of PT jobs.

The Part-Time Work Directive came into effect in July 2000. This stipulated that PT workers must not be treated less favourably than comparable FT workers; should receive equal hourly rates of pay; should receive equal

Table 4.3. Levels of Satisfaction

(sorted by female FT)	Percentage 'satisfied' in 2006						Percentage 'satisfied' in 2012					
	Women				Men		Women				Men	
	PT	FT	PT 1-19	PT 20-29	PT	FT	PT	FT	PT 1-19	PT 20-29	PT	FT
Friendliness of the people	93.4	94.0	94.0	92.9	87.8	92.3**	89.8	92.6	94.2	85.8***	82.6	90.7***
Being able to use initiative	87.5	87.9*	86.1	88.8	77.5	90.0***	85.9	89.9**	85.1	85.1	66.0	83.6***
Opportunity to use abilities	83.9	86.2***	80.5	86.6**	71.7	86.0***	81.6	88.8***	80.5	82.0	59.0	82.5***
Work itself	89.4	88.1*	89.6	89.1	82.7	87.2**	87.0	86.1	86.7	87.4	70.8	84.9***
Variety	83.2	85.2**	79.1	86.1***	81.9	84.0	80.8	85.4**	80.2	81.9	54.9	79.5***
The job	88.5	86.0**	88.9	88.0	86.5	85.3*	86.9	83.2**	87.2	85.4	62.5	83.1***
Relationship with boss	84.9	83.5**	82.5	87.0**	81.4	79.3	84.1	81.1***	87.1	80.6*	74.7	78.3
Job security	82.5	82.0	82.9	83.0*	70.9	78.5***	77.4	77.9*	82.6	72.3***	63.2	70.8***
Hours worked	90.9	78.0***	90.7	91.1	87.3	76.8***	87.9	76.6***	88.8	88.1	68.1	72.6
Amount of work	80.0	72.1***	80.1	80.2*	81.9	76.9*	78.6	70.4***	81.0	74.3	65.3	71.6**
Training provided	66.1	69.6*	61.8	69.7***	54.4	64.2***	64.4	69.0**	63.1	66.5	50.0	64.5***
Ability and efficiency of manager	72.5	68.3***	71.0	73.8**	64.6	62.7	71.3	67.1	75.7	66.8*	52.5	64.5*
Pay	64.0	65.1	63.8	63.7	62.7	67.0***	65.3	60.6	67.2	63.1**	50.0	62.7***
Promotion prospects	45.3	51.9***	40.6	49.5**	28.7	48.8***	40.9	47.1***	40.5	41.5	36.1	47.9***
Fringe benefits	44.2	41.3*	38.4	49.2***	33.3	49.4***	35.8	41.8***	33.5	40.0**	31.3	44.3***

Notes: Difference between the two categories (PT vs. FT, Long PT vs. Short PT); level of significance: *** = 1 per cent, ** = 5 per cent; * = 10 per cent.

Source: SES

overtime pay, as well as equal enhanced rates of pay for working outside normal contractual hours; should get equal access to any company pension scheme, training, and career development; rights to career breaks; rights to receive enhanced sick, maternity, paternity, and adoption leave and pay; parental leave rights; consideration for promotion; and should receive contractual benefits pro-rata. This chapter has traced the quality of PT jobs in Britain both before and up to twelve years after the Directive came into force. It showed that in the dominant depiction of PT work in Britain, part-timers are overly concentrated in poor-quality jobs that require few skills and low levels of education and training. These jobs, in return, offer workers low wage rates and restricted opportunities for advancement. Women with caring responsibilities have borne the heavy burden of this PT disadvantage in Britain as they account for the vast majority of PT workers. The purpose of the chapter was to interrogate this dominant depiction and explore trends over time in the quality of PT jobs.

The analysis showed stability over time in the overall proportions of working women with PT hours, and the persistence of female-dominated PT working in Britain. A notable change by 2012 was in the proportion of men working PT, reducing women's dominance of PT hours somewhat, although the small numbers of male part-timers in the samples restrict what we can say about the men themselves.

Women's PT jobs were sharply divided according to the hours worked: short PT hours were associated with lower-level jobs in particular sectors and occupations, whereas longer PT hours tended to be worked more by women in middle or senior roles. There was some evidence of a growing number of female part timers in higher-level jobs over time, raising hopes that more PT jobs were being opened up in more senior-level positions. On the other hand, there is a possibility that the large majority of these jobs were being done by 'high-value' female workers who had previously worked FT in the same position and negotiated reduced hours for a period of time in order to cope with caring responsibilities such as pre-school children (Tilly, 1996).

The chapter has confirmed that PT jobs continued to require lower levels of skills and training, in comparison with FT. Women in FT jobs appeared to fare better than female part timers more generally, longer-hours part timers better than shorter, and men working PT did particularly badly. Satisfaction with jobs fell after the recession. Unlike some other aspects of work, there was evidence here of narrowing gaps between the shorter-hours and the longer-hours part timers. In some cases such as job security, shorter-hours female part-timers overtook those working longer hours in levels of satisfaction, due primarily to a sharp drop in satisfaction for the longer-hours group, rather than a large rise among the shorter-hours group.

In conclusion, we saw some evidence of improvement over time in the quality of PT jobs in Britain up until 2012. Amongst female employees, more longer-hours part-timers were working in higher-level occupations in 2012, there was a narrowing over time of PT/FT gaps in education and learning times, and there were signs of improvement in levels of discretion for part-timers. A PT disadvantage nevertheless remained, and was most pronounced for those women working shorter-PT hours. Male PT workers appeared to be a distinct group and due to small numbers, we are unable to make any longer-term projections about the quality of male PT jobs. The 'hierarchy of job quality' among the various groups under consideration here would place male part-timers at the bottom of all workers, followed by female shorter-hours part-timers, longer-hours female part timers, then male full-timers and finally female full-timers. However, we would argue that, at one extreme, the female full timers are paying for their quality advantage by working harder and under more pressure, whereas at the other end of the hierarchy, the male part timers are likely to revert to better FT jobs once the labour market strengthens. What is likely to endure is the well-established poorer quality of shorter-hours PT jobs for women.

Why women continue to dominate the short-hours, lower-quality PT job market is in no small part related to a lack of affordable childcare in the UK, which limits many women's opportunities to work longer hours. In addition, women remain normatively associated with domestic work and caring, which serves to perpetuate gender-stereotypical behaviours both within the home and in the labour market. Until men are willing to share more housework and care responsibilities, it seems likely that large numbers of women will continue to work part time in the UK. At the same time, employers are often unwilling to offer higher-level jobs on a PT basis, so restricting the types of work available with reduced hours. There was some optimism that the recession may serve to challenge this inflexibility (e.g. Lewis and Rapoport, 2009), with employers using flexible working to help with budgetary constraints. There is some evidence of an increase in (longer-hours) PT jobs in senior positions, but only time will tell if this translates into better PT jobs on a wider scale.

5

Temporary Work and Job Quality

Hande Inanc

5.1. INTRODUCTION

This chapter investigates the trends in job quality among temporary workers in Britain covering the period between 1992 and 2012. This period was marked with important changes in labour market institutions and in the economy that may well have had significant implications for the quality of jobs and employment. The first part of this period witnessed a process of labour market flexibilization and deregulation of employment contracts. After recovery from recession in the early 1990s, there was a prolonged period of economic growth until the 2008–2009 global economic crisis. The central concern of the chapter is to investigate whether these changes, particularly the global economic crisis, resulted in a divergence or a convergence between the job quality of temporary and permanent employees.

The analysis of job quality differentiates between two distinct types of temporary workers—those in longer contracts (referred to as fixed-term workers hereinafter) and those on shorter-term contracts (referred to as casual workers hereinafter). It focuses on five major aspects of jobs: opportunities to use job skills, learning and training opportunities, work intensity, job control, pay and job security. The chapter starts with a discussion of contrasting theoretical positions (section 5.2), before providing an overview of the employment protection legislation in Britain that regulates the hiring and firing of employees (section 5.3). It then goes on with a review of the changes in the skill structure of temporary employees (section 5.4). Section 5.5 presents the trends in job quality from the analysis of the Skills and Employment Surveys (SES). In addition to examining trends in each aspect of job quality, it presents the changes in subjective responses to temporary contracts, concentrating on subjective job insecurity and job satisfaction. The chapter concludes with a general discussion on the hypotheses of divergence, convergence, and an internal divide within the temporary workforce, and discusses the potential drivers of the changes observed (section 5.6).

5.2. CONTRASTING THEORETICAL SCENARIOS

Different predictions can be made concerning the trends in temporary work-ers' job quality, based on the arguments in the literature. A *divergence* between temporary and permanent workers could be expected with a deterioration in the job quality of temporary workers after the economic crisis, resulting from an increase in employer power. Alternatively, a positive picture can be drawn linked to a possible upward shift in the skill structure of temporary employees, resulting from a process of destruction of low-quality jobs in the most backward industries that disproportionately employ temporary employees. This, together with the changes in the regulative controls of temporary work, could be expected to lead to a *convergence* in job quality of permanent and temporary employees. It is also plausible to expect an internal divide within the temporary workforce, and heterogeneous trends between those on fixed-term contracts and those on casual contracts.

Turning now to these predictions in more detail, first, the flexibilization hypothesis predicts a polarization of the workforce, thereby an increasing *divergence* between temporary and permanent employees' job quality. Tem-porary work grew in European labour markets in the early 1980s as a conse-quence of the policies of labour market flexibilization, which were adopted in order to combat mass unemployment, to foster economic growth and effi-ciency, and to provide employment opportunities for groups who were trad-itionally weakly attached to the labour market. But at the same time they were seen as leading to a major new divide in the conditions of work. While full-time permanent employees constitute a core workforce, enjoying high-quality jobs with learning and training opportunities, involvement in decision-making, job security, and decent pay, temporary employees are at the periph-ery in jobs with little scope for learning, skill development, and decision-making, poor pay, and job insecurity (e.g. Purcell et al., 1999).

In many European countries labour market flexibilization resulted in a rapid increase in the share of workers employed with non-standard contracts, particularly temporary workers, which consequently led to a segmented labour market. However, Britain's weak employment protection for permanent em-ployees provided little incentive for British employers to use temporary contracts extensively. While the share of temporary workers remained between 5.5 and *c.* 8 per cent of all employees between 1992 and 2012 (see Figure 5.1), questions of whether these flexible staffing arrangements were a new phenomenon or the extent to which there was a polarization in the British labour market have been subjects of sharp debate (Atkinson, 1987; Casey, 1991; Marginson 1991; Pollert, 1988).

More recent studies have focused on the trends in different forms of temporary work. They have consistently highlighted an increase in temporary agency work throughout the 1990s that eventually became the most common

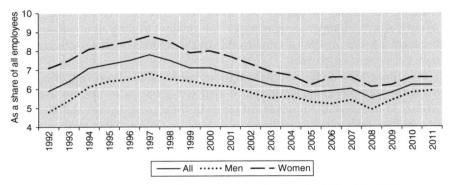

Figure 5.1. Percentage of Temporary Workers in the UK, 1992–2012
Source: UK Labour Force Surveys, unweighted percentages

form of temporary work, while the share of temporary jobs remained stable (e.g. Forde, 2001; Ward et al., 2001). With respect to the polarization of the workforce, in the early 1990s it was the professionals and managers for whom the growth of temporary contracts in absolute terms had been the greatest (Heather et al., 1996; Heery and Salmon, 2000; Millward et al., 2000; Robinson, 2000). Some argued that negative consequences of temporary work were not as prominent for these highly skilled employees (Cam et al., 2003; Tregaskis, 1997). Others have shown that managerial and professional non-standard workers experienced different treatment in their workplace (Gallie et al., 1998; Mallon and Duberley, 2000). Another study pointed out that while temporary employees in many occupations report lower job satisfaction, earn lower wages, and are less likely to receive work-related training, there was a differential effect of contract type on job quality (Booth et al., 2002). Those working in seasonal/casual jobs compared to those working with fixed-term contracts suffered a larger wage growth penalty.

Regardless of the extent of earlier polarization, the global economic crisis of 2008–2009 could be expected to have accentuated the divide between the temporary and permanent workforce, as employers gained more power and sought ways of shifting risk onto employees, especially onto those whose labour market situation was more vulnerable. Therefore, these arguments point to a divergence and a widening of the gap between permanent and temporary employees' job quality.

In contrast, a more positive account can be drawn following the idea of economic crisis as a source of creative destruction, increasing the job quality of temporary employees by disproportionately eliminating poor-quality jobs held by temporary employees. This destruction process leads to an upward shift in the quality of jobs held by temporary workers, hence, narrowing the gap between permanent and temporary workers' job quality. The changes introduced in British employment protection legislation in 2011 regarding the working conditions of agency workers could also have contributed to an upward shift in temporary employees' job quality, leading to a convergence between the two groups of employees, with temporary workers catching up with permanent employees.

Turning to the divide within temporary work, it has been suggested that fixed-term employees in Britain are a mixed group who are, on average, similar to permanent employees in terms of their composition and the sorts of jobs they do. On the other hand, it is those on shorter-term contracts who are actually on the periphery, and effectively occupying jobs of poorer quality. Therefore, a sharper divide between the two types of temporary workers can be expected. Casual, agency, and seasonal workers whose job contracts are much shorter may enjoy much lower job quality than both fixed-term employees and permanent employees. The divergence and convergence hypotheses could both apply to casual workers versus the rest. There could be an even wider gap with the economic crisis as employers push this relatively vulnerable group towards ever poorer-quality jobs, widening the gap between casual workers and other employees. Or alternatively, an upward shift in the quality of casual workers' jobs could be expected due to a selection effect of those who survived the crisis, as well as the changes in the employment protection legislation concerning agency workers that were introduced in 2011.

5.3. EMPLOYMENT PROTECTION LEGISLATION

Employment protection legislation (EPL) is crucial to understanding the degree of polarization between regular and temporary workers, as this depends largely on the level of labour market protection for the former and the degree of regulation of the latter. A more profound polarization will be found in countries that adopt strong employment protection for permanent employees whilst liberalizing the use of temporary contracts. Due to smaller termination costs attached to temporary contracts, firms will substitute permanent workers with temporary ones. Meanwhile, a large gap in job protection that provides better protection for permanent workers will reduce the conversion rate from temporary to open-ended contracts, creating a duality in the labour market in which temporary employees are trapped in the periphery (Boeri, 2011). On the contrary, polarization will be less accentuated in countries with weak protection for permanent workers and flexible regulations with respect to workers with fixed-term contracts.

The Organisation for Economic Co-operation and Development's (OECD) EPL indicators show that Britain adopts relatively light regulations on temporary contracts and at the same time weak protection for permanent

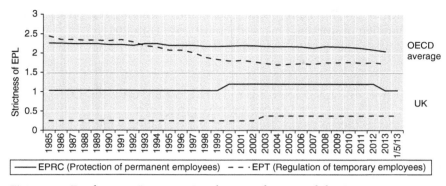

Figure 5.2. Employment Protection Legislation in the UK and the OECD, 1983–2013

Notes: The EPL indicator has two main dimensions: EPRC refers to the regulations governing the individual or collective dismissal of regular workers and includes rules on notification procedures, length of notice period depending on job tenure, severance pay by tenure, and definitions of justified and unfair dismissals. EPT is the regulations on the hiring and firing of temporary employees and includes rules on definitions for valid cases to use fixed-term contracts and for temporary working agencies (TWAs), maximum number of (cumulative) fixed-term contracts (and of TWAs), authorization or reporting obligations for TWAs, and procedures of equal treatment of agency workers at the user firm (for details on the EPL indicators see OECD EPL database; OECD 2013c). Each of these dimensions varies between 0 and 6, 0 indicating the least restrictions and 6 indicating the most restrictions in the regulation of temporary and protection of permanent employees.

Source: OECD EPL Database, <http://www.oecd.org/els/emp/EPL-timeseries.xlsx>

employees (Figure 5.2). Thus, standard fixed-term contract and regular workers in Britain are subject to relatively similar regulations with respect to the cost and difficulty of dismissals. The same definition of fair and unfair treatment applies for both groups. Fixed-term and regular workers alike are entitled to the same level of compensation and possibility of reinstatement following unfair dismissal. The length of trial period for both groups has to be agreed between the employer and the employee and the same notice and severance pay procedures apply to all (OECD, 2013a; 2014b).

In the period between 1985 and 2013 EPL in Britain remained relatively stable, at a lower level compared to the OECD average. Regarding protection of permanent employees, the only change implemented has been on the length of trial period, which in 2000 was reduced from twenty-four months to nine months, increasing back to twenty-four months in 2012. Similarly, slight restrictions were introduced with respect to the regulation of temporary employees after the millennium. Until 2002, there was no limit to the maximum cumulative duration of successive fixed-term contracts, meaning that individuals could be employed with a series of temporary contracts without being offered a permanent contract. However, in 2003 the maximum duration was set to four years, after which fixed-term employees had to be treated as permanent employees. Another change was introduced also regarding agency workers. Agency Worker Regulations 2010, that became effective as of 1 October 2011, ensures equal treatment of regular and agency workers in areas such as pay and basic working conditions including rest breaks, night work, duration of working time, and annual leave (BIS, 2011).

5.4. TRENDS IN THE SKILL STRUCTURE OF TEMPORARY WORKERS

Skills are highly correlated with job quality: jobs with low skills tend to be of poorer quality. Changes in the skill distribution in the workforce, or among a certain group of employees, are likely to have important implications for workers' level of job quality, and for the differences in job quality across groups.

There is a long-standing perception in Britain that temporary jobs are low skilled. Empirical studies lend support to this idea that temporary workers are less skilled than permanent workers in terms of a number of criteria, for example educational credentials and occupational group. Additionally, there is also some evidence concerning the differences in skill requirements and demands of the jobs held by temporary and permanent workers, with the former work in less skilled and less demanding jobs (Felstead et al., 2001). Moreover, there is a considerable variation within the temporary group, with casual/agency/seasonal jobs particularly low skilled, whereas fixed-term jobs are closer to permanent jobs in terms of level of skill requirement and job demands (Felstead and Gallie, 2004).

Figure 5.3 shows the skill structure of permanent, fixed-term, and casual workers between 1992 and 2011 for the five years the SES were conducted, measured in terms of occupational group taking the SOC 2000 classification.[1] Overall, there are remarkable differences in the skill structure of the three types of employees, and with respect to the changes that took place after the 2008–2009 economic crisis. The share of high-skilled jobs, represented by managerial and professional occupations, is the highest among fixed-term employees, followed by permanent employees, and with a remarkable gap, by casual workers. The reverse applies with respect to the share of low-skilled jobs. Sales, operative, and elementary jobs are most common among casual workers, followed by permanent workers and fixed-term workers (Labour Force Surveys, 1992–2011).

With respect to the changes in skill structure, there was a visible change for all employees between 2001 and 2006. The share of high-skilled occupations

[1] The skill levels are defined using SOC 2000 from LFS quarterly data. LFS does not provide SOC 2000 in 2012; therefore the latest year included in this figure is for 2011. Note that there is a continuity in trends in skill distribution from 2009 onwards, thus 2011 figures are believed to represent skill structure of 2012.

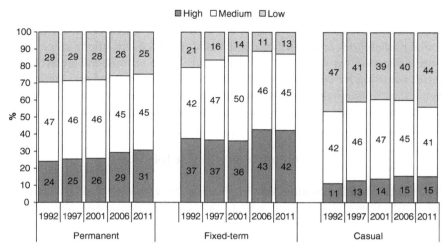

Figure 5.3. Changes in the Skill Distribution of Employees by Contract Type, 1992–2011

Notes: Skills groups based on SOC 2000. High-skilled jobs are e.g. managers and professionals, medium-skilled jobs are e.g. associate professionals and technicians, administrative and secretarial occupations, skilled trades, and personal services, and low-skilled jobs are e.g. sales, operative, and elementary occupations.

Source: UK LFS, unweighted distributions

increased, while there was a decline in the share of low-skilled occupations. The change was particularly striking for fixed-term workers. The share of high-skilled occupations increased from 37 per cent to 43 per cent. After the economic crisis, the upskilling trend continued for permanent employees; however, there was a slight downskilling for temporary workers. Among fixed-term employees the share of low-skilled occupations increased from 11 to 13 per cent, and the share of high-skilled jobs dropped from 43 to 42 per cent. The downward trend for casual workers was more drastic. While the share of high-skill jobs remained at 15 per cent, there was a four percentage point increase in the share of low-skilled jobs (from 40 to 44 per cent).

5.5. TRENDS IN JOB QUALITY: FINDINGS FROM THE SES

This section examines how the quality of jobs held by employees with different contractual arrangements changed over time, and investigates whether there has been a convergence or a divergence in trends between 1992 and 2012 using the five waves of the SES. A short discussion of trends in absolute levels of job quality for each job quality indicator is followed by results from multivariate analysis with pairwise comparisons of fixed-term vs. permanent employees, casual vs. permanent employees, and casual vs. fixed-term employees. Gross differences between groups of employees are calculated for each survey year separately. For each survey, weights are used to take into account for differential probabilities of sample selection, based on LFS distributions of sex, age, and occupation for each corresponding year. These estimations are recalculated, adjusting for compositional differences with controls for skill level, age, gender, part-time status, and ownership sector of the workplace (see Technical Appendix). Both gross and adjusted differences are presented in tables.

5.5.1. Opportunity to Use Job Skills

The use of job skills has important implications for employees' self-realization, job satisfaction, and well-being, whilst enhancing their employment prospects. Having a job that allows the use of one's current job skills helps prevent skill depreciation. Hence, employees who find themselves in jobs with little scope for using their competencies will be frustrated, demotivated, and less competitive in the job market.

The opportunity to use job skills is derived from the SES question asking respondents whether in their job they have enough opportunity to use the knowledge and skills that they have. Those who agree or strongly agree with the statement are considered to have the opportunity to use job skills. There has been a mild increase between 2001 and 2012 in the percentage of permanent and fixed-term employees who have enough opportunities to use their knowledge and skills at work (from around 80 per cent to 86 per cent). The share of casual workers with the opportunity to use their skills at work has been somewhat lower than the other two groups, with a sharp decrease in 2006 and a recovery in 2012.

Multivariate models (Table 5.1) show that only some of these differences remain statistically significant, after compositional controls are introduced. Permanent and fixed-term workers did not differ in terms of opportunity to use skills even after adjusting for compositional differences. In the gross models, a disadvantage for casual workers was evident with respect to both fixed-term and permanent employees throughout the 2000s. In 2001 these differences were due to compositional differences of casual workers, hence disappearing once these factors were taken into account. In 2006, the strong negative effect of casual contracts on opportunities for using job skills remained in adjusted models, signalling an inherent disadvantage in this regard. After the economic crisis casual workers still fared worse compared to permanent employees, yet the gap between casual and fixed-term employees disappeared, after controlling for compositional factors. In other words, the difference in levels of opportunity to use job skills between the two types of temporary workers was due to the differences in their composition. Once these factors are controlled for, there was a clear convergence between these two groups.

Table 5.1. Temporary vs. Permanent Employees: Differences in Opportunity to Use Job Skills

Has enough opportunity to use the knowledge and skills that one has

	Gross differences			Adjusted differences		
	2001	2006	2012	2001	2006	2012
Fixed-term vs. permanent	−0.016	0.032	−0.147	0.052	−0.198	−0.182
Casual vs. permanent	−0.803**	−2.099***	−1.224**	−0.496	−1.878***	−1.052**
Casual vs. fixed-term	−0.787*	−2.131***	−1.077*	−0.548	−1.680***	−0.871
N	3925	5468	2386	3925	5468	2386

Notes: Analyses carried out for each year separately. Adjusted models control for gender, age, occupational skill level, part-time work, and ownership sector. Significant at * = 10 per cent, ** = 5 per cent,*** =1 per cent.

Source: SES

5.5.2. Learning and Training Opportunities

Temporary employees are repeatedly found to lag behind in the learning and training opportunities provided to them by their employers or by their job settings. It is assumed that employers are most often not willing to invest in the training of their temporary staff because of the inability to benefit later on from their skill improvements. A lack of learning and training opportunities effectively hinders the employment prospects of temporary workers, who may then be trapped in a series of short-term contracts and unemployment spells. In contrast, those who are able to attend training and work in jobs that allow them to learn new things become more employable: they are less likely to experience unemployment and more likely to move to permanent jobs.

We examine first the importance of 'competencies' or 'practical expertise', that, in contrast to formal training, could be acquired through a process of *informal learning* based primarily on experience on the job. Job settings that provide workers with opportunities for learning on the job enhance their competencies and may increase job satisfaction, engagement, motivation, productivity, and career prospects. The SES question 'My job requires that I keep learning new things' is a useful indicator of informal learning.

With respect to employees who agreed or strongly agreed that their job required learning new things, the differences between permanent, fixed-term, and casual workers are rather trivial in 1992, with a relatively small gap between casual workers on the one hand and fixed-term and permanent workers on the other. The gap widens between 1992 and 2006 due to a sharp decline in informal learning for casual workers, which is followed by a recovery after the economic crisis. There is also an increase in the share of fixed-term workers with informal learning opportunities in 2012, exceeding the share of permanent workers.

Multivariate models show that indeed in 1992 there were no statistically significant differences in informal learning among the three groups (Table 5.2). Between 2001 and 2012, the gap between casual workers and others is large. These differences are also statistically significant in both gross and adjusted models, with one exception: once compositional differences are taken into account, the difference between casual and fixed-term employees are no longer significant in 2006.

We next investigate three different aspects of training opportunities, all of which are of significance for skills development: its *incidence* (i.e. whether or not someone has received work-related training in a given time period), its *duration* (i.e. the total length of training spells in a given time period), and its *quality* (i.e. usefulness of training for skill improvement). The SES introduced a large set of questions on all three aspects of training in 2006. Training incidence is captured with an item asking respondents whether or not they participated over the previous year in each of the following forms of training: training from someone which took you away from your normal job; instructions whilst performing the normal job; self-teaching from a book, manual, video, computer, DVD, or the internet; correspondence or internet course, evening classes; and other work-related training. Those who participated in one of these training activities were then asked how many separate days they had spent on each activity, providing a measure of training duration. Trainees were also asked a number of questions reflecting the quality of these training spells. They were asked if the training: improved their skills; was useful for another job in the same industry; was useful for another job in a different industry; led to a credit towards a qualification; and helped to improve the way that one works. A standardized index item is used here for training quality. This extended set of training questions was only available in the 2006 and 2012 surveys.

Similar to opportunities for skill use and informal training, the levels of training are rather similar for fixed-term and permanent employees, with fixed-term workers scoring slightly higher on all indicators. Casual workers are disadvantaged in both 2006 and 2012; however, they drew closer to the rest in 2012.

The share of permanent and fixed-term workers who had training in the previous twelve months remained stable over the period, at around 65 per cent for permanent and 68 per cent for fixed-term employees. In contrast, there was a remarkable increase in the share of casual workers who received training, rising from 40 per cent to 62 per cent. In contrast to the stability in training incidence experienced by fixed-term and permanent employees, there was a decline in its volume. Both absolute numbers of days spent in training

Table 5.2. Temporary vs. Permanent Employees: Differences in Learning Opportunities

Job requires learning new things

	Gross differences				Adjusted differences			
	1992	2001	2006	2012	1992	2001	2006	2012
Fixed-term vs. permanent	0.008	0.23	0.087	0.639	−0.205	0.189	−0.548	0.334
Casual vs. permanent	−0.329	−0.913***	−1.708***	−1.130**	−0.176	−0.627*	−1.257***	−1.043**
Casual vs. fixed-term	−0.337	−1.143**	−1.794***	−1.770***	0.029	−0.815*	−0.709	−1.376*
N	3239	3930	5469	2387	3239	3930	5469	2387

Notes: Analyses carried out for each year separately. Adjusted models control for gender, age, education, part-time work, and industry. Significance of temporary/permanent gap at * = 10 per cent, ** = 5 per cent, *** = 1 per cent.

Source: SES

and the share of those receiving training for ten days or longer decreased in 2012. Casual workers also experienced a decline in the number of days spent in training; however, the share of those receiving 'long' training increased slightly. Finally, there was an improvement in the quality of training for all types of employee, but especially for casual workers.

Multivariate models suggest that casual workers' poorer training opportunities were statistically significant in 2006, both in gross and composition-adjusted models (Table 5.3). Only for training incidence was the difference between fixed-term and casual workers attributable to the compositional differences between the two groups. The results for 2012 indicate a remarkable convergence in training opportunities between casual workers, on the one hand, and workers with fixed-term and permanent contracts, on the other hand. The 'casual vs. the rest' gap is significant for the incidence of long training in gross models, but this gap also disappears once controls are added in the models.

Table 5.3. Temporary vs. Permanent Employees: Differences in Training Opportunities

	Gross differences		Adjusted differences	
	2006	2012	2006	2012
Training incidence				
Fixed-term vs. permanent	0.368	0.141	−0.231	−0.074
Casual vs. permanent	−1.203***	−0.400	−0.880***	−0.276
Casual vs. fixed-term	−1.571***	−0.541	−0.649	−0.203
N	5458	2383	5458	2383
Training duration				
Fixed-term vs. permanent	12.597	8.185	−0.892	5.099
Casual vs. permanent	−32.180***	−24.951	−25.778**	−19.744
Casual vs. fixed-term	−44.777***	−33.136	−24.886*	−24.844
N	5323	2205	5323	2205
Incidence of long training (ten days or more)				
Fixed-term vs. permanent	0.432*	0.230	0.037	0.185
Casual vs. permanent	−1.314***	−0.825*	−1.077***	−0.575
Casual vs. fixed-term	−1.746***	−1.054*	−1.114**	−0.760
N	5323	2205	5323	2205
Training quality				
Fixed-term vs. permanent	0.151*	0.123	−0.055	0.074
Casual vs. permanent	−0.458***	−0.157	−0.302***	−0.085
Casual vs. fixed-term	−0.609***	−0.280	−0.247**	−0.159
N	5458	2382	5458	2382

Notes: Analyses carried out for each year separately. Adjusted models control for gender, age, occupational skill level, part-time work, and ownership sector. Significant at * = 10 per cent, ** = 5 per cent, *** = 1 per cent.

Source: SES

5.5.3. Work Intensity

Even though sustained work intensity can have adverse effects on workers' well-being, especially when it is accompanied with poor work organization (see OECD, 2014a for a review), it can also be stimulating, rewarding, and induce productivity. The SES include a number of items to capture the level of work effort and intensity covering a period of twenty years. It asks respondents whether (1) their job requires working very hard, (2) work involves working at very high speeds, or (3) to tight deadlines, (4) if they have to work extra hours to get through the work, and (5) if they work under a great deal of pressure. A standardized work intensity index is constructed using these five items.

Throughout the period 1992 to 2012, permanent employees worked in jobs with the highest intensity level, followed by fixed-term workers. Jobs held by casual workers involved relatively less intensity. All employees experienced an increase in work intensity. For permanent workers there was a sharp rise in the period between 1992 and 2001 which levelled off after 2006, but then increased slightly after the economic crisis. Work intensity for fixed-term contract holders increased gradually between 1992 and 2006, and remained stable in 2012. For casual workers the work intensity index remained low and stable until 2006, after which there has been a slight increase. There remained, however, a significant gap between casual and permanent employees even in 2012.

The gross differences in work intensity between casual workers and the other two groups are statistically significant throughout this period (Table 5.4). What is notable, however, is that once compositional differences are controlled for, there are no differences in work intensity between the jobs held by casual workers and those held by fixed-term workers. There is, however, a gap between fixed-term and permanent workers in both 2001 and 2006, even after we control for compositional factors. In both years, fixed-term workers had less work intensity than permanent workers, but this gap disappeared in 2012.

The implications of work intensity for career and employment opportunities are important. While low work intensity faced by temporary workers could potentially reduce the risk of stress-related ill-health, it is worth noting that low-intensity jobs are negatively correlated with employee motivation and productivity, which in turn could have negative repercussions on temporary employees' career advancement.

5.5.4. Job Control

Job control refers to the level of influence workers have over their immediate work tasks and wider decisions concerning their work. It not only gives them control, it also buffers the potential negative consequences on the well-being of excessive work intensity (Karasek 1979; Karasek and Theorell 1992). Job

Table 5.4. Temporary vs. Permanent Employees: Differences in Work Intensity

Work intensity index

	Gross differences				Adjusted differences			
	1992	2001	2006	2012	1992	2001	2006	2012
Fixed-term vs. permanent	−0.069	−0.187***	−0.018	−0.104	−0.078	−0.183***	−0.127*	−0.125
Casual vs. permanent	−0.206***	−0.390***	−0.427***	−0.404***	−0.160***	−0.280***	−0.237***	−0.321***
Casual vs. fixed-term	−0.137*	−0.202*	−0.409***	−0.300*	−0.083	−0.097	−0.110	−0.197
N	3254	3932	5470	2391	3254	3932	5470	2391

Notes: Analyses carried out for each year separately. Net models control for gender, age, education, part-time work, and industry. Significance of temporary/permanent gap at * = 10 per cent, ** = 5 per cent, *** = 1 per cent.

Source: SES

control, in itself, is also crucial for opportunities for self-development and self-realization as well as for employee motivation and well-being, thereby constituting a particularly important aspect of intrinsic job quality.

We investigate two aspects of job control: task discretion and workplace voice. To measure the former, the SES ask four questions designed to assess how much personal influence workers have over specific aspects of their daily work tasks: over how hard they work; deciding what tasks they are to do; deciding how they are to do the task; and the quality standards to which they work to. These items are measured with a four-point response scale ranging from 'not at all' to 'a great deal'. A task discretion index is constructed by standardizing the four items.

Trends in task discretion indicate a decline between 1992 and 2012—a decline which was steepest for casual workers, followed by fixed-term workers. There has been a partial recovery in task discretion among fixed-term workers between 2001 and 2012, and among casual workers after 2006.

The multivariate models for task discretion are presented in Table 5.5. Even though there were differences in task discretion among three groups until the mid-2000s, a convergence in task discretion is observed in 2012. Composition-adjusted models show that there was a divide between both types of temporary workers and permanent workers in 2001. This turned into a contrast between casual workers and the rest in 2006. These differences disappeared altogether after the economic crisis, due to an increase in task discretion among temporary, and particularly casual, workers.

With respect to workplace voice, respondents were initially asked 'Suppose there was going to be some decision made at your place of work that changed the way you do your job. Do you think that you personally would have any say in the decision about the change or not?' Those who think they would have a say were then asked how much say or chance they would have to influence that decision. In contrast to the recovery in temporary workers' task discretion, there has been a downward trend in their influence over work decisions at organizational level, which continued between 2006 and 2012.

This trend in influence over work decisions is exceptional in the sense that this is one of the few aspects of job quality in which there has been a divergence between both types of temporary workers and permanent workers, rather than between casual workers and the rest. Temporary workers had less influence over work decisions than permanent workers between 1992 and 2012. Their influence eroded further after the economic crisis.

5.5.5. Pay and Unemployment Experience

Earnings from employment and labour market insecurity are the other important aspects of job quality. We take gross hourly pay as the measure of

Table 5.5. Temporary vs. Permanent Employees: Differences in Task Discretion and Workplace Voice

Task discretion index

	Gross differences					Adjusted differences				
	1992	1997	2001	2006	2012	1992	1997	2001	2006	2012
Fixed-term vs. permanent	−0.084	0.030	−0.198***	−0.034	−0.024	−0.086	−0.004	−0.176***	−0.090	−0.064
Casual vs. permanent	−0.020	−0.205*	−0.336***	−0.547***	−0.190*	0.029	−0.066	−0.242**	−0.333***	−0.163
Casual vs. fixed-term	0.063	−0.235*	−0.138	−0.513***	−0.166	0.114	−0.061	−0.066	−0.243***	−0.099
N	3197	2149	3926	5460	2382	3197	2149	3926	5460	2382

Has quite a lot/great deal of influence over decisions at work

	Gross differences				Adjusted differences			
	1992	2001	2006	2012	1992	2001	2006	2012
Fixed-term vs. permanent	−0.044	−0.569*	−0.377	−1.073**	−0.086	−0.472	−0.428	−1.060**
Casual vs. permanent	−0.523**	−1.216**	−1.034**	−1.648**	−0.379	−0.975*	−0.614	−1.522**
Casual vs. fixed-term	−0.479	−0.648	−0.657	−0.574	−0.293	−0.503	−0.186	−0.461
N	3214	3917	5456	2384	3214	3917	5456	2384

Notes: Analyses carried out for each year separately. Adjusted models control for gender, age, education, part-time work, and industry. Significance of temporary/permanent gap at * = 10 per cent, ** = 5 per cent, *** = 1 per cent.

Source: SES

earnings. But differences in hourly pay need to be considered in conjunction with unemployment experience as the latter effectively determines the amount of yearly earnings.

There was an increase in gross hourly wages for all groups between 1992 and 2012; however, the increase was more modest for casual workers, creating a divergence in pay. These differences in hourly pay among casual workers and the rest are explained by compositional differences. Gross differences indicate a significant and increasing gap—a gap that disappears when skill level, age, gender, part-time status, and ownership sector are controlled for.

With respect to unemployment experience, the SES asks respondents whether they were unemployed for a month or more at any time in the previous year. Both fixed-term and casual workers were more likely to have had an unemployment spell. Around one-fifth to one-quarter of temporary workers had been unemployed in the twelve months as opposed to one in twenty permanent employees.

Moreover, the differences between temporary and permanent workers' probability of having had unemployment experience remain statistically significant throughout the period, including in the composition-adjusted models, except for differences between casual and permanent workers in 2001 (Table 5.6).

Overall, the analyses show that there is no hourly wage penalty for workers in temporary contracts, net of compositional differences. Workers with similar characteristics but with different contractual arrangements are paid similar hourly wages. However, both fixed-term and casual workers are more likely to have been unemployed within the previous twelve months. This effectively reduces the yearly earnings of temporary workers. This is equally true of fixed-term and casual workers.

5.5.6. Subjective Responses to Temporary Work: Fear of Job Loss and Job Satisfaction

The results from the SES 1992–2012 showed that there are remarkable differences in job quality between temporary and permanent workers, with those on casual contracts in particular lagging far behind others. Fixed-term workers are also disadvantaged with respect to workplace voice and unemployment experience. Are there differences among the employees' subjective responses to their contractual arrangements? This section examines the trends in fear of job loss and job satisfaction. Fear of job loss is measured with a question asking respondents whether they think they would lose their job in the next twelve months, and if so, the likelihood of this happening. Overall job satisfaction is measured with a 1–7 answer scale that is reverse coded, with 1 representing completely dissatisfied and 7 representing completely satisfied.

Table 5.6. Temporary vs. Permanent Employees: Differences in Pay and Unemployment Experience

Gross hourly pay

	Gross differences					Adjusted differences				
	1992	1997	2001	2006	2012	1992	1997	2001	2006	2012
Fixed-term vs. permanent	0.454	0.888*	0.177	0.402	1.520	0.320	0.680	1.039	−0.83	1.591
Casual vs. permanent	−0.603*	−1.467**	−1.901	−3.710**	−3.528*	−0.374	0.019	−0.163	−0.124	−2.101
Casual vs. fixed-term	−1.057**	−2.355***	−2.078	−4.112*	−5.048*	−0.694*	−0.661	−1.202	0.706	−3.692
N	2616	1969	3632	4816	2065	2616	1969	3632	4816	2065

Unemployed in the last twelve months

	Gross differences			Adjusted differences		
	2001	2006	2012	2001	2006	2012
Fixed-term vs. permanent	1.403***	1.627***	1.291***	1.785***	1.967***	1.664***
Casual vs. permanent	0.981*	1.994***	1.753***	0.817	1.307***	1.778***
Casual vs. fixed-term	−0.423	0.366	0.462	−0.968	−0.66	0.114
N	2838	5460	2381	2838	5460	2381

Notes: Analyses carried out for each year separately. Adjusted models control for gender, age, education, part-time work, and industry. Significance of temporary/permanent gap at * = 10 per cent, ** = 5 per cent, *** = 1 per cent.

Source: SES

Starting with subjective job insecurity, there is a large gap between permanent and temporary employees' levels of fear of job loss (Table 5.7). While only 5 per cent of the former think it is likely that they will lose their job and become unemployed, it is much higher among casual and fixed-term workers. In 1997 almost half of those on casual contracts and one quarter of those in fixed-term contracts felt subjective insecurity. The gap narrowed in 2001 with a sharp decline of job insecurity among casual workers. There was a further but smaller decline for this group between 2006 and 2012 whereas job insecurity increased for fixed-term workers. The multivariate models show that the differences in 1997 were statistically significant in both gross and adjusted models. Fixed-term workers were more fearful than permanent workers of losing their job, whereas casual workers were more fearful than both fixed-term and permanent workers. The differences between casual and fixed-term workers disappeared between 2001 and 2012 but remain statistically significant for temporary workers vs. permanent employees.

Turning finally to job satisfaction, there was a decline in job satisfaction between 1992 and 2001 for all employees. The levels of job satisfaction somewhat recovered for fixed-term and permanent workers between 2001 and 2006 while remaining much lower among casual workers. After the economic crisis there was a small decline in the job satisfaction of fixed-term and permanent workers but it increased slightly for casual workers, indicating a converging trend. Indeed, the differences between casual and other workers became statistically insignificant in 2012, in both gross and composition-adjusted models, supporting the idea of a convergence in job satisfaction after the economic crisis.

5.6. CONCLUSION

Turning back to the initial theoretical expectations, the first prediction was a divergence between permanent and temporary workers over time, due to employers gaining more power after the economic crisis and shifting the risks to peripheral workers. This negative scenario was contrasted with a positive one, arguing that a process of creative destruction could have taken place as a result of the recession, eliminating the worst-quality jobs in poor industries, which were disproportionately held by temporary workers, effectively leading to an upward shift in their average job quality. In addition to this, the arrangements in EU regulations on temporary workers, which were also adopted in Britain, were expected to lead to a convergence in job quality between permanent and temporary workers. A third argument pointed to the heterogeneity of temporary workers and expected a cleavage

Table 5.7. Temporary *vs.* Permanent Employees: Differences in Fear of Job Loss and Job Satisfaction

Fear of job loss

	Gross differences				Adjusted differences			
	1997	2001	2006	2012	1997	2001	2006	2012
Fixed-term vs. permanent	0.222***	0.160***	0.217***	0.241***	0.225***	0.167***	0.227***	0.251***
Casual vs. permanent	0.433***	0.191***	0.272***	0.173***	0.426***	0.185***	0.263***	0.186***
Casual vs. fixed-term	0.211***	0.030	0.056*	−0.068	0.201***	0.018	0.035	−0.065
N	2117	3839	5370	2222	2117	3839	5370	2222

Job satisfaction

	Gross differences				Adjusted differences			
	1992	2001	2006	2012	1992	2001	2006	2012
Fixed-term vs. permanent	−0.193*	−0.035	0.026	0.069	−0.204*	−0.070	−0.032	−0.017
Casual vs. permanent	−0.217*	−0.467**	−0.638***	−0.294	−0.211*	−0.454**	−0.594***	−0.341
Casual vs. fixed-term	−0.024	−0.432*	−0.664***	−0.363	−0.008	−0.383*	−0.562***	−0.324
N	3237	3917	5457	2391	3237	3917	5457	2391

Notes: Analyses carried out for each year separately. Adjusted models control for gender, age, education, part-time work, and industry. Significance of temporary/permanent gap at * = 10 per cent, ** = 5 per cent, *** = 1 per cent.

Source: SES

between those on shorter-term contracts, referred to as casual workers throughout the chapter, and those on longer-term contracts, referred to as fixed-term workers.

The analyses above showed that there were remarkable differences in levels and trends of job quality between permanent, fixed-term, and casual workers. There was clear evidence that jobs held by casual workers were the poorest in quality in terms of all the indicators discussed. Fixed-term workers shared similar levels of job quality with permanent workers with respect to opportunities for use of job skills, learning opportunities, task discretion, pay, and job satisfaction. They had better training opportunities than permanent workers but they fell short with respect to workplace voice, they were more likely to have been unemployed, and they felt more insecure about their jobs. These findings point to a divide within the temporary workforce and also lend some support to the arguments that fixed-term jobs were, in many respects, of similar quality to permanent jobs.

In terms of the convergence or divergence debate, there was one result that provided some support for the divergence hypothesis, which predicted an increased polarization of the workforce due to a shift in power balance in employer–employee relations after the recession. This divergence was the decreased workplace voice in 2012 among both fixed-term and casual workers.

But there was more substantial support for a convergence in job quality by contract type. The analyses also indicated a convergence after the economic crisis between the three types of contracts, mainly resulting from a remarkable increase in the job quality of casual workers. What could have driven this convergence?

The 'creative destruction' thesis pointed to the possibility of an upskilling among temporary workers that could have led to improvements in other aspects of job quality. However, as was seen in section 5.3, there was a downskilling among casual workers, while the share of high-skilled occupations among permanent workers increased slightly. Moreover, the analyses of the SES data on trends in job quality controlled for skill level of respondents.[2] Therefore, it seems implausible that the improvement in job quality among casual workers resulted from an upskilling of this type of work.

An alternative argument was that regulatory change may have led to an improvement in the working conditions of casual workers. Turning back to the changes in EPL, in 2003 there was an improvement with respect to the regulation of fixed-term contracts: a limit was brought to the maximum cumulative duration of successive open-ended contracts. Further improvement in temporary work took place with the adoption of the Agency Worker

---

[2] The estimations also included weights in order to take into account differential probabilities of sample selection (calculated with LFS distributions of sex, age, and occupation).

Regulations that ensured equal treatment of agency workers in terms of pay and basic working conditions. This was followed by a weakening of the protection of permanent workers with the trial time being increased back to twenty-four months. These two regulatory changes in 2011 and 2012 narrowed the EPL gap between permanent and temporary employees to its smallest point during the twenty-eight years for which data is available. Therefore, it is possible that the convergence in job quality was driven, at least partially, by the recent statutory changes.

6

Job Quality and the Self-Employed

Is It Still Better to Work for Yourself?

Ben Baumberg and Nigel Meager

6.1. INTRODUCTION

This chapter focuses on self-employment, drawing on the Skills Employment Surveys (SES) to examine the intrinsic quality of the jobs undertaken by the self-employed. In doing this, it offers a far fuller picture of the quality of self-employed work in Britain and how it has been changing over time than has hitherto been available. Most of the previous literature—selected features of which are highlighted below—has focused on changes in the extent of self-employment, the personal characteristics of the self-employed, and some key characteristics of their jobs (for example, occupation, sector, working time, and income), rather than the actual intrinsic quality of self-employment.

The literature highlights some 'positive' and 'negative' features of this form of work and how the balance between them may have changed over time. This includes examining factors such as the level and stability of self-employed incomes, and the extent to which spells of self-employment during a working career increase or reduce individuals' economic well-being over the life cycle. For the most part, however, it does not focus on what it is like to work as a self-employed person—how intensively the self-employed work, how much autonomy and discretion they really have in their work tasks, what skills they deploy, and how their work makes them feel. Such questions are addressed for the first time through the findings from the SES surveys reported below.

The chapter begins by considering what is and what is not known about self-employment in Britain. In the context of these debates, the contributions of this chapter are twofold. First, the chapter builds on existing literature which highlights greater levels of happiness and job satisfaction among the self-employed than among employees, to ask whether these differences are also reflected, as is often assumed, in more objective measures of intrinsic job quality.[1] Specifically, given the debate about whether self-employment represents marginalized or privileged workers, we examine whether self-employment is on average 'better' or 'worse' than working as an employee—or more precisely, we look at the differences between wage employment and self-employment across a number of different aspects of intrinsic job quality. Second, given the suggestion that rises since the recession in self-employment are primarily in 'bad' self-employment, we examine whether self-employment has 'improved' or 'deteriorated' over time, in particular focusing on changes since the recession in 2008–2009. Throughout the chapter we focus in particular on the various aspects of intrinsic job quality that are uniquely available in the SES series.

6.2. EXISTING LITERATURE

There has been a long-standing debate about the intrinsic job quality of self-employment, and whether it represents 'good work' (new opportunities for autonomy and fulfilling work), or 'bad work' (the erosion of security among marginalized workers). This has variously been called 'portfolio' vs. 'marginalization' self-employment (Smeaton, 2003) or 'necessity' vs. 'opportunity' self-employment (Binder and Coad, 2013). Much of this is couched in terms of long-term economic impacts. On the positive side, some have suggested that spells of self-employment are advantageous: partly as they help to keep people attached to the labour market who might otherwise exit, partly to acquire human capital which enhances their future labour market chances, and partly as a 'signal' of positive characteristics towards future employers. Conversely, on the negative side, self-employment may be associated with worse outcomes than other kinds of transitions, resulting in low incomes and social exclusion.

   In practice, the self-employed tend to have much more polarized incomes than do employees, and once other characteristics are controlled for, the impact of being self-employed is to increase an individual's likelihood of falling into the lower deciles of the overall income distribution, while not increasing the likelihood of moving up into the higher deciles (Meager and Bates, 2001). More generally, it seems from the UK data that that there is a 'scarring' effect from self-employment, in the sense that even when individuals leave self-employment, having self-employment experience can have a significant negative impact on employment and income prospects later in life. As Meager (2008, 200) concludes, 'the presence of self-employed spells in the

---

[1] This literature has both academic (Benz and Frey, 2008; Binder and Coad, 2013; Millán et al., 2013, Sutherland, 2013) and policy-oriented strands (D'Arcy and Gardiner, 2014; Dellot, 2014).

previous work history does increase chances of poverty, low savings levels and poor pension entitlement in later life'. Similar findings are also observed from longitudinal data sets in the USA (see, for example, Bruce and Schuetze, 2004; Williams, 2000). The picture is, however, complex, with the impact of self-employment varying according to the length of time over which outcomes are measured.

Evidence of negative impacts, especially for groups of the workforce not traditionally well represented in self-employment, has led to scepticism regarding the promotion of self-employment to disadvantaged groups and the unemployed as a policy tool. One policy rationale for such schemes is that even if subsidized start-ups quickly 'fail', the experience of self-employment will enhance the participants' subsequent labour market chances (measured by employment rates or earning levels). A rare UK example of a longitudinal evaluation of such subsequent impacts, based on a matched control group comparison examined a self-employment scheme targeted at unemployed youth (Meager et al., 2003). It found that participation in such a scheme had no significant impact on subsequent employment chances or earnings levels, and that during the period of self-employment, the participants were worse off in financial terms than their counterparts in the control group. Once again, there was little or no evidence that the transitions into self-employment supported by this kind of programme were generally 'good' ones.

Despite these findings, it is notable that such schemes became the subject of renewed policy interest in the early 2010s. The UK government, for example, launched the 'New Enterprise Allowance Scheme' in October 2013, once again providing subsidized support for the unemployed to take up self-employment. In the policy discussions, as Meager et al. (2011) note, there is often a lack of clarity about whether the underlying rationale for self-employment promotion is mainly to move the unemployed into work (as self-employed), thereby possibly also enhancing their human capital, or whether it is mainly an instrument of enterprise policy, aiming to increase the number of small businesses and the number of private sector jobs as the newly self-employed subsequently go on to employ others.[2] In much policy commentary, at both national and European levels, there is a strong emphasis on the latter. For example, the European Commission claims that: 'Self-employment is an important driver of entrepreneurship and job creation and thus contributes to the European Union's goals of more growth and better jobs' (European Commission, 2010, 5). This policy emphasis relates, in turn, to a long-standing debate in the academic literature (Storey, 1994) about whether supporting start-ups (in general, or among the unemployed in particular) is an effective policy tool to stimulate private sector growth. Many argue (Henrekson and

---

[2] The distinction between sole traders and the self-employed with employees is explored in section 6.4, below.

Johansson, 2010; Shane, 2009) that the latter would be more appropriately served by an emphasis on supporting existing small businesses with high growth potential.

6.2.1. Trends in Self-Employment: 1980s and 1990s

Early work on the changing nature of self-employment in the UK was stimulated by the unusual trajectory of self-employment observed during the 1980s (Meager and Bates, 2004), a period which saw the previous post-war trend of declining self-employment go into reverse. During this period the UK, unlike most other developed economies, experienced rapid self-employment growth, with the level of self-employment almost doubling to 3.5 million between 1979 and 1989, and the self-employment rate (as a percentage of all employment) growing almost as fast from 7.3 to 13.1 per cent.

The consensus from the literature (Bryson and White, 1997; Campbell and Daly, 1992; Meager, 1993; Meager et al., 1992) was that the surge in self-employment reflected an unusual configuration of mutually reinforcing influences. These included an 'unemployment push' in the 1980s recession; a structural shift towards services; the growth of outsourcing and franchising (Felstead, 1991; 1992); a rise in 'bogus self-employment' (driven by tax avoidance), especially in construction (HM Treasury and HM Revenue and Customs, 2009; Winch, 1998): the impact of financial deregulation and easy credit for business start-ups (Cowling and Mitchell, 1997); and public policy initiatives to subsidize the unemployed to enter self-employment (Meager, 1996). The early literature, including work on self-employment using data from the SES series (Burchell and Rubery, 1992; Rubery et al., 1993), had already highlighted the heterogeneity of the self-employed, including many with low levels of independence and autonomy in practice. The subsequent research evidence increasingly suggested that much of the new growth in self-employment was concentrated among those with lower incomes, and that one impact of the growth was to further increase that heterogeneity (see Meager and Bates, 2004).

In the post-2000 period, aggregate self-employment resumed its upward growth (Figure 6.1), which persisted uninterrupted during the economic downturn following the recession in 2008–2009. However, the composition of the self-employed has been changing. One such change relates to the working time of the self-employed. It is well documented in the existing literature that the self-employed (in the UK and most other countries: Parent-Thirion et al., 2007) exhibit much longer average weekly working hours than do employees. There has been debate (Ajayi-Obe and Parker, 2005) about the extent to which this can be seen as a 'good' feature of self-employment, reflecting choice, autonomy, and satisfaction with working life

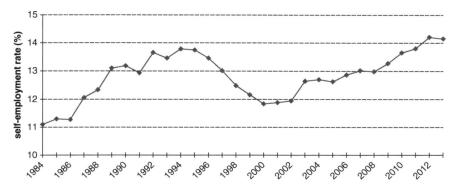

Figure 6.1. Self-Employment Rate, 1984–2013

Source: ONS/Labour Force Survey (seasonally-adjusted data, Annual = four quarter average)

among the self-employed, unconstrained by formal employment contracts and legal regulation of working time. The alternative is that it reflects 'bad' features such as low hourly earnings among large segments of the self-employed who, as a result, work much longer hours to secure a desired level of overall labour income.

6.2.2. Trends in Self-Employment: Post-2000

One striking feature of post-2000 self-employment growth, however, especially during the period of rapid growth since 2000, has been the strongly growing proportion of the self-employed working on a part-time basis (Figure 6.2); since 1984 the number of self-employed part timers has increased by more than 2.5 times, and the share of part timers among the self-employed has increased from 17.0 to 28.4 per cent. As Figure 6.2 shows, the growth in part-time self-employment first became evident during the 1990s, accelerated after 2000, and has been particularly rapid following the onset of the economic crisis in 2008, to the extent that since 2011, for the first time, the share of part-time work among the self-employed is actually higher than among employees.[3]

The sectoral and occupational make-up of post-2000 self-employment growth also suggests some difference between the pre- and post-2008 periods. During the 2001–2008 period, the pattern of self-employment growth had several characteristics familiar from the earlier self-employment boom in the

---

[3] As D'Arcy and Gardiner (2014, 18) note, analysis of the Labour Force Surveys also reveals a growth in the period 2005–2013 in the number of people combining self-employment in their main job (typically part time) with a second job as an employee, although by 2013 this accounted for only a small proportion (around 2 per cent) of total self-employment, and most of this growth occurred in the period immediately prior to the 2008 recession.

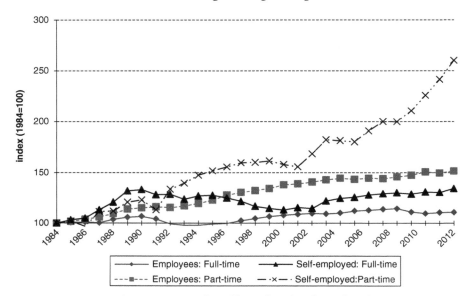

Figure 6.2. Growth Rates among the Self-Employed and Employed, 1984–2012

1980s. In particular, nearly two fifths of self-employment growth was in the construction sector, and at an occupational level a similar proportion was in skilled trades (with a considerable overlap between the two). By contrast, the composition was very different during the period immediately following the recession (2008–2013), although the overall rate of growth of self-employment was similarly fast. At a sectoral level, construction self-employment hardly grew at all (only 5.1 per cent of self-employment growth in this period was in construction), while at an occupational level, traditional self-employment in skilled trades actually fell, despite the overall growth in self-employment. In this latter period, self-employment growth was more evenly distributed sectorally, and somewhat polarized among occupations (with the biggest concentrations in managerial and associate professional occupations on the one hand, and personal services and elementary occupations on the other).

There is therefore a hypothesis that the post-economic crisis surge in self-employment, embodying as it does a continuation of the spread into non-traditional (for self-employment) sectors and occupations and non-traditional (for self-employment) working patterns, might represent a further shift in the balance of self-employment towards 'bad' self-employment. This is reinforced by data from the Family Resources Survey (Levy, 2013) that record a dramatic fall in the median real incomes of the self-employed, which dropped by 16 per cent in the three-year period from 2007–2008 to 2010–2011 (much faster than the recessionary fall in the real incomes of employees).

There are therefore no conclusive explanations for the post-2008 developments in self-employment, and it remains unclear how far the evidence supports some of the contemporary commentary around this topic, exemplified by the Chartered Institute for Personnel and Development which has argued that: 'It is far from clear that the recent rise in self-employment marks a resurgence in British enterprise culture, with many of those taking the self-employed route back to work looking more like an army of part-time "odd jobbers" desperate to avoid unemployment' (CIPD, 2012, 1).

What is nevertheless clear from the data presented above is that, while aggregate self-employment has grown continuously since around 2000, there has been a major discontinuity during that period, and the profile of the new self-employed in the post-2008 period looks rather different from that which preceded it, with an acceleration in the shift towards part-time self-employment, a fall in the median income of the self-employed, and a change in the sectoral and occupational composition of the self-employed. Some of these changes are at least broadly consistent with the hypothesis that the post-crisis growth includes a component of relatively less advantaged self-employment, exhibiting short hours and low incomes and including many in lower-skilled service activities not traditionally the preserve of the self-employed. Self-employment growth in the 1980s and 1990s may have been associated with negative impacts on career and income prospects for a growing segment of those experiencing spells of self-employment. Given the apparent further intensification of such changes since 2000, particularly following the economic crisis in 2007–2008, the data raise important questions about whether there has been a further shift in the balance of 'good' and 'bad' self-employment towards the latter. Finally, however, in examining these questions, it is worth stressing that the previous literature makes it clear that a crude 'good'–'bad' typology is likely to be over-simple, and that in some forms of self-employment there may well be significant trade-offs between positive aspects of this form of work (independence and autonomy) and its more negative aspects (lower incomes and high levels of work intensity). Blanchflower (2004), for example, collating a range of data sources from Organisation for Economic Co-operation and Development countries, highlights such a trade-off. Binder and Coad (2013) provide a more nuanced picture from British Household Panal Survey data, using a distinction (common in the literature) between 'necessity' self-employment (driven by unemployment and a lack of alternatives) and 'opportunity' self-employment, with the latter exhibiting higher levels of life satisfaction than the former.

6.3. THE INTRINSIC QUALITY OF SELF-EMPLOYMENT

To see if self-employment on average is 'better' than working as an employee, we pool the two most recent surveys in the SES series (there are only 399 self-employed people aged 20–60 in the 2012 sample, but a further 868 in the larger 2006 sample, giving us a greater ability to tease apart genuine differences). Throughout this chapter, 'self-employment' is measured by a simple self-reported measure available in all the years of the SES surveys: 'Are you working as an employee or are you self-employed?', and on this definition, 14.4 per cent of workers were self-employed in 2012. We return to the different working arrangements captured by this broad definition of self-employment later.

We focus on four key dimensions of intrinsic job quality: task quality (including discretion, variety, and skill match); skill requirements (training and learning); generic skills; and work effort (both intensity and hours). This enables us to compare dimensions where we would expect—on the basis of the prior literature—the self-employed to have better job quality (e.g. task discretion), worse job quality (e.g. exhaustion), and areas that have not been investigated in detail previously (e.g. generic job skills). We return to the issue below about which of these characteristics can be considered 'better', given that certain dimensions of job quality are ambiguous. Before exploring whether these effects are causal or compositional, we begin by making simple comparisons between self-employed people and employees.[4]

The first area we focus on is task quality, starting with a task discretion scale. This is based on questions about respondents' personal influence over how hard they work, what tasks they do, how they do their job, and the quality standards they work to. For each of these, responses are given on a four-point scale from 0 (no influence at all) to 3 (a great deal of influence); the summary scale simply averages these four responses. We also examine job variety (based on a question asking 'How much variety is there in your job?') and skills match (how much opportunity they have to use their past skills, experience, and abilities in their present job). Using the task-discretion scale, we find that the self-employed have noticeably more discretion than employees, scoring around half a point higher (2.66 vs. 2.18) on a 0–3 scale. The self-employed also report more job variety than employees (44.9 per cent of self-employed people say they have 'a great deal' of variety vs. 30.8 per cent of employees) and greater skill match (57.0 per cent of the self-employed say they can use almost all of their past skills/experience/abilities in their present job, compared with only 39.4 per cent of employees). In this respect, self-employment has higher intrinsic job quality than working as an employee.

The second area we look at is skill requirements, as captured by two questions: (1) whether people have had any training after leaving full-time education for the type of work they currently do, and (2) how long it took people to learn how to do their job well. On the one hand, 44.7 per cent of

---

[4] Estimates in this chapter are weighted (and differences statistically significant) unless otherwise specified. Variables with 7+ response categories are treated as continuous, while those with fewer categories are treated as ordinal.

self-employed people say that it would take them more than two years to learn to do their job well compared with only 23.5 per cent of employees. Yet self-employed people also report *lower* levels of training for the type of work they currently do.

The previous paragraph refers to *broad* skill requirements, but a particular strength of the SES Series is that we can disaggregate this into a range of *generic* skills, for which we use the eleven indices derived by the survey team based on over forty questions on the importance of a type of skill in respondents' jobs: computer use (importance and complexity separately), literacy, numeracy, physical, influence, self-planning, client communication, problem-solving, and emotional and aesthetic skills. When doing this, we can see that there are:

- skills which are similar between employees and the self-employed (numeracy, emotional, and aesthetic skills);
- skills which are used to a greater degree by employees (importance of computer use, complexity of computer use, verbal skills, and influence skills);
- skills which are used to a greater degree by the self-employed (physical, self-planning, client communication, and problem-solving skills).

It is perhaps surprising that physical skills are noticeably higher among the self-employed (2.39 for the self-employed vs. 1.86 for employees on a scale from 0 ('not important') to 4 ('essential')). This may partly be because self-employment is more common in some industries that are more physically demanding (e.g. construction), which is explored below, and partly because self-employed people report greater levels of task variety (as we have already seen above), meaning that even primarily non-physical jobs have a greater physical component. This suggests no simple answer to the question as to whether self-employment is higher quality than working as an employee in terms of skill use and training.

Another critical aspect of intrinsic job quality is work effort, and again, rather than finding that self-employment or working as an employee is of higher quality in all regards, we instead find a different pattern for different measures of work effort. Employees have slightly more intense jobs in terms of how often their job requires them to work at high speed (and to a slight and non-significant degree, also how often their job requires them to work to tight deadlines). However, both of these measures better capture work intensity in some settings than others (high speed better captures assembly line work, while tight deadlines better captures non-manual work). Looking across more general measures, though, it is the self-employed who have noticeably greater work effort, including (1) whether their job requires them to work very hard, (2) how much effort they put into their job beyond what is required, and

(3) the usual hours that they work, including overtime. These differences can be moderately large; for example, 52.7 per cent of the self-employed say that their job requires them to work very hard against only 41.8 per cent of employees, while the reported average hours of employees at 36.6 hours per week compares to 40.6 hours per week among the self-employed.

We also look at several measures that can be thought of as *consequences* of high work effort—although the additional effort of self-employed people may (for some consequences) be somewhat compensated for by greater discretion. Hence we find no difference between the employed and self-employed in terms of whether people say that they work under a great deal of tension, nor in whether they say they come home from work exhausted. We can also look at 'negative job carry-over' using a scale from Warr (1990), based on averaging responses to how often people (1) find it difficult to unwind at the end of a work day, (2) feel used up at the end of a work day, and (3) keep worrying about job problems after they leave work. Reflecting the greater effort levels above (and possibly also the responsibility that self-employed people have for their own business), self-employed people have slightly higher negative job carry-over, although this is only marginally significant (p<0.10). We can summarize this by saying that employees report having to work faster (and with less task discretion), but the self-employed report having to work harder, for longer, with more negative job carry-over; these result in roughly equal levels of reported tension and exhaustion. However, we should bear in mind that many of these questions ask about what is 'required' in the job, which may be interpreted differently by self-employed people (where require-ments will typically be in terms of client expectations and income) compared with employees (where requirements will typically be in terms of a formal job specification and the expectations of managers).

6.3.1. Intrinsic Job Quality and Job Satisfaction

A final area we look at is job satisfaction, but it is important to stress that this is *not* a direct summary measure of 'job quality' (Brown et al., 2012). Satisfaction is an individual's assessment of the quality of their job compared to their expectations and compared to the other possibilities available to them. So we find that some people express satisfaction with low-quality jobs because of the paucity of alternatives, and that job satisfaction often rises in an economic downturn, not because job quality improves, but because people become more grateful to have any job whatsoever. Nevertheless, it is interesting to look at whether job satisfaction is higher among the employed or the self-employed, partly because the existing literature on self-employment above tends to focus on satisfaction, partly because people's evaluations of their jobs is of interest in itself (Brown et al., 2012), and partly because there are dimensions of job quality that may not be fully captured in other measures. For example, in Smeaton's (2000) analysis of the 1992 Employment in Britain and 2000 Working in Britain surveys, the most common reason for people becoming self-employed is that they 'prefer to be my own boss'. Still, readers should be aware throughout that job satisfaction must not be treated as a direct measure of job quality.

To measure job satisfaction, and bearing this caveat in mind, we look at one overall measure ('all in all, how satisfied are you with your job?—responses here rescaled to be from 1 'completely dissatisfied' to 7 'completely satisfied'), and satisfaction with eight different aspects of the job on the same scale (pay, job security, opportunity to use abilities, being able to use own initiative, hours of work, the work itself, the amount of work, and the variety in the work). Put simply, in nearly every aspect of work, the self-employed are significantly more satisfied than employees—often to the extent of 0.4–0.5 more points on this 1–7 scale. Only for satisfaction with job security are employees more satisfied than the self-employed (by 0.2 points). Following the discussion above, this may suggest that there is something *intrinsically* higher quality about self-employment—but equally it may suggest that job satisfaction is higher because of the measured aspects of job quality above (particularly autonomy); that self-employed people have different expectations about job quality; and/or that they have less appealing alternative jobs to which to compare.

6.3.2. Genuine or Spurious Differences in Intrinsic Job Characteristics?

These differences in the quality of self-employment and employment may not be due to anything about self-employment itself—they may simply reflect that these are different kinds of people doing different kinds of jobs. As data in Appendix 6.A show (Table 6.A2), self-employed people are more likely than other employees to be male, older, and have 2+ dependent children, and are more likely to work in agriculture/mining/fishing, construction or real estate while less likely to work in manufacturing, wholesale/retail, or public administration/education/health.

To see if these differences explain the findings above, we therefore test whether there are statistically significant differences between employees and the self-employed net of a range of controls. Beyond the year of the survey, this includes:

- socio-demographics, including gender, age (quadratic), region (thirteen categories), ethnicity (white/black/Asian/other), living with a partner, and dependent children under sixteen (none/1/2+);

- human capital, both in terms of highest qualifications (NVQ levels 0/1/2/ 3/4–5 combined) and years in paid work since leaving full-time education (quadratic);
- the type of work being done, as measured by a relatively detailed industrial classification (a grouped version of the two-digit Standard Industrial Classification 1992).
- In the main analyses we do not control for occupation, because whether someone is self-employed can influence whether their occupation is classified as 'managerial'. However, in sensitivity analyses we do use occupation (one-digit SOC2000) alongside a simpler industrial classification (one-digit SIC92); see Appendix 6.B for further details and results.

It must be stressed here that there is still a lingering possibility of residual confounding, despite the number of controls used. In particular, people have different opportunities and desires to move into self-employment and this selection process is not captured well by the available controls. Nevertheless, adjusting for these controls enables us to see how far the unadjusted differences between employees and the self-employed simply reflect differences in sociodemographics, human capital, or the work being done.

Net of these controls, the remaining differences between self-employed and employed people are shown in Table 6.1. A few parts of the picture do change when controls are added. Notably, the difference in the usual hours of work becomes much smaller (1.6 hours rather than 4.0 hours per week), and indeed, in a sensitivity analysis controlling for occupation as well as industry the difference becomes even smaller (0.8 hours per week) and non-significant (see Appendix 6.B). This suggests that part of the reason that self-employed people seem to work longer hours is because of the type of person they are and the type of job involved, rather than anything about self-employment per se. We return to these findings about hours of work when looking at trends below.

Taking account of these confounding factors also influences the results above in more minor ways. This includes working under tension and working to tight deadlines (which the self-employed are now significantly less likely to do, marginally significantly ($p < 0.10$) in the latter case), aesthetic skills ('looking the part' and 'sounding the part', which the self-employed are now significantly more likely than employees to say are important), and for problem-solving skills (where the difference becomes non-significant after adding controls).

Yet, in general, nearly all of the patterns identified above are unchanged when adding controls. Compared with employees, the self-employed still have greater task discretion, variety, skills match, and learning time, although less training; use certain generic skills more (physical, self-planning, and client communication skills) and other skills less (computer, literacy, and influencing skills); and work noticeably harder and longer hours but slightly slower. They are also still slightly less satisfied with their job security but more satisfied with every other aspect of their job.

Table 6.1. Intrinsic Job Quality of the Self-Employed vs. Employees (Net of Controls), 2006–2012

	Self-employed vs. employees		Self-employed vs. employees
Task quality		**Work effort**	
Discretion index	0.437**	Work at high speed	−0.192**
Job variety	0.592**	Work to deadlines	−0.137+
Use of past skills/experience	0.504**	Work hard	0.367**
		Work beyond what is required	0.437**
Skill requirements		Usual hours of work	1.583*
Job training after f/t education	−0.418**	Work under tension	−0.172*
Time to learn job	0.669**	Exhausted at end of day	−0.046
		Negative job carry-over scale	0.014+
Generic skills			
Computers-importance	−0.383**	**Job satisfaction**	
Computers-complexity	−0.106*	Pay	0.216**
Literacy	−0.183**	Job security	−0.116*
Numeracy	−0.015	Use of abilities	0.389**
Physical	0.351**	Use of initiative	0.547**
Influence	−0.264**	Hours of work	0.167**
Self-planning	0.329**	The work itself	0.391**
Client communication	0.331**	Amount of work	0.185**
Problem-solving	0.043	Variety in the job	0.290**
Emotional	0.063	Overall satisfaction	0.399**
Aesthetic	0.143**		

Notes: *** = p<0.001. ** = p<0.01. * = p<0.05. For full list of controls, see text. Models are either OLS (discretion index, generic skills, hours of work, feeling scales, job satisfaction) or binary/ordinal logit models.

Source: SES

It is worth noting, however, that the benefits of self-employment seem to be greater among women. Compared to employed women, and taking into account the controls above, self-employed women are less likely to work at high speed and have lower negative job carry-over (and are more satisfied with the amount of work), none of which show any differences for men. Moreover, the gap between working as an employee and being self-employed is greater for women than men for several aspects of job satisfaction (with each of the use of abilities, use of initiative, the work itself, and the variety of work). For further discussion of the gendered quality of work, see Chapters 3 and 4.

6.4. FORMS OF SELF-EMPLOYMENT

So far we have compared employment to 'self-employment' as if the latter were a single, homogeneous form of work—but as section 6.2 highlights, there are clearly several different forms of self-employment, which are likely to have somewhat different characteristics. In particular, most self-employed people are sole traders (78.3 per cent of self-employed in 2012) but a noticeable minority have people working for them (21.7 per cent). Sole traders are different kinds of people than the self-employed-with-staff: for example, they are noticeably younger. Even taking these differences into account, though, it is striking how different these two forms of self-employment tend to be:

- sole traders have lower skill use and particularly skills match than the self-employed-with-staff. Nearly every generic skill is also significantly less important for sole traders than the self-employed-with-staff (with the exceptions of physical and self-planning skills), the difference being greatest for influence skills (0.85 points on a four-point scale);[5]

- sole traders and the self-employed-with-staff are alike in terms of their task discretion;

- the self-employed-with-staff have the greatest work effort, the longest hours of work, and the most exhaustion, compared with *both* sole traders and employees. The extent of this is striking: the self-employed-with-staff work 45 hours per week on average, 10 hours longer than sole traders and 8 hours longer than employees;

- despite this, the self-employed-with-staff report similar levels of overall job satisfaction than sole traders—they are less satisfied with their hours, but more satisfied with their job security, pay, use of skills, variety, and opportunity to use their initiative (contradicting the findings of Sutherland 2013 using the 2006 Skills Survey).

These differences—and the comparison of both types of self-employment with employed people—are shown in Table 6.2.

As before, though, there is still a chance that there are further differences in the nature of work or the process of selection into self-employment that explain these differences. For example, sole traders are much more likely to have been unemployed in the past five years (19.7 per cent vs. 13.4 per cent of the self-employed-with-staff), and on average have been self-employed for a shorter period (7.9 years vs. 10.3 years). It seems likely that the self-employed-with-staff are a subset of people who set out as sole traders, who over time became more successful and were also motivated to expand, and it might be differences in these types of people (rather than differences in the types of self-employment per se) that partly explain these differences.

---

[5] The difference in complexity of computer use between sole traders and the self-employed is only significant at $p = 0.06$.

Table 6.2. Estimated Intrinsic Job Quality (Net of Controls) for Sole Traders *vs.* Others, 2006–2012

	Employed	Self-employed with staff	Sole trader
Task quality			
Discretion index (0–3 scale)	2.19	2.67	2.61
Job variety (a great deal)	30.8%	48.1%	41.5%
Can use 'almost all' skills	40.2%	60.5%	48.6%
Skill requirements			
Job training after f/t education	59.8%	53.0%	50.0%
<1 mth to learn job	20.2%	10.3%	13.2%
Generic skills (1–4 scale)			
Computers - importance	2.72	2.68	2.20
Computers - complexity	1.72	1.84	1.53
Literacy	2.64	2.68	2.37
Numeracy	1.96	2.20	1.85
Physical	1.88	2.19	2.25
Influence	2.32	2.67	1.82
Self-planning	3.03	3.39	3.35
Client communication	2.66	3.26	2.89
Problem-solving	2.83	3.11	2.78
Emotional	2.90	3.16	2.89
Aesthetic	2.63	2.95	2.71

	Employed	Self-employed with staff	Sole trader
Work effort			
Work at high speed (1–7 scale)	4.08	4.39	3.70
Work to deadlines (1–7 scale)	4.70	4.82	4.47
Work hard (strongly agree)	42.1%	60.5%	47.2%
Work beyond required (strongly agree)	69.3%	84.7%	74.7%
Usual hours of work	36.9	45.4	35.8
Work under tension (strongly agree)	20.8%	26.9%	15.4%
Exhausted at end of day (always)	17.0%	24.9%	13.8%
Negative job carry-over (0–1 scale)	0.425	0.518	0.409
Job satisfaction (1–7 scale)			
Pay	4.57	4.99	4.72
Job security	5.29	5.41	5.09
Use of abilities	5.44	5.96	5.78
Use of initiative	5.58	6.30	6.06
Hours of work	5.19	5.05	5.48
The work itself	5.40	5.79	5.80
Amount of work	4.99	5.21	5.16
Variety in the job	5.37	5.79	5.61
Overall satisfaction	5.31	5.71	5.71

Notes: Estimates refer to average marginal effects—that is, estimating the outcome for each person in the combined 2006–2012 sample, varying only their self-employment status, and then averaging these predicted outcomes. For statistical significance of contrasts between groups, and for full list of controls, see text.

Source: SES

6.5. TRENDS IN THE QUALITY
OF SELF-EMPLOYMENT

This chapter so far has shown how the current picture of self-employment compares to employment. But how has this picture changed in the past two decades? For many of these variables we can look at changes from 1992–2012, giving us a twenty-year perspective on the changing nature of self-employment in Britain.

6.5.1. Trends in Self-Employment Itself

As set out in section 6.2, there has been a marked increase in the prevalence of self-employment (although the SES and Labour Force Surveys (LFS) trends differ slightly).[6] The sorts of people and the sorts of jobs that make up the population of the self-employed has also changed (see Table 6.A2 in Appendix 6.A, and Smeaton (2003) for 1992–2000). Partly there have been changes in self-employment that are similar to those among the rest of the labour force: the workforce is more female, older, better educated, contains slightly more ethnic minorities and fewer workers with 2+ children; there has also been a rise in the real estate sector and a fall in manufacturing work. However, there are also changes that seem to be concentrated among the self-employed, such as fewer people not living with a partner and a decline in self-employment in the wholesale and retail trade industry.

To concentrate on changes in the nature of self-employment (rather than its composition), we concentrate on changes in the intrinsic job characteristics of self-employment *after* controlling for the changing make-up of self-employment in Britain.

6.5.2. Trends in the Intrinsic Job Quality of Self-Employment

Looking first at the period up to 2006, this was a mixed period for the quality of self-employment. Task discretion fell, some forms of work effort rose (working fast, working to tight deadlines, hours of work), and tension at

---

[6] The SES trends differ from the LFS in that (1) 1992–2006 the SES shows a flat prevalence of self-employment, whereas the LFS shows a 0.8 per cent fall; and (2) the rise in self-employment 2006–2012 is greater in SES (11.1 per cent to 14.3 per cent) than the LFS (12.9 per cent to 14.1 per cent). The difference in the 1992 figure seems most likely to be due to differences in the timing of interviews. Note also that the definitions of self-employment in LFS and SES differ slightly—if we use the LFS definition in SES (excluding agency staff and sub-contractors), then the prevalence of self-employment drops from 14.3 per cent to 12.1 per cent in 2012, and from 11.1 per cent to 9.5 per cent in 2006 (this definition is not available at earlier waves).

work rose, but use of past skills and certain generic skills (computers, literacy, physical, and problem-solving skills) also rose, with most of these changes occurring in the 1990s rather than the early 2000s. While not a direct measure of job quality (as discussed above), it is worth noting there was also a rise in *every* type of job satisfaction 1992–2006.[7]

The period from 2006 to 2012, however, tells a different story. Job quality fell as measured by task discretion, skill match, time taken to learn the job, and use of problem-solving skills; hours of work also fell. Job satisfaction followed these trends in objective job quality: nearly every measure of job satisfaction fell significantly at conventional levels (p<0.05), other than a marginally significant fall in satisfaction with the amount of work (p<0.10) and stability in satisfaction with hours. Changes in job variety and other measures of work intensity were not statistically significant, however.

The decline in job quality 2006–2012 suggests that the rise in self-employment in this period has indeed been in 'distressed self-employment', as we discussed in section 6.1. The workforce's recent experiences of unemployment also supports this interpretation, as shown in Table 6.3. In 2006, only 12.9 per cent of the self-employed had been unemployed in the past five years, and 6.2 per cent had been unemployed in the past twelve months. By 2012, these figures had more than doubled to 26.5 per cent and 14.5 per cent, respectively. By way of contrast, the proportions of those with unemployment experience among the employed stayed almost constant (unemployment in the past five years rising from 14.8 per cent to 17.4 per cent, and unemployment in the past twelve months rising only from 6.1 per cent to 6.5 per cent).

Further measures also suggest a shift towards newer, less established forms of self-employment from 2006 to 2012. Tenure among self-employed people—i.e. how long they have been self-employed—hovered around nine years between 1997 and 2006, but then dropped in 2012 to 7.6 years (see Table 6.3). Furthermore, the rise in self-employment 2006–2012 is entirely among sole traders (7.7 per cent to 11.2 per cent of the population); the proportion of the self-employed-with-staff actually fell (3.4 per cent to 3.1 per cent). In addition, as shown in Table 6.A2 (Appendix 6.A), a greater proportion of self-employed people were younger and female (although the declining job quality in Table 6.3 is net of age). This suggests that the increase in self-employment is primarily due to younger, newly self-employed sole traders.

---

[7] We do not have measures of most specific aspects of job satisfaction between 1992 and 2006, but the trend in overall job satisfaction suggests that this took place in the early 2000s rather than in the 1990s.

Table 6.3. Trends in the Quality of Self-Employment, 1992–2012 (Net of Controls)

Task quality	1992	1997	2001	2006	2012
Discretion index (0–3 scale)		2.64	2.65	2.65	2.53
Job variety (a great deal)		48.5%	48.6%	44.6%	38.6%
Can use 'almost all' skills	47.7%		53.0%	53.8%	43.7%
Skill requirements					
<one mth to learn job	14.3%	8.8%	11.0%	11.4%	17.7%
Job training after f/t education		45.7%	52.3%	50.4%	52.2%
Generic skills (1–4 scale)					
Computers - importance		1.63	2.06	2.23	2.34
Computers - complexity		1.18	1.39	1.53	1.65
Literacy		2.31	2.46	2.47	2.32
Numeracy		1.95	1.97	1.97	1.88
Physical		2.07	2.16	2.27	2.25
Influence		1.94	2.07	2.03	2.01
Self-planning		3.32	3.34	3.36	3.28
Client communication		2.80	2.96	2.98	2.91
Problem-solving		2.73	2.87	2.96	2.68
Characteristics of self-employed					
Unemployed in past five years				12.9%	26.5%
Unemployed in past twelve months				6.2%	14.5%
Tenure of self-employment (years)		9.14	9.32	9.14	7.56

Work effort	1992	1997	2001	2006	2012
Work at high speed (1–7 scale)	3.02		3.83	3.91	3.83
Work to deadlines (1–7 scale)			4.31	4.53	4.60
Work hard (strongly agree)	45.5%	53.6%	50.5%	52.2%	48.0%
Work >required (strongly agree)	80.7%	81.3%	81.7%	79.8%	73.7%
Usual hours of work		45.0	41.7	39.9	36.0
Full-time (vs. part-time)		79.3%	76.9%	75.2%	62.3%
Under tension (strongly agree)	14.1%		19.2%	18.7%	17.1%
Exhausted at day end (always)		19.9%	16.6%	17.3%	15.1%
Negative carry-over (0–1 scale)	0.454		0.446	0.441	0.431
Job satisfaction (1–7 scale)					
Pay	4.61			4.91	4.63
Job security	4.80			5.33	4.97
Use of abilities	5.67			5.90	5.61
Use of initiative	6.03			6.19	5.90
Hours of work	5.09			5.37	5.36
The work itself	5.67			5.87	5.63
Amount of work	4.88			5.26	5.09
Variety in the job	5.51			5.76	5.42
Overall satisfaction	5.61		5.63	5.80	5.56

Notes: Estimates refer to average marginal effects—that is, estimating the outcome for each person in the combined 1992–2012 sample, varying only their self-employment status and the survey year, and then averaging these predicted outcomes. For statistical significance of contrasts between groups, and full list of controls, see text.

Source: SES

6.5.3. The Changing Gap between the Employed and Self-Employed

Finally, it is worth asking whether these trends in self-employment—the improvements in job quality to 2006 and the deterioration since—increase or lessen the gaps shown in Section 6.3 between employment and self-employment per se. Indeed, if the changes in self-employment are similar to the considerable changes among employees in this period (Felstead et al., 2007; Green, 2006), then considerable change could coexist with an unchanging gap. This is shown in Table 6.4, which shows the gap between employment and self-employment each year, and also (in the final column) shows whether the gap has statistically significantly changed over time. We consider the respective trends firstly for the period up to 2006, and then for 2006–2012.

From the early 1990s to 2006, task discretion fell and some aspects of work effort rose among employees as well as the self-employed, although the shifts in work effort tended to be significantly greater for employees. The timing for the drop in task discretion also differs; it fell for both groups 1992–1997, but then fell further for employees 1997–2001, while only falling for the self-employed in the later 2006–2012 period covered below. In contrast, computer use rose among both groups, but more among the self-employed; and self-employees also saw notable drops in average working hours. Overall job satisfaction was also declining among employees at the same time as it was rising among the self-employed.

Likewise, from 2006 to 2012 there are some similarities between employees and the self-employed, but in general the trends have been different. Employees have seen a rise in negative job carry-over that is not found among the self-employed. In contrast, the self-employed saw a fall in the importance of problem-solving skills and hours of work from 2006 to 2012 that were not seen among employees, and a fall in skill requirements that is much greater and consistent across measures than that seen for employees. Overall, while nearly every measure of job satisfaction fell among employees 2006–2012, it fell by around twice as much as among the self-employed.

Taken together, this means that the gap between the self-employed and employees has changed for some aspects of work but stayed the same for others, as shown in Table 6.4. Generally, the position of self-employment seems to have improved over time relative to that of employment—work effort in self-employment is relatively less, the previous differences in negative job carry-over have evaporated, and certain aspects of job satisfaction have improved compared with employees. And as shown in the LFS data above, part-time work has become more prevalent among the self-employed than employees for the first time and the previous differences in average hours worked have disappeared. However, as the earlier results suggest, the relative

Table 6.4. Gap between Employees and the Self-Employed, 1992–2012 (Net of Controls)

Task quality	1992	1997	2001	2006	2012	Sig. of diff trend
Task quality						
Discretion index (0–3 scale)		0.347**	0.468**	0.481**	0.370**	**0.00**
Job variety (a great deal)		0.117**	0.146**	0.144**	0.095**	0.50
Can use 'almost all' skills	0.067*		0.111**	0.141**	0.044	**0.04**
Skill requirements						
<one mth to learn job	−0.072**	−0.105**	−0.093**	−0.087**	−0.058**	0.05
Job training after f/t education		0.096**	0.091**	0.088**	0.096**	0.99
Job training after f/t education		0.096**	0.091**	0.088**	0.096**	0.99
Generic skills (1–4 scale)						
Computers-importance		−0.627**	−0.401**	−0.401**	−0.389**	0.15
Computers-complexity		−0.289**	−0.172**	−0.134**	−0.080	0.11
Literacy		−0.222**	−0.074	−0.134*	−0.258**	0.16
Numeracy		0.068	0.068	0.047	−0.056	0.66
Physical		0.226**	0.176**	0.353**	0.354**	0.05
influence		−0.241**	−0.113*	−0.254**	−0.284**	0.11
Self-planning		0.394**	0.369**	0.342**	0.311**	0.68
Client communication		0.193**	0.387**	0.356**	0.254**	**0.04**
Problem-solving		−0.067	0.054	0.142**	−0.095	**0.01**

Work effort	1992	1997	2001	2006	2012	Sig. of diff trend
Work effort						
Work at high speed (1–7 scale)	−0.039		−0.221*	−0.151+	−0.321**	0.34
Work to deadlines (1–7 scale)			−0.248*	−0.125	−0.202	0.66
Work hard (strongly agree)	0.128**	0.145**	0.129**	0.124**	0.051	0.36
Work >required (strongly agree)	0.127**	0.100**	0.125**	0.112**	0.042	0.23
Usual hours of work		6.672**	3.807**	2.785**	−0.537	0.00
Full-time (vs. part-time)		0.008	−0.021	−0.037+	−0.165**	0.00
Under tension (strongly agree)	−0.013		−0.018	−0.018	−0.037+	0.90
Exhausted at day end (always)		0.000		0.007	−0.024	0.56
Negative carry-over (0–1 scale)	0.048**		0.030**	0.030**	−0.012	0.00
Job satisfaction (1–7 scale)						
pay	−0.044			0.327**	0.111	0.00
Job security	−0.267**			−0.043	−0.167+	0.11
Use of abilities	0.207**			0.435**	0.252**	0.02
Use of initiative	0.459**			0.571**	0.448**	0.18
Hours of work	−0.099			0.145*	0.193*	0.02
The work itself	0.150*			0.437**	0.305**	0.00
Amount of work	−0.217**			0.221**	0.163*	0.00
Variety in the job	0.097			0.377**	0.139+	0.00
Overall satisfaction	0.184**		0.450**	0.455**	0.337**	0.00

Notes: Estimates are the scale or percentage point differences for self-employment (vs. employees) in each year.
'Sig of difference trend' column tests whether gaps in 1992, 1997, 2001, and 2006 (where available) are *jointly* significantly different from the gap in 2012. Italics indicate statistical significance in difference trend. For full list of controls, see text.

benefits of self-employment in some aspects of job satisfaction fell back from 2006 to 2012.

6.6. CONCLUSION

There has been a long-standing debate about the intrinsic job quality of self-employment, and whether it represents 'good work'. However, while previous studies have looked at the characteristics of self-employed workers and measures such as job satisfaction and hours worked, few studies have been able to look directly at intrinsic job quality in any detail. This is particularly the case for self-employment following the 2008–2009 recession, which we know has risen sharply, particularly part-time self-employment among older workers. Some have therefore suggested it is a rise in 'bad' self-employment, out of necessity when there are two few employee jobs available. The unique data in the SES therefore offer a rare opportunity to speak to these debates directly.

The chapter has three main findings. First, self-employment in general involves a higher intrinsic job quality than working as an employee, even taking into account the differences in the sort of person who is self-employed and the sort of work that they do. Compared with employees, the self-employed have greater task discretion, variety at work and skills match, greater time taken to learn to do their job well, and a slightly slower pace of work; they are also more satisfied with nearly every aspect of their job. Self-employed people work noticeably harder and have less training; they are also less satisfied with their job security, and as described in the literature review, self-employment has further possible pecuniary disadvantages around the chances of low pay and the impact on future earnings. Beyond this, there are further differences in the nature of self-employment that are hard to construe as simply 'good' or 'bad', with the self-employed using certain generic skills more (physical, self-planning, and client communication skills) and other skills less (computer, literacy, and influence skills).

The second finding, though, is that this average picture hides considerable heterogeneity within the ranks of the self-employed. Previous research has shown that the differences between sole traders and the self-employed-with-staff are considerable, and we likewise find that while overall job satisfaction is similar for both forms of self-employment, the intrinsic quality of work otherwise differs substantially between them. In particular, compared with sole traders, the self-employed-with-staff work harder (they work longer hours and more intensely); they do, however, have more satisfaction with the other aspects of their job (greater use of past skills and more satisfaction with most aspects of the work itself). We should bear in mind that the self-employed-with-staff are not necessarily different people from sole traders, but rather, are the subset of sole traders who want to—and are successful enough to—expand to take on more staff as their business develops. Nevertheless, this is a reminder that the *average* characteristics of self-employment include a great many different forms of work in practice.

Finally, over the 2006–2012 period, the quality of self-employment has deteriorated, providing support for those who have argued that these rises in self-employment are not necessarily the 'good' self-employment that many people hold as prototypical. Job quality among self-employed people fell in terms of task discretion, skill use, and use of problem-solving skills, and while work effort fell, it seems that this reflects a change towards less intense and less rewarding work, with nearly every measure of job satisfaction falling between 2006 and 2012. More generally, the rise in self-employment was among new sole traders and people with recent experiences of unemployment, which fits the idea that self-employment is a response to the scarcity of work. However, the extent to which self-employment is now 'bad work' should not be overstated—compared with those working as employees, the intrinsic quality of self-employment generally improved over the past two decades, even if the relative advantages have fallen since 2006.

APPENDIX 6.A. CHARACTERISTICS OF THE SELF-EMPLOYED

Table 6.A1. The Changing Characteristics of the Self-Employed, 1992–2012

Industrial sector SIC 2007	Change Apr–Jun 2001 to Jan–Mar 2008 (000s)	Change Jan–Mar 2008 to Oct–Dec 2013 (000s)
All self-employed	*601*	*528*
Agriculture, forestry, fishing, mining, energy, water	34	33
Manufacturing	6	20
Construction	236	27
Wholesale, retail and repair of motor vehicles	−28	−8
Transport and storage	35	27
Accommodation and food services	18	11
Information and communication	16	63
Financial and insurance services	1	30
Real estate activities	8	14
Professional, scientific and insurance services	71	54
Admin and support services	43	57
Public admin and defence; social security	11	3
Education	57	54

Health and social work	13	52
Other services	78	77

Occupation SOC 2000	Change Apr–Jun 2001 to Jan–Mar 2008 (000s)	Change Jan–Mar 2008 to Oct–Dec 13 (000s)
All self-employed	*601*	*528*
Managers	74	137
Professional	79	41
Associate professional	126	101
Admin and secretarial	−1	37
Skilled trades	232	−49
Personal services	8	99
Sales and customer services	−29	18
Process, plant and machine operatives	44	54
Elementary occupations	67	84

Note: The LFS data used in Table 6.A1 start from June 2001 because this is the point at which the occupational classification used by ONS in the publicly available data changed to SOC 2000.

Source: ONS/Labour Force Survey (quarterly data, not seasonally adjusted)

Table 6.A2. The Changing Characteristics of the Self-Employed and the Employed, 1992–2012

	Self-employed					Employees				
	1992	1997	2001	2006	2012	1992	1997	2001	2006	2012
Gender										
Female	28%	27%	31%	28%	32%	47%	47%	47%	49%	49%
Male	72%	73%	69%	72%	68%	53%	53%	53%	51%	51%
Age group										
20–29	17%	15%	11%	10%	16%	29%	25%	24%	24%	25%
30–44	46%	44%	40%	43%	40%	40%	43%	44%	43%	39%
45–59	37%	41%	49%	48%	43%	31%	32%	33%	34%	36%
Ethnicity										
White	92%	96%	92%	94%	90%	95%	95%	95%	93%	89%
Black	1%	1%	1%	1%	1%	2%	2%	2%	2%	3%
Asian	7%	3%	5%	5%	8%	3%	2%	2%	3%	6%
Other	0%	1%	2%	1%	1%	0%	1%	1%	2%	3%
Living with partner										
Yes	83%	82%	79%	76%	74%	74%	73%	72%	70%	72%
No	17%	18%	21%	24%	26%	26%	27%	28%	30%	28%
Dependent children										
None	39%	54%	54%	56%	55%	50%	60%	59%	60%	58%
One	22%	16%	20%	18%	17%	18%	17%	17%	17%	21%
Two or more	39%	29%	26%	26%	29%	31%	23%	24%	22%	21%

(*continued*)

Table 6.A2. Continued

	Self-employed					Employees				
	1992	1997	2001	2006	2012	1992	1997	2001	2006	2012
Highest quals										
None	16%	20%	16%	13%	6%	21%	18%	13%	9%	5%
NVQ Level 1	7%	10%	9%	8%	11%	6%	8%	10%	10%	10%
NVQ Level 2	24%	27%	19%	16%	14%	25%	29%	22%	20%	20%
NVQ Level 3	28%	20%	25%	29%	25%	22%	18%	23%	23%	22%
NVQ Level 4/5	26%	22%	31%	35%	43%	25%	27%	32%	38%	43%
Industrial sector										
Agriculture, fishing, and mining	7%	7%	4%	4%	7%	2%	1%	1%	1%	1%
Manufacturing and elec/gas/ water	14%	8%	9%	8%	6%	25%	23%	20%	16%	13%
Construction	18%	25%	18%	21%	22%	4%	5%	5%	4%	4%
Wholesale and retail trade	17%	14%	16%	12%	5%	14%	14%	15%	13%	15%
Hotels and restaurants	6%	5%	3%	3%	3%	3%	4%	3%	4%	5%
Transport/communication	5%	6%	6%	7%	6%	7%	8%	6%	6%	5%
Financial intermediation	0%	2%	2%	2%	2%	5%	5%	5%	4%	4%
Real estate	10%	11%	19%	19%	24%	9%	9%	12%	12%	14%
Public administration	0%	0%	1%	1%	0%	10%	7%	8%	10%	7%
Education	4%	2%	2%	5%	6%	10%	9%	10%	10%	11%
Health and social work	5%	8%	8%	10%	6%	11%	12%	12%	14%	15%
Other service activities	14%	12%	12%	10%	13%	3%	4%	4%	4%	4%

Source: SES

APPENDIX 6.B. OCCUPATIONAL AND INDUSTRIAL CLASSIFICATION

6.B.1. Sensitivity Analysis

In the main analysis, we control for two-digit industry (see below). If we control for one-digit occupation and one-digit industry (rather than two-digit industry), then the substantive differences between employment and self-employment are effectively identical, other than the difference in hours of work mentioned in the main text in this chapter. Beyond this, there are only two occasions where the level of statistical significance differs slightly (differences in working to deadlines become slightly more significant ($p<0.05$ rather than $p<0.10$) and differences in negative job carry-over become slightly less significant (ns rather than $p<0.10$).

The same is true for the analysis of trends. In general, the same trends are observed in this sensitivity analysis; the only findings that differ slightly in the sensitivity analysis are that trends in training, verbal, and physical skills are no longer significant at the 5 per cent level.

The picture is different, however, for our comparison of sole traders vs. the self-employed-with-staff. In general, the differences between these are less pronounced in our sensitivity analysis that controls for one-digit occupation; unsurprisingly, many people who are self-employed-with-employees are categorized in the occupational structure as 'managers', even if they are otherwise doing the same type of work as a sole trader. Given that the occupational classification arguably captures self-perceptions and social status more than the type of work, the main results above do *not* control for occupation.

6.B.2. Two-Digit Sic92 for Main Analyses

The two-digit SIC92 classification includes some large (n = 3.5k) and small (n = 1) groups. Groups with n<30 were combined with similar groups in SIC92 until n> = 30 as shown in Table 6.B1.

6.B.3. One-Digit Sic92 for Sensitivity Analyses

We merge small groups in the one-digit version of SIC92 as follows: agriculture/ fishing/mining merged with one another; electricity/gas/water supply merged with manufacturing; private household work merged with other services.

Table 6.B1. Occupational Reclassification

Original code	Merged categories
2 Forestry, logging, etc.	1 Agriculture, hunting, etc.
5 Fishing, fish farms, hatcheries, etc.	
10 Coal, lignite mining, peat extraction	11 Oil, gas extraction (not surveying)
12 Uranium, thorium ore mining	
13 Mining of metal ores	
14 Other mining, quarrying	
16 Tobacco products manufacture	15 Food, beverage manufacture
18 Clothing, fur manufacture	17 Textile manufacture
19 Leather, leather goods manufacture	
20 Wood, straw, cork, wood products (not furniture)	21 Pulp, paper, paper products manufacture
23 Coke, petrol products, nuclear fuel manufacture	24 Chemicals, chemical products manufacture
32 Radio, TV, communication equipment manufacture	31 Electrical machinery, equipment manufacture
37 Recycling	36 Furniture, etc. manufacture
41 Water collection, purification, supply, etc.	40 Electricity, gas, steam, etc. supply
61 Water transport	60 Transport by land, pipeline
62 Air transport	
71 Personal, household, machinery, equipment rental (no op)	70 Real estate activities
90 Sanitation, sewage, refuse disposal, etc.	93 Other service activities
95 Private households with employed persons	

7

Unions and Job Quality

Alex Bryson and Francis Green

7.1. INTRODUCTION

Since the start of the 1980s there has been a transformation in the system of employment relations in Britain. The dominant model in the post-war period, which had been based 'on the shared values of the legitimacy of representation by independent trade unions and of joint regulation' (Millward et al., 2000, 234), was substituted by an emerging system in which management communicates directly with employees via team briefings, town hall meetings, and email, where employees look to their individual statutory rights for protection, and where an employer-driven discourse on productivity growth via human resource management is the dominant paradigm (Dickens and Hall, 2009; Van Wanrooy et al., 2013; Willman et al., 2009; Wood and Bryson, 2009).

In this chapter we ask: what are the implications of this transformation for the level and distribution of job quality? Unions have typically been regarded as a force for equality and fairness at work. A decline in the relative size of the union sector means a decline in union 'reach', and perhaps also of the extent to which unions can make a difference within that reach. It may also entail a reduction in any impact unions might have on the non-union sector.

The restructuring of employment relations is indeed reflected in falling union density: between 1986 and 2012 across the economy the proportion of employees who were union members declined by over one-third from 45.6 per cent to 29.0 per cent (Skills Employment Surveys (SES)). The percentage of employees in the unionized sector also declined, albeit less dramatically, whether one defines the sector in terms of the workplace presence of unions or of workplace recognition for pay bargaining (see Figure 7.1). Both the levels of unionization and the pattern of decline shown in the SES broadly confirm what is known from other sources: a substantial de-unionization in the 1980s and 1990s followed by a somewhat slower rate of decline in the 2000s (Blanchflower and Bryson, 2009; Brown et al., 2009; Bryson and Forth, 2011;

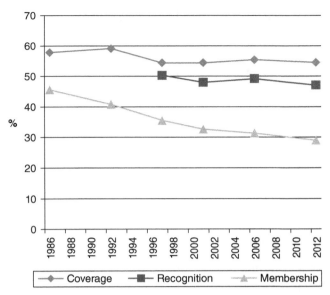

Figure 7.1. Union Coverage, Recognition, and Membership, 1986–2012
Source: SES

van Wanrooy et al., 2013). Schnabel (2013) shows that Britain is by no means unusual in this respect: there has also been falling union density in much of the advanced industrialized world over the last three decades.

It would be wrong, however, to imagine that unions have become a spent force in the British economy. Even after this sustained period of union decline, nearly half of all employees are working in a workplace where at least one union is recognized for pay bargaining, while close to one-third of all employees are union members. Furthermore, where unions remain in situ the trend for union influence is theoretically open: it is likely to depend on the degree of bargaining power unions wield in negotiations with employers. Only if there is a reduction in bargaining power will there be a predicted reduction in influence; according to some theories such a reduction is predicted by increasing market competition, and by the loss of legal protections. Evidence from workplace surveys point to a bifurcation in union strength in workplaces where they still have a presence (Millward et al., 2000, chapter 5). In many instances, where unions remain they are quite weak: negotiations with employers are less common than they once were and, where they do occur, the number of issues over which negotiation occurs has been falling (van Wanrooy et al., 2013, 80–5). Yet many unions have maintained their organizational strength on the ground. Union representation appears to have been remarkably resilient in the face of recession (van Wanrooy et al., 2013, 65–7).

Against this backdrop, the aim of this chapter is to study the changing association of unions with job quality, thereby to improve understanding of the implications of union decline for inequality in the workplace. We draw on a literature that has been primarily focused on unions' effects on wages. A broad aim of our analysis, beyond that of previous studies, is to examine the changing associations between unions and several core domains of intrinsic job quality, as well as the association with job security. Given unions' traditional effects on pay, we also contribute new analyses of unions' effects on wages, using the SES: we address the question of whether, as expected following the posited reduction in bargaining power, the union wage premium has declined over time; we also ask whether, along with union decline, there has been a reduction in the extent to which trade unions reduce wage inequality.

We begin the chapter by reflecting on the changing nature of unionized employment in Britain: we show that unionized employees are increasingly likely to be found in the public service industries and that a growing proportion are engaged in professional occupations. Taking note of, and controlling for, these changes is important for the union/non-union comparisons to follow. In section 7.3 we begin with the standard measure of union influence, namely the union wage premium, and extend our analysis with a measure of union influence over wage dispersion. Building up towards our broader analysis of job quality other than pay, we then examine how employee perceptions of unions' influence on work organization have been changing. Finding that, where they remain, unions' perceived influence on work organization may even have increased since the early 1990s, we turn in section 7.5 to the core part of the chapter: the associations of union coverage with work intensity, task discretion, opportunities for skill use, job insecurity, and job learning requirements. Our findings enable us to draw some general conclusions about how the changing employment relations system has been associated with changing workplace inequalities.

7.2. WHO ARE UNION MEMBERS?

Not only has the union sector shrunk in the last quarter century, its composition has changed considerably, as is shown in Table 7.1. As earlier studies have testified (e.g. Department for Business, Innovation and Skills, 2013; Machin, 2000), union members have aged relative to their non-member counterparts because unions have found it increasingly difficult to organize young workers. Whereas in 1986 less than half (48.5 per cent) of union members were over forty, this proportion had risen to 62.9 per cent by 2012. What was once a male-dominated movement, with 64.4 per cent male in 1986, evolved into one with a male minority (47.0 per cent). The latter is partly

Table 7.1. Trends in the Characteristics of Union Members (Percentage of All Union Members)

	Aged forty or more	Male	Public service industries**	Professional*
1986	48.5	64.4	32.1	25.6
1992	50.4	58.2	43.6	29.6
1997	53.2	54.2	43.8	34.8
2001	58.6	52.5	49.4	37.9
2006	61.4	48.4	57.8	41.8
2012	62.9	47.0	58.7	47.9

Notes: *professional or associate professional occupation; ** health, education, and public administration.

Source: SES

associated with the increased concentration of union members in the public service industries (health, education, and public administration) (from 32.3 per cent in 1986 to 59.3 per cent in 2012). These changes may be especially salient when studying relationships between unionization and a range of economic and social outcomes.

But perhaps most significant for the study of job quality is the fact that the type of occupations that are unionized has changed radically. The trade union movement in Britain, like elsewhere, had its origins in manual labour jobs, such as coal mining and machine operatives, and in craft workers such as shoemakers and typesetters. Already by the mid-1980s this had begun to change: by 1986, one quarter (25.6 per cent) of union members were in professional or associate professional occupations (this compared with less than one in six non-members). Economic forces, most notably skills-biased technological change and the shift to services which has characterized most advanced Western economies, has led to increased demand for professional occupations. This is apparent in the increased proportion of all employees in professional or associate professional occupations. However, the penetration of professional occupations is much more apparent in the union sector than it is in the non-union sector. In 2012, whereas under a quarter of union non-members were drawn from the ranks of the professions, this was the case for nearly one half (47.9 per cent) of union members. What is more, this professionalization of unionized employees occurred in both the public and the private sectors: it is not solely due to the increased concentration of members in the public sector.

7.3. THE UNIONS AND WAGES

With the prevalence of unions in long-term decline over the last quarter century, and the character of their membership changing, what has been happening to their association with job quality? Before examining unions' associations with broader, non-pay aspects of job quality, we look first at the links with wages.

7.3.1. The Union Wage Premium

Unions' ability to procure a wage premium for covered employees is often regarded as the touchstone for union influence among economists and scholars of industrial relations, primarily because it is a chief objective of union bargaining. The empirical literature addressing this issue is considerable (for a review, see Bryson, 2014), and one of the issues in comparing studies has been that heterogeneous findings can be attributed either to differences in specifications or to data differences. To examine whether the union wage premium has been changing over time, therefore, it is useful to be able to use consistent data and adopt the same methodology with successive cross-sectional waves of data. The SES series is one that affords a further opportunity for such an analysis.

Table 7.2 presents union wage effects for the quarter century ending in 2012, first for the whole economy and then for the public service and 'private' (i.e. other) industries separately. In each case the first column presents the raw wage gap between covered and uncovered employees (columns 1, 3, and 5). The next column (columns 2, 4, and 6) presents the union wage premium, which is the wage gap adjusting for observable differences in the demographic and job attributes of covered and uncovered employees.

Table 7.2. The Union Coverage Wage Premium

	All	All	Public service industries		Other industries	
	(1) Raw wage gap	(2) With controls	(3) Raw wage gap	(4) With controls	(5) Raw wage gap	(6) With controls
1986	0.204***	0.084***	0.398***	0.144***	0.168***	0.052***
1992	0.214***	0.104***	0.334***	0.154***	0.179***	0.078***
1997	0.226***	0.093***	0.441***	0.112***	0.180***	0.079***
2001	0.117***	0.039***	0.321***	0.116***	0.046**	0.007
2006	0.143***	0.026**	0.301***	0.093***	0.079***	−0.006
2012	0.166***	0.040**	0.238***	0.094***	0.119***	0.022

Notes: The dependent variable is the log of the hourly wage; controls in columns (2), (4), and (6) are for the highest education level, a quadratic in work experience, gender, white/non-white, size (four categories), one-digit occupation, region, and one-digit industry; asterisks give the significance of union/non-union gap, at * = 10 per cent, ** = 5 per cent, *** = 1 per cent.

Source: SES

Back in 1986 the raw union wage gap was 0.204 log points (that is, 22.6 per cent) in the whole economy (row 1, column 1), but the premium is only two fifths of this (0.084 log points) having adjusted for the wage-enhancing attributes of covered employees relative to uncovered employees. By 2012 the raw wage gap had fallen a little to 0.166 log points, but the regression-adjusted premium had fallen more sharply to 0.04 log points, a gap which is only statistically significant at a 10 per cent confidence interval.[1] Similar patterns of decline are apparent in both the private and public industries, indicating that the trend is not simply due to the changing composition of jobs. However, the premium tends to be larger in the public service industries than elsewhere. Furthermore, whereas the public services union wage premium remained statistically significant throughout the period, the union wage premium elsewhere in the economy disappeared in the late 1990s and has never resurfaced.

These findings are consistent with other studies for Britain showing a substantial decline in the union wage premium in recent decades (e.g. Blanchflower and Bryson, 2007, 2009, 2010; Bryson and Forth, 2011; Forth and Millward, 2002; Hildreth, 1999). However, many of these studies focus on the premium attached to union membership, as opposed to union coverage, and a number find that a significant, if reduced, premium persists.[2]

7.3.2. Unions and Wage Dispersion

The union wage premium is one channel through which unions might impinge on wage inequalities between jobs. In addition, unions' wage policies may be directly aimed at reducing inequalities in the workplaces where they have bargaining influence. Their wage policies are often guided by the principle of a 'fair day's pay for a fair day's work', such that wages are attached to jobs rather than individuals' attributes. This wage standardization policy, coupled with concerns to tackle wage discrimination on grounds of race, gender, and disability, can compress wage differentials. Yet, with unions' prevalence falling, the wage premium lower, and, potentially, unions' reduced power to impose solidarity-preserving settlements on employers, it could be expected that unions' overall effect on wage inequality has declined.

---

[1] The uptick in the premium between 2006 and 2012 is consistent with counter-cyclical movement in the wage premium, as discussed by Blanchflower and Bryson (2007).

[2] We obtained results that are similar to those presented in Table 7.2 by replacing the union coverage measure—which is based on whether a union or staff association is present at the workplace—with a measure of union recognition identifying whether a union or staff association is recognized by management for negotiating pay and/or conditions of employment. The union recognition measure is not available prior to 1997.

Examining the practical force of unions' solidarity policies is, however, by no means straightforward. It is difficult to disentangle the causal effect of unions on wage compression from the fact that unions may be more likely to organize homogeneous workers, and these may be drawn from the middle of the wage distribution. Whether unions actually compress wage differentials depends on the position of unionized workers in the pay distribution, the union wage premium attached to different types of worker, and the degree of centralization and coordination in collective bargaining. Notwithstanding these methodological issues, there is evidence that unions have contributed substantially to wage compression, both in the UK and elsewhere, and that they continue to do so (Bryson and Forth, 2011; Card et al., 2004; Gosling and Machin, 1995). Moreover, the decline in unionization is found to have contributed substantially to the growth in wage inequality in the United States (Frandsen, 2012) and in Germany (Dustmann et al., 2009), and there is some evidence that union decline in Britain was a factor (in addition to rising relative demand for highly educated labour) behind the rapidly increased wage inequality that occurred in Britain from the early 1980s onwards (Leslie and Pu, 1995; Lindley and Machin, 2013; Machin, 1997).

To establish the effect of union coverage on the changes in wage dispersion over time in Britain we compare the dispersion of wages in the covered and uncovered sectors at the start and end of the SES series. Having combined the datasets for 1986 and 1992 for the early period, and the 2006–2012 data for the end period, we use the reweighting estimator originally deployed by DiNardo et al. (1996) to construct counterfactual wage distributions for uncovered employees which proxy the wage distribution that would have obtained in the absence of unions in the economy. This is achieved by reweighting uncovered employees such that their observable characteristics closely resemble those of their covered counterparts.[3] One can then recover the 'effect' of union coverage at different parts of the wage distribution by comparing the actual distribution of wages to the counterfactual distribution which would have obtained if uncovered employees were observationally equivalent to those who are covered. Comparisons of the actual wage distribution and the counterfactual wage distribution allow us to identify that part of the wage gap between covered and uncovered employees that is attributable to union coverage, as opposed to differences in their observable characteristics.

The results from this exercise are presented in Table 7.3. The top half of Table 7.3 presents results for the 90/50 percentile wage ratio, a measure of wage dispersion at the top end of the distribution. The first row in Table 7.3 indicates that, back in 1986–1992 the 90/50 percentile ratio was considerably

---

[3] This is achieved by running a probit estimate for the probability of being covered by a union and then using the predicted probabilities to reweight the uncovered employees in such a way as to give additional weight to those with high estimated probabilities of being covered.

Table 7.3. Union Coverage and Wage Dispersion, 1986–2012 (Ratios of Hourly Wages)

Percentile ratio	Waves	(1) Covered	(2) Not covered	(3) Not covered, counterfactual	(4) Non-union/union dispersion gap (3)–(1)
90th/50th	1986/92	1.798	2.007	2.017	0.220
	2006/12	1.860	2.379	2.162	0.303
50th/10th	1986/92	1.626	1.640	1.754	0.129
	2006/12	1.720	1.601	1.830	0.103
50th/5th	1986/92	1.848	1.922	2.189	0.342
	2006/12	1.896	1.684	1.964	0.067

Notes: The probit to construct the weights for the 'not covered/counterfactual' sample uses for covariates the same controls as in Table 7.2. All estimates are based on a sample with non-missing values for wages and all controls (n = 7,205 for 1986/1992; n = 9,031 for 2006/2012).

Source: SES

higher among uncovered employees than it was among covered employees (2.01 vs. 1.80). The third column of the row shows the ratio in the uncovered sector rises to 2.02 once uncovered employees are reweighted such that they resemble covered employees on their observable attributes. Having made this adjustment the covered/uncovered gap in the 90/50 hourly wage distribution is 0.22 (final column of row 1).

The second row indicates that wages had become more unequal in the top half of the wage distribution by 2006–2012 in both the covered and uncovered sectors: the 90/50 ratios are 1.86 and 2.38, respectively. The growth in wage dispersion was more pronounced among uncovered employees, but much of this was driven by the characteristics of employees in the uncovered sector. Once uncovered employees are reweighted so that they are observationally equivalent to covered employees, the 90/50 ratio in 2006/2012 among uncovered employees is 2.16. Comparing the 90/50 ratio in the covered sector with the counterfactual distribution among uncovered employees (see column (4)), it is apparent that the non-union/union dispersion gap had risen from twenty-two to thirty percentage points over the period. Thus, in the upper half of the distribution, union presence seems to have been a break upon the rising dispersion of wages.

A contrasting story is shown in the second panel of Table 7.3, where the bottom half of the wage distribution is captured by the 50/10 percentile ratio. Back in the late 1980s/early 1990s the distribution of wages in the bottom half of the distribution was very similar in the covered and uncovered sectors (with 50/10 percentile ratios of 1.63 and 1.64, respectively). However, the counterfactual 50/10 distribution for uncovered employees was more dispersed (1.75), indicating that uncovered employees possessed observable traits which led to lower wage dispersion than the characteristics possessed by covered employees in that part of the wage distribution. Consequently, having reweighted un-covered employees so that they shared the characteristics of covered employ-ees, the 50/10 percentile ratio was around thirteen percentage points greater among uncovered employees compared with that for covered employees. By 2006/12, however, this non-union/union dispersion gap had fallen a little to ten percentage points over the period.

One potential reason for this relative closing of the non-union/union dispersion gap as indicated by the 50/10 ratio could be the differential impact the national minimum wage had on lower earners, particularly those in the uncovered sector. To test this explanation, we also examined the 50/5 per-centile ratio, since the minimum wage is directly relevant at the 5th percentile, but only applies at the 10th percentile in so far as its effects are extended to those earning above the minimum. As expected, the non-union/union disper-sion gap for the 50/5 ratio fell by a much greater extent, from thirty-four to just seven percentage points over the period.

7.4. DO UNIONS STILL INFLUENCE THE WAY WORK IS ORGANIZED?

While unions' influence over pay has declined, it remains possible that they have retained or even increased their influence on other aspects of job quality, by changing the emphasis of their activities, for example by increasing their involvement through representing and supporting their members directly in forms of workplace participation, or in their personal development through training, or in grievance procedures.

Unions' influence over work organization is of course by no means new. For a number of years lower labour productivity in the unionized sector relative to the non-unionized sector was attributed by many to unions' 'restrictive prac-tices', union-negotiated rules which limited managers' ambit for reorganizing work. Some of these practices were intended to protect craft skills while others maintained what appeared to be fairly arbitrary distinctions between occupa-tional classes at the workplace. Such negative effects were set against possible productivity-enhancing effects of efficient union communication—the conse-quence of 'union voice'. Many studies of unions' productivity effects have ensued, with heterogeneous findings across countries, though the balance of evidence from past British studies appears to support a negative effect (Doucouliagos and Laroche, 2003).

Arguably, however, these effects have been changing. In the mid-1980s there were signs that unions were finding it increasingly difficult to maintain restrictive practices (Metcalf, 1989). More recently, it has been commonly maintained that the closure of the labour productivity gap between the union and non-union sectors is attributable, at least in part, to the reassertion of management's 'right-to-manage' in the union sector (Blanchflower and Bryson, 2009). Throughout the 2000s unions have devoted resources—with the help of government subsidies—to supporting and facilitating training via their union learning representatives. In short, with the declining prevalence and bargaining power of unions, and with the evolution of unions' policies, it is of interest to ask how unions' influence over matters of work organization has been changing, as a preliminary to investigating unions' relationship to broader, non-wage aspects of job quality that are associated with work organization.

The SES series provides some direct evidence of employees' perceptions about trade union influence which, though it may be coloured by employees' limited awareness of what unions may be achieving, is nonetheless informative. Respondents in union-covered workplaces were asked (in 1992 and from 2001): 'How much influence do the trade unions in your establishment have over the way work is organized?' In 1992 a quarter responded that unions had 'a great deal' or 'a fair amount' of influence. By 2001 this proportion had risen to 36.1 per cent, and thereafter reported influence changed rather little. In short it seems that, where they have remained present, many unions have continued to make their presence felt. The rise in perceived influence between 1992 and the 2000s occurred largely within industries and was not associated in any way with changes in industrial structure.

There were also plenty of employees in covered workplaces at the other end of the scale who perceived that unions had no influence at all—32.2 per cent in 1992, falling to 27.0 per cent in 2012.[4] This evidence of heterogeneity in perceived union influence on work organization is consistent with the evidence from the Workplace Employment Relations Study (WERS) surveys (Millward et al., 2000). We investigated whether the pattern of heterogeneity varied much between industries, finding some notable variation. Taking the 2001–2012 period as a whole, the proportion reporting no trade union influence over work organization, which averaged 26.1 per cent over the decade, was high in the hotels industry (44.9 per cent) and low in transport and communications (16.6 per cent). Among occupations, the groups with the most reporting no trade union influence were sales (30.6 per cent) and personal services (32.6 per cent).

What might account for the rise in the 1990s and subsequent resilience of perceived union influence over work organization? One possibility is that many unions have learned to compensate for a possible decline in their

---

[4] These proportions at the low end of the scale include those answering 'don't know'. From 2001 onwards, while the item and scale were identical to those of 1992, the item was part of a smaller batch of items than in 1992.

bargaining power by becoming more efficient—perhaps learning to do more with less. Unions' policies may also be evolving to cope with and compensate for their declining bargaining power. Whatever the reason, evidence from elsewhere confirms that unions remain capable of having a substantial influence in the workplace. For example, the WERS indicate that around half of employees agree that the unions at their workplace are 'taken seriously by management', a figure that has not changed significantly since the late 1990s (Bryson and Forth, forthcoming). The British Social Attitudes Survey indicates that the percentage of employees saying the workplace union is doing its job well has been rising since 1997 and stood at seven in ten by 2008 (Bryson and Forth, 2011, 264).

7.5. THE NON-WAGE QUALITY OF UNION AND NON-UNION JOBS

If unions persist in their effects on work organization, it seems worth asking whether there are significant differences between unionized and non-unionized jobs in respect of important aspects of job quality other than pay, and if so whether this link has been decreasing alongside unions' diminishing influence on pay, or conversely rising in partial compensation.

A priori it is unclear whether one might expect union jobs to be of higher or lower non-wage quality than the jobs undertaken by those in the uncovered sector. On the one hand, it is known that poor job quality and bad management are strongly linked with the desire for union representation in the United States and Britain (Bryson and Freeman, 2013). Although poor non-wage job quality can be addressed by unions through their influence over work organization, their determination and power to do so may be weak. In the case of job security, unions start off at a disadvantage in that jobs growth is traditionally slower among unionized workplaces compared with non-unionized workplaces (Bryson, 2004); in such circumstances attempts by unions to obtain job security guarantee clauses are no more than a rearguard action to ameliorate an already weak situation. Traditionally, unions sought instead to obtain compensating financial rewards for poor working conditions through the wage–effort bargain. Even if unions were concerned about aspects of job quality, one could anticipate that their reduced bargaining power has diminished their ability to engineer improvements in all aspects of job quality, not just wages. Thus one might expect unionized employees to be subject to poorer job quality than non-unionized employees, and that this difference would increase as their bargaining power declines.

On the other hand, a contrasting hypothesis is that unions have shifted their attention away from pay bargaining (van Wanrooy et al., 2013, 86–7, 91–4), and started to focus more on improving other aspects of job quality, such as access to training or safe working conditions. Employers might also welcome union interest in non-pay job quality if it leads to higher productivity, either directly through 'smarter' working or indirectly via higher employee well-being.[5] There is evidence, also, that unions did indeed start to help managers innovate through the adoption of productivity-enhancing high involvement management practices—practices, such as autonomous team working, which aim to engage workers more fully in the tasks they are performing (Wood and Bryson, 2009). Opportunities for union influence were still apparent in 2011 since employers were significantly more likely to negotiate or consult over labour-related organizational changes where employee representatives were present at the workplace (van Wanrooy et al., 2013, 72–3). To the extent that this influence has been effective, one might expect that unionized workers would enjoy higher non-wage job quality than their non-union counterparts.

The association between unionization and non-wage job quality is, then, theoretically ambivalent. Yet the relationship has attracted much less attention in empirical studies than the links between unions and pay. For example, in a recent broad-ranging follow-up to Freeman and Medoff's (1984) seminal *What Do Unions Do?* (Bennett and Kaufman, 2007), references to non-wage job quality are rare. Instead, a large part of the volume is devoted to the relationship between unionization and job satisfaction. Job satisfaction is often treated as a proxy for overall job quality in the union literature and elsewhere (for a discussion see Brown et al., 2007). This can be problematic because employee responses to job satisfaction questions are informed not just by the quality of their jobs but by other considerations such as their expectations (Brown et al., 2012; Green, 2006). Furthermore, any relationship between unionization and job satisfaction is hard to interpret as a job quality effect because, by offering employees an opportunity to address poor job quality via bargaining and worker voice, dissatisfied union employees are less likely to quit than dissatisfied non-union employees (Freeman and Medoff, 1984). Consequently, the stock of dissatisfied employees is likely to be higher in a unionized environment than a non-unionized environment, even if under-lying job quality is similar. This is not to say we learn nothing about union effects on job quality from the job satisfaction literature. Recent studies for Britain which account for fixed unobservable differences between union and non-union employees indicate that union-covered employees are more

---

[5] There is evidence that organizational changes are associated with increased job-related anxiety and lower job satisfaction, but that these effects are ameliorated when employees work in a unionized workplace and are involved in the introduction of the changes (Bryson et al., 2013).

satisfied with their pay and hours of work than 'like' uncovered employees, although they appear less satisfied with their job security and there are some indications of adaptation to coverage over time (Bryson and White, 2013; Powdthavee, 2011).

Another strand of the literature finds that unions are associated with better fringe benefits such as holiday entitlements, pension provision, and extra-statutory sick pay (Bryson and Forth, forthcoming; Forth and Millward, 2000; Green and Potepan, 1988). Fringe benefits were often subject to union bargaining, but the scope of bargaining on such issues has declined in the private sector since the early 2000s (Van Wanrooy et al., 2013, 80–2), which may be another indicator of diminishing union influence at the workplace.

Much less is known about differences in the intrinsic job quality of unionized and non-unionized jobs. Often union status may appear in an analysis of job quality as a background control variable occasioning little comment. Nevertheless, there is a growing realization that unions can play an important role in affecting job quality via both their voice and bargaining roles at the workplace. For example, using linked employer–employee data from WERS 2004 Green and Whitfield (2009) find that, other things equal, employees in workplaces with recognized unions are more likely to say they have no time to complete tasks and are less likely to agree that they have influence over the pace of work and how tasks are done. They concur with C. Wright Mills' observation that unions are often 'managers of discontent' (Green and Whitfield, 2009, 228).

The focus of the evidence presented in Table 7.4, derived from the SES data, is on four core aspects of intrinsic job quality: the effort required to undertake the job, the degree of control the employee has over when and how the job tasks are performed, and the degree to which the employee can use or develop his or her skills in the job. We also examine the association with job security.

The indicators for the five facets of job quality are defined in the notes below Table 7.4. The levels of job quality in the union-covered and uncovered sectors are provided in columns 1 and 2, respectively, with the raw gap between the two sectors presented in column 3. The regression-adjusted gap in job quality between covered and uncovered employees is presented in the final column, which conditions on the same control variables that were used to estimate the union wage premium. We take each of the five facets of job quality in turn.

Effort: the effort–reward trade-off is, arguably, at the core of collective bargaining. Unions traditionally sought to limit work intensification on the part of employers to improve their members' health and safety and to counter 'ratchet effects' whereby employers paying piece rates continually cut piece rates for a given level of output (Carmichael and MacLeod, 2000). The top panel of Table 7.4 shows the proportion of union- and non-union-covered employees who strongly agreed that 'My job requires that I work very hard'.

Table 7.4. Unions and Non-Wage Job Quality

	(1)	(2)	(3)	(4)
	Non-union	Union	Raw gap ((2)–(1))	With controls
Effort[a]				
1992	0.307	0.290	−0.017	−0.038*
1997	0.379	0.404	0.025	−0.013
2001	0.368	0.384	0.016	−0.007
2006	0.388	0.432	0.043***	0.018
2012	0.396	0.505	0.110***	0.093***
Task discretion[b]				
1992	2.48	2.43	−0.057***	−0.077***
1997	2.32	2.23	−0.089***	−0.152***
2001	2.25	2.14	−0.109***	−0.086***
2006	2.22	2.16	−0.069***	−0.055**
2012	2.25	2.18	−0.074**	−0.053*
Opportunity for skill use[c]				
2001	0.338	0.330	−0.0089	−0.0475***
2006	0.399	0.405	0.0066	−0.0387**
2012	0.392	0.455	0.0629	0.0212
Insecurity[d]				
1986	0.212	0.209	−0.0026	0.0118
1997	0.224	0.238	0.0141	0.0232
2001	0.160	0.181	0.0213	0.0287**
2006	0.172	0.187	0.0153	0.0272**
2012	0.220	0.271	0.0514***	0.0278
Learning requirement[e]				
1992	0.239	0.270	0.0310*	−0.0204
2001	0.259	0.334	0.0741***	0.0258
2006	0.305	0.379	0.0746***	0.0174
2012	0.278	0.424	0.1458***	0.0597**

Notes: For column (4), each job quality indicator was regressed against union coverage and the control variables from Table 7.2. Asterisks give significance of union/non-union gap, at * = 10 per cent, ** = 5 per cent, *** = 1 per cent. The job quality indicators are defined as follows:

   a. The proportion who strongly agree that 'my job requires that I work very hard'.
   b. The task discretion index combines the responses to four items capturing worker influence over tasks performed. The index ranges from 0 to 3.
   c. Opportunity for skills use: proportion who strongly agree that 'In my current job I have enough opportunity to use the knowledge and skills that I have'.
   d. The proportion who report that there is 'any chance at all' of losing their job and becoming unemployed in the next twelve months.
   e. The proportion who strongly agree that 'my job requires that I keep learning new things'.

Source: SES

This proportion has been rising over time among both union-covered and uncovered employees, a trend that can be attributed to effort-biased techno-logical change and to closer monitoring of work effort (Green, 2006). How-ever, intensification has been more rapid among covered employees such that, by the early 2000s, unionized jobs were statistically significantly more

demanding of hard work than non-unionized jobs. This difference is accounted for by other observable differences between union and non-union employees. However, by 2012 unionized jobs had become even more hard-working,
and the difference could no more be attributed to differences in individual and
job characteristics.[6] This increased intensity of unionized labour relative to
non-unionized labour does not seem to have been compensated for by a
higher union wage premium (see section 7.3), and is consistent with declining
union power within the effort–wage bargain.

Task discretion: the second panel in Table 7.4 records the degree to which
employees have task discretion, as measured by their personal influence over
how hard they work, which tasks they perform, the order they perform them
in and the quality standards to which the employee works (see Technical
Appendix). Task discretion declined in the 1990s in both union and non-
union jobs, a fall noted in earlier work (Gallie et al., 2004) and attributable to
multiple factors, including the evolving culture of management through tight
targets. Over and above the theoretical ambivalence surrounding unions'
association with non-wage job quality, an additional consideration is that
employers may feel a greater need to monitor and control employees when
they are unionized and are thus less likely to cede discretion to them relative
to 'like' non-unionized employees. In the event, throughout the period task
discretion has been lower in unionized jobs than it was in non-unionized jobs.
The size of this gap in column 3 moves around from year to year but follows
no clear pattern. The same is true when controls are added, and the controls
make little difference to the size of the gap.

Opportunities for skills use: opportunities for employees to use their knowledge and skills have been rising since 2001 in both union and non-union jobs
(third panel in Table 7.4). In the early 2000s there was virtually no difference
in the raw skills use gap between union and non-union employees. However,
controlling for demographic and job traits union jobs offered significantly
fewer opportunities to use skills than non-union jobs in both 2001 and 2006.
This had changed by 2012: opportunities to use skills continued to grow after
2006 in unionized jobs whereas they remained static in non-union jobs. The
regression-adjusted gap favours union jobs but it is not statistically significant.

Job insecurity: as can be seen from the fourth panel in Table 7.4, employee
perceptions of job insecurity tend to move counter-cyclically reflecting the
reality that job loss is more likely in recession, though 1997 is an exception
with rather high insecurity (Green et al., 2000). In the two decades through to
2006 there is no significant difference in perceived job insecurity between
union-covered and uncovered employees; however, after having controlling

---

[6] The same story of unionized jobs getting harder in the 2000s is also found when using a
broader index of effort. However, this index is not available before 2001, so to get a longer
historical sweep, we use the single catch-all item.

for differences in the demographic and work characteristics of unionized and non-unionized employees, those in the covered sector experienced greater insecurity than their uncovered counterparts in 2001 and 2006. Thereafter, there emerged a substantive union–non-union gap in job insecurity which, however, is much lower and insignificant after controls (including for public sector employment) are added. The squeeze on public spending, which led to big rises in job insecurity in the public sector (Gallie et al., 2013; van Wanrooy et al., 2013) may account for this pattern.

Job learning requirements: the final panel in Table 7.4 shows that the proportion of jobs with high learning requirements increased between 1992 and 2006, a trend consistent with skill-biased technological change and with theories of the knowledge economy (Felstead et al., 2007, 2014a). It has sometimes been suggested that 'unions, through narrow job classifications and restrictive work rules, limit union workers' full use of their skills and abilities, and offer few opportunities for challenge, achievement, autonomy and promotions' (Hammer and Avgar, 2007, 349). Yet Table 7.4 also shows that union jobs tend to be more stretching than non-union jobs in terms of the need to keep learning new things. The growth in learning requirements has been faster in unionized workplaces, implying that the raw gap in the learning requirement has been growing; this might have helped spawn the growth of union learning reps (Wallis et al., 2005). Nevertheless, the changing character of the union sector accounts for the gap until 2006, since the regression-adjusted gap remained insignificant. Thereafter, the regression-adjusted difference becomes statistically significant for the first time in 2012.

7.6. CONCLUSION

In this chapter we have examined the changing relationship of trade unions with several core aspects of job quality, including wages, in order to add to understanding about how workplace inequalities have been evolving over the last quarter century.

There are two main limitations to our analyses and the conclusions that can be drawn. First, the associations, even after controlling for many observed differences between union and non-union workplaces, cannot be claimed as unbiased measures of the causal influence of unions; in the case of some aspects of non-wage job quality there are good reasons to expect that unionization is partly a reflection of poor conditions rather than the other way round.

Second, our analysis has been focused on individual effects, and therefore captures neither the spill-over effect of unions on non-union workplaces, nor the indirect political influence of unions on the formation of employment rights legislation. Since the latter was an important part of the changing regulatory environment during the period of the Labour government following 1997, the (contested) influence of unions on Labour party policy in this period would need to be taken into account in a broader analysis of unions' influence on job quality. Even though unions' political influence is undoubtedly much reduced from its earlier high points, the significance for job quality of the 1998 minimum wages regulation, and of the subsequent legislation for fair treatment of part-time, fixed-term, and agency workers (whose formulation will have been influenced to some extent by trade union pressures) would form part of such a comprehensive account.

Despite these caveats, the evidence is consistent with the view that the declining bargaining power and reach of unions has reduced but by no means eliminated the extent to which they can have an impact on job quality and on workplace inequality. Summarizing our findings, unionized jobs began the period with a significant advantage over non-unionized jobs in wages, somewhat lower effort, and no disadvantage in security. Matters deteriorated for union-covered workers during the 1990s. Effort has greatly intensified in union jobs since 1992, and these jobs were also beginning by the end of our period to look relatively less secure than in the non-union sector. Unionized jobs were subject to lower task discretion, perhaps reflecting the fact that management had asserted greater control, where once they had been weak. There is, however, some evidence of compensatory relative improvement in their position in respect of skill use and increased exposure to a learning requirement. By the end of the period the wage premium had also been substantially eroded, averaging at around 4 per cent and becoming vanishingly small outside the public service industries.

Nevertheless, throughout the period wage dispersion was lower among covered employees than it was among similar uncovered employees. In the upper half of the distribution, union coverage acted as a break on increasing wage dispersion, in that the rise in pay inequality was greater where unions were absent. In the lower half of the wage distribution the wage-compressing effect of union coverage diminished. This reduction in wage compression is most apparent in respect of the 50th/5th percentile of the wage distribution, and hence seems likely to have been associated with the introduction of the union-supported national minimum wage.

8

Is the Public Sector Pay Advantage Explained by Differences in Work Quality?

David Blackaby, Alan Felstead, Melanie Jones, Gerry Makepeace, Philip Murphy, and Victoria Wass

8.1. INTRODUCTION

This chapter addresses the common perception that work in the public sector confers a 'double premium' of better quality work and better pay (Bellante and Long, 1981), leading to feelings of 'sector envy' (Dolton and Makepeace, 2011). In the past, these feelings have been exacerbated by evidence which claimed to show that, in some cases, the pay of public sector workers is 35 per cent higher than those working in the private sector. Furthermore, it has also been claimed that equalizing the pay and pensions of the public sector with the private sector would reduce public expenditure (Holmes and Oakley, 2011, 2012). Although the evidence has been hotly disputed, it has been used to promote the case for local 'market-facing' pay deals in the public sector (Damant and Jenkins, 2011; Incomes Data Services, 2011).

In addition to being wasteful of public expenditure, it has also been argued that higher average levels of pay in the public sector have a number of other damaging consequences. These include making it difficult for private sector business to compete with higher pay levels offered in the public sector; sustaining variations in pay unrelated to public sector service quality; and reducing the number of jobs that the public sector can support with any given level of expenditure (Lambert, 2010). These claims are also widely contested (Algan et al., 2002; Faggio and Overman, 2012).

Yet, to ensure that public sector pay is fair the government seeks independent advice from seven Pay Review Bodies (PRBs). They are tasked to review pay levels and recommend annual pay rises given to public sector workers such as teachers, doctors, nurses, police officers, and senior civil servants. The first PRB was set up in 1971 and the latest in 2014 (Home Office, 2013). Together their remit covers 2.25 million workers, which accounts for 40 per cent of the 6.3 million strong public sector workforce, and their decisions have an impact on a pay bill of £93 billion. Each PRB is given an annual remit which varies according to a number of factors. These include the state of public finances and hence the affordability of any recommendations; recruitment and retention issues; and varying the size of the pay award by grade or pay level in order to favour the low paid (see NHS Pay Review Body, 2014, appendix A).

However, while pay and other features of work such as final salary pension schemes—which have been phased out more slowly in the public sector—have attracted much attention, little is known about the comparative non-pecuniary advantages and disadvantages of working in the public as opposed to the private sector. The notion of the public sector as a 'good employer' suggests that one would expect to see a public sector advantage here as well as in relation to pay. This chapter tests this notion by examining inter-sector differences in the intrinsic quality of work which are evident in data collected by surveys carried out in 1997, 2001, 2006, and 2012 as part of the Skills and Employment Survey (SES) series (see Technical Appendix). It also examines how the sector gaps have changed over time. The chapter then goes on to explore what effect the inter-sector differences identified have on the public sector wage premium.

The chapter proceeds as follows. Section 8.2 outlines the theory of compensating wage differentials as a framework within which to understand inter-sector wage differences. Section 8.3 examines the possible sources of the public sector pay premium as well as the limited evidential basis that public sector jobs are better in other ways too. Section 8.4 outlines our twofold analytical approach and the evidence base on which the chapter draws. Section 8.5 outlines the bivariate findings on intrinsic features of work which are rarely collected by official datasets—such as the Quarterly Labour Force Survey (QLFS) and the Annual Survey of Hours and Earnings (ASHE)—on which most of the public–private sector pay gap literature is based. Section 8.6 presents the results of a series of regressions which explore the extent to which the public sector pay premium can be explained in terms of the theory of compensating wage differentials. By carrying out separate analyses by gender and at different points in the pay distribution we identify for whom and at what pay levels there is evidence of a public sector wage premium after accounting for differences in intrinsic work quality. Section 8.7 ends the chapter with a summary and an outline of the implications for policy-makers who have used the raw pay gap data to justify political interventions into pay-setting arrangements and for labour market analysts who monitor movements in pay differentials.

8.2. COMPENSATING WAGE DIFFERENTIALS

The theory of compensating wage differentials was conceived by Adam Smith nearly 250 years ago. Simply stated, it argues that jobs which are more costly to undertake, more disagreeable, involve more effort, or require more training will command a higher wage because 'the whole of the advantages and disadvantages of the different employments of labour and stock must, in the same neighbourhood, be either perfectly equal or continually tending toward equality' (Smith, 1976, 111). This is expressed in equation (1), where undesirable non-pay benefits of working in sector 1 such as high work intensity and low levels of autonomy are compensated by higher pay than in sector 2 where non-pay benefits are more desirable, and vice versa. In other words, if one job has *ceteris paribus* a better (traditionally unobservable) attribute such as greater autonomy or less stress, then the wages for that job will be lower in order to compensate for the better non-pecuniary benefits. Workers move between jobs until net advantages are eliminated. In this model, wage rates embody a set of implicit prices for different job characteristics. Any resulting pay differences simply reflect differences in non-monetary characteristics of jobs, thereby equalizing 'net advantages'.

$$
\begin{array}{lcl}
\text{Pay in sector 1} & & \text{Pay in sector 2} \\
\text{+ net value of non-monetary benefits of} & = & \text{+ net value of non-monetary benefits of} \\
\text{work in sector 1} & & \text{work in sector 2}
\end{array} \qquad (1)
$$

Duncan and Holmlund (1983, 366) note that there are few propositions in labour economics with greater intuitive appeal than compensating wage differentials. However, empirical results are mixed so that, while there is 'some clear support for the theory', there are also 'an uncomfortable number of exceptions' (Brown, 1980, 118, quoted in Duncan and Holmlund, 1983, 367). Econometric difficulties turn on the inability to adequately control for all relevant worker and job characteristics in typical cross-sectional datasets and notably the non-monetary aspects of work, as contained in the Skills and Employment Surveys (SES).

As an extension to this approach some researchers have advocated modelling the determinants of total reward (e.g. Danzer and Dolton, 2012; Leslie, 2008). This refers to the total present value of a number of items, including pay as well as pensions and other benefits in kind over the life course. While the dataset used here measures whether or not the employer contributes to a pension on behalf of respondents,[1] the level of detail needed to pursue the total

---

[1] This shows a marked and, if anything, widening sector difference with those in the public sector more likely to report that their employer contributes to their pension. In 2012, 79.6 per cent of public sector workers reported that employer pension contributions were made on their behalf compared to 45.6 per cent of private sector workers.

150   *David Blackaby, Et al.*

rewards approach is not available—as its advocates acknowledge 'data requirements for this research are high' (Danzer and Dolton, 2012, 589). These
include pension membership rules, pension scheme parameters, the value of
employee and employer contributions, and scheme tenure. So, in line with
existing research on public–private sector pay comparison, differences in
pension arrangements are not factored into the analysis which follows.

8.3. EXPLANATIONS FOR SECTOR DIFFERENCES

There are reasons one might expect the non-pay quality of work to be higher
in the public sector. Historically, the public sector has striven to be a 'good
employer'. This notion has roots extending back to the formation of the civil
service in the mid-19th century (Davies, 2012; Horton, 2006; Morgan and
Allington, 2002). The *Royal Commission on the Civil Service*, for example,
stated that while a 'good employer' need not necessarily offer its employees
high rates of pay, it did have to provide job security, joint consultation in the
form of collective bargaining and 'carr[y] out a range of practices that would
today constitute good management, whether they be in the form of joint
consultation along civil service lines, fairness and equal opportunities'
(Priestley, 1955, paragraph 172). This idea was echoed a quarter of a century
later by Beaumont (1981), who attributed superior pay and conditions in the
public sector to the government pursuing model employment practices and
treating employees as stakeholders in the productive process. Almost three
decades later, the Black Review (2008) cited the public sector as a beacon of
good employment practice and looked to it to take forward the agenda of
enhancing health and well-being at work.

   However, the evidence of superior working conditions in the public sector
tends to be inferred rather than based on direct evidence. The institutional
environment tends to be better in the public sector with higher union density,
and tighter regulation of employment practices and working conditions (see
Chapter 7 of this book; Bellante and Long, 1981; Jones et al., 2014). The latter
includes the 1997 Single Status Agreement which ensures that all local government staff receive equal pay for work of equal value, changes resulting from
the NHS Agenda for Change 2004 and the additional demands stemming
from the Public Sector Equality Duty which came into force in 2010. Using
employee rights in relation to equality as a marker of superior working
conditions, the public sector is seen to be a clear leader over the private sector.
According to the Workplace Employment Relations Survey 2011, the presence
of an equal opportunities policy was almost universal in the public sector—99
per cent of workplaces had one in 2011—compared to 74 per cent of private
sector workplaces (Bach et al., 2009; van Wanrooy et al., 2013, 116–18). More

importantly, perhaps, the equality policies in the public sector are more likely to be supported by substantive workplace practices, for example, the monitoring of jobs by gender and ethnicity, flexible working, and practices in relation to requests for disability related adjustments (Hoque and Noon, 2004). Furthermore, it is argued that there is positive interaction between regulation and unionization in the enforcement of individual rights in relation to equality, a factor which has greatest impact in the public sector given its relatively high levels of unionization (Hoque and Bacon, 2014).

There are also reasons why public sector workers are better paid. The employment profiles of each sector are very different (Incomes Data Services, 2011). For example, professionals with specific service roles and high-level qualifications are over-represented in the public sector, especially within healthcare and education. Indeed, much of the pay gap disappears when controls for the qualifications held by employees are included in wage equations. By taking these structural differences into account, Emmerson and Jin (2012) report an overall 8 per cent pay differential, which varies according to the time period chosen, how the model is specified, and where in the earnings distribution the gap is measured. In subsequent studies, Blackaby et al. (2012) and ONS (2012) include further controls, including establishment size, and the pay gap disappears completely for men and shrinks significantly for women. Studies by Disney and Gosling (1998), Blackaby et al. (1999), and Lucifora and Meurs (2006) have also found that the adjusted public–private sector pay premium decreases the further up the wage distribution you move, and that for men this gap becomes negative for high-income earners. The public sector pay premium favours women and the low paid and can therefore be regarded as a force for reducing inequalities in pay. This has sometimes been recognized in the remits given to the PRBs which exempt those towards the bottom of the earnings distribution from stringencies and/or suggest tighter controls on the pay awards for those at the top (e.g. NHS Pay Review Body, 2014, appendix A).

There are grounds, then, for expecting that the intrinsic quality of work is higher in the public sector and most empirical work indicates a public sector pay premium. The coincidence of both better pay and better job quality in the public sector presents a challenge to the compensating wage differential model and therefore an important and interesting subject of study. However, there is little quantitative evidence to substantiate many of the differences in non-monetary benefits of work in each sector. This chapter aims to fill that gap by addressing four aspects of intrinsic job quality. These include inter-sector differences in the skill content of jobs; differences in discretion and autonomy over job tasks; differences in work effort and work intensity; and differences in perceived risk of job loss and anxiety about this and other aspects of work. A distinctive feature of the SES data series is that most of these measures are focused on the job and not the individual. We explore how inter-sector differences have evolved over time (1997–2012) and, in particular, whether they have widened or narrowed. These differences in job quality are then included as controls in the compensating wage differentials framework, which allows us to evaluate whether there is a 'double premium' or whether the wage differences can be accounted for by non-pay variations in the quality of work.

8.4. EMPIRICAL APPROACH

The chapter is based on data collected in surveys of the working adult population carried out in 1997, 2001, 2006, and 2012.[2] We follow as far as possible the Office for National Statistics' (ONS) definition of the public sector as comprising organizations which are wholly or mainly owned and controlled by the government. Private sector firms, on the other hand, are organizations which are mainly owned by private persons or shareholders who exercise control over how these businesses are run. The ONS then goes on to list the evidence on which this decision can be based. However, individuals are often not in possession of such detailed information. Self-reporting by respondents of sector is therefore subject to some error. In the surveys reported here—as in many others—respondents are asked: 'Is your organization a private sector organization such as a company, or a public sector body such as local or national government, schools, or the health service, or a non-profit organization such as a charity?' Respondents are grouped into three categories according to the responses given.[3] The official definition of the public–private sector divide puts non-profit organizations into the private sector (Matthews, 2010) and we follow this practice. The empirical work is based on a total pooled sample of 15,896 employees of whom 30.8 per cent work in the public sector.[4]

The empirical analysis is carried out in two ways. First, we examine inter-sector differences in the non-monetary characteristics of work and assess if workers in the public sector are privileged or disadvantaged in these terms. We focus on four features of work which provide a potential source of a compensating wage differential: job skills; discretion and autonomy; work intensity; and insecurity and anxiety at work. These measures are focused on the job and not the individual so, for example, job skills cover what qualifications, skills, training, and learning are required to do the job. Some aspects are desirable,

---

[2] A consistent public sector identifier is available from 1997 onwards.

[3] While the 1986 and 1992 surveys collected self-reported sector data, they did not provide respondents with a three-option response or give examples of the type of organization. For this reason, the 1986 and 1992 public–private sector variable is not consistent with later years. In other publications such adjustments were not made (e.g. Felstead et al., 2013c; Gallie et al., 2013).

[4] For each of the data points the comparative LFS estimates for public sector employment are two percentage points lower than SES estimates.

some less so. Autonomy and discretion at work, for example, are often regarded as desirable features of work and are thought to be key characteristics of professional roles, especially those involving the delivery of public services. Similarly, protection from job insecurity (referred to by Adam Smith as the constancy of employment) is a non-pecuniary and intangible benefit which might give rise to a compensating wage differential. Work intensity, on the other hand, is commonly regarded as less desirable and may therefore be compensated for in higher wages, other things being equal. We examine these four features of work by reporting a set of simple summary statistics which highlight significant inter-sector differences and how these differences in work quality have changed between 1997 and 2012.

Our analysis goes on to explore the public–private sector pay gap in the context of a series of compensating wage models. These produce increasingly like-for-like comparisons, so that the inter-sector wage differential is progressively measured net of all measured differences in characteristics and requirements both at the level of the individual, the employment context, and the job. The analysis presented in this chapter provides a much stronger test of the contention that public sector workers are overpaid than a comparison based on unadjusted averages which fails to take into account the differences outlined earlier. Furthermore, the data series allows us to take into account a much more extensive range of characteristics and requirements than is typical. Datasets traditionally used to measure pay gaps (such as LFS and ASHE) collect data on individual characteristics and gather rather less on the nature of the job itself. While the effects of inter-sector differences in workplace characteristics (such as pay-setting, management structure, human relations policies) have been taken into account using the management data collected by the Workplace Employment Relations Survey alongside individual-level employee data (e.g. Chatterji et al., 2011), we have a richer set of data on job quality at our disposal. Returning to equation (1), greater work intensity, for example, is an undesirable feature of work which will manifest itself in higher wages, so inter-sector differences in work intensity will be 'compensated' for by an inter-sector wage differential. Therefore, by introducing a set of controls associated with the non-monetary characteristics of work, we may uncover sector-related 'compensating differentials' not captured in previous analyses.

The SES series contains pay data along with data on a range of intrinsic features of work. Based on the pay data alone, there is a *prima facia* case for the public sector pay premium as reported in Table 8.1. Here, we compare the raw percentage pay differential estimated from our data series with estimates from ASHE and LFS. While there is variation between the figures generated from different surveys, which is expected given differences in the sample, measurement of earnings, and classification of sector, the raw gap is in the order of 10–15 per cent and there is consistent evidence that the gap is much

Table 8.1. Public–Private Sector Percentage Pay Gaps, Gross Hourly Pay, 1997–2012

	1997			2001			2006			2012		
	SES	ASHE	LFS	SES	ASHE	LFS	SES	ASHE	LFS	SES	ASHE	LFS
All	14.4	8.1	15.7	10.7	3.3	8.4	11.7	9.5	10.4	12.9	15.7	10.0
Men	12.1	8.1	13.5	11.4	4.0	8.7	8.0	11.7	10.2	13.9	18.3	8.5
Women	33.8	25.6	31.6	24.1	19.3	20.3	26.8	23.6	22.3	19.5	28.7	22.2

Notes: The above figures are a percentage differential which is calculated as (public sector average wage – private sector average wage) / (private sector average wage)*100. SES estimates are trimmed (1 per cent top and bottom) throughout.

greater for women. This suggests that the pay data at our disposal are comparable to data collected by much larger sample surveys.

8.5. SECTOR DIFFERENCES IN THE NON-PAY QUALITY OF WORK

8.5.1. Skill Requirements

The skill requirements of jobs are captured by three broad indicators: qualifications required on entry to the job, prior training for that type of work, and initial post-entry learning while on the job. The first draws data from a survey question which asks respondents 'if they were applying today, what qualifications, if any, would someone need to get the type of job you now have?' We rank the qualifications given and put them into five categories. These range from degree or equivalent to those who said that no qualifications would be needed. Each level is given a score, with '4' at the top and '0' at the bottom. The derived qualification index is the average of these scores. We subtract the private sector score from the public sector score in order to highlight sector differences. We also examine: (a) whether the public–private sector gaps are significant at each data point; and (b) if these gaps have changed significantly over time in order to assess to what extent sector differences have contributed to the evolution of non-pay inequalities at work. This analytical approach is applied throughout this section.

The results show that jobs in the public sector demand higher skills than the private sector as measured by the level of qualifications required on entry. For example, degree-level jobs rose by ten percentage points in both the public and private sectors—rising from 25.2 per cent in 1997 to 35.5 per cent in 2012 in the public sector and from 12.1 per cent in 1997 to 22.7 per cent in 2012 in the private sector (percentages not shown in Table 8.2). The gap in the required

Table 8.2. Public–Private Sector Gaps in the Non-Pay Quality of Work, 1997–2012

Dimensions of the quality of work (1)	1997 Public–private sector gap (2)	2001 Public–private sector gap (3)	2006 Public–private sector gap (4)	2012 Public–private sector gap (5)	2012 Interaction coefficient (6)
A. Skill requirements (scale differences)					
Required qualifications	0.667***	0.615***	0.774***	0.702***	0.035
Training time	0.758***	1.108***	1.256***	1.086***	0.328
Learning time	0.370***	0.374***	0.468***	0.605***	0.235*
Literacy	0.470***	0.434***	0.480***	0.456***	−0.014
Numeracy	−0.290***	−0.289***	−0.184***	−0.183***	0.107
Physical skills	−0.328***	−0.117***	−0.177***	−0.134**	0.194**
Influence skills	0.357***	0.308***	0.331***	0.329***	−0.028
Planning skills	0.291***	0.236***	0.244***	0.253***	−0.038
Client communication skills	0.011	−0.083**	−0.096***	−0.177***	−0.188***
Problem-solving skills	0.061	−0.018	0.040	−0.037	−0.098
Checking skills	−0.043	−0.056*	0.030	na	0.073
Emotional skills	na	na	0.362***	0.398***	0.036
Aesthetic skills	na	na	0.226***	0.245***	0.019
Computer-use skills	0.153*	0.158**	0.433***	0.307***	0.153
Sophisticated computer-use skills	0.087	0.098**	0.240***	0.148***	0.060
B. Discretion at work (scale and percentage point item differences)					
Task discretion index	0.069**	0.006	−0.001	0.020	−0.049
Supervision index	−0.017	0.061**	0.127***	0.006	0.023
A great deal of say in decisions which change the way you do your job	na	−4.3***	−8.0***	−7.4***	0.661*
Should you have more say in decisions which affect work?	na	2.3	10.7***	8.9***	1.31**
C. Work intensity (percentage point item differences)					
Strongly agree: 'my job requires that I work very hard'	9.2***	8.6***	12.3***	11.8***	1.09
Strongly agree: puts a lot of effort into job beyond what is required	2.1	2.8	4.0**	5.3**	1.17
D. Perceptions and experiences of insecurity (percentage point item differences)					
A chance of job loss	0.7	−7.2***	−3.7***	3.9*	1.18
Recent work reorganization	na	7.1***	5.7***	10.0***	1.14
In future may have less say in job	na	na	na	11.2***	na
In future may have less ability to use skills	na	na	na	5.2**	na

(continued)

Table 8.2. Continued

Dimensions of the quality of work (1)	1997 Public–private sector gap (2)	2001 Public–private sector gap (3)	2006 Public–private sector gap (4)	2012 Public–private sector gap (5)	2012 Interaction coefficient (6)
In future may have pay reduced	na	na	na	10.7***	na
In future may be moved to a less interesting job	na	na	na	5.3**	na

Notes: Both the descriptive data (columns 2–5) and regression results (column 6) are weighted. Columns 2–5 report t-tests of the public–private sector from the private sector differences, while column 6 reports the 2012* sector interaction variable (i.e. whether the public–private sector gap in 2012 is significantly larger than the gap in 1997 or the earliest year for which data are available). For linear regressions, the interaction coefficient equates, subject to rounding, to the difference between columns 5 and 2. For logistic regressions (where items are reported using percentages), the interaction coefficient presented in column 6 is the odds ratio. *, **, *** indicate statistical significance at the 10 per cent, 5 per cent, and 1 per cent levels, respectively; 'na' denotes question not available at the survey point.

Source: SES

qualification index has remained more or less unchanged at around 0.7 for most of the period (see Table 8.2, panel A).

The second broad skills indicator, prior training, comes from the question: 'Since completing full-time education, have you ever had, or are you currently undertaking, training for the type of work that you currently do?' If 'yes', 'How long, in total, did (or will) that training last?' Eight responses were possible ranging from no prior training (scoring '0') needed at one end of the spectrum to over two years (scoring '7') at the other. The training time index refers to an average of these scores. This produces evidence to suggest that public sector jobs are associated with longer periods of prior training with a significant sector gap in the index at all dates in the series. In 2012, for example, three out of ten public sector workers (31.0 per cent) spent more than two years training for the job compared to two of ten private sector workers (20.7 per cent). Although the absolute sector gap has widened over time—in 1997 it was 0.758 but, by 2012, it had risen to 1.086—the rise was not large enough to be statistically significant (note the positive, but insignificant, 2012 interaction term in column 6 of Table 8.2).

The third broad skills indicator, initial post-entry learning, is based on the question: 'How long did it take for you after you first started doing this type of job to learn to do it well?' Six responses were possible ranging from 'less than a month' (scoring '1') to 'over two years' (scoring '6'). The learning time index refers to an average of these scores. Again, the public–private sector differences in job skills at each data point are significant with public sector jobs requiring longer initial post-entry learning. On these three measures, then, public sector jobs are substantially more skilled than those in the private sector, on average. This is true in all four years in the series. Furthermore, the sector gap on this skill measure increases significantly over time (see positive and significant 2012 interaction term in column 6 of Table 8.2).

Respondents to the four surveys were also asked: 'in your job, how important is [a particular job activity]?' Examples of the activities included: 'using a computer'; 'analysing complex problems'; and 'adding, subtracting, multiplying, or dividing numbers'. The 2012 questionnaire covered forty-four activities with previous surveys carrying somewhat fewer. Respondents were asked to pick from a five-point scale which ranged from 'essential' (scoring '4') to 'not at all important' (scoring '0'). Factor analysis produced the ten types of generic skills. To these we add two measures of generic computer use. The first measures the importance of computer use at work. The second asks respondents whether they draw on 'advanced', 'complex', 'moderate', or 'straightforward' computer skills with each level accompanied by concrete examples of such use. From this we derive a computer skills sophistication index. This ranges from no use at all (scoring '0') to 'advanced' use (scoring '4').

Examination of these data reveals that public and private sector jobs are different in terms of the type of skills that are required and, once again, the suggestion is that public sector jobs require higher skills. Public sector jobs require higher skills in terms of literacy, influencing abilities, planning, emotional labour, aesthetic labour, and computer use. However, private sector jobs require significantly more from workers in terms of numeracy skills, physical effort, and client communication (such as selling products and services and advising customers). Out of twelve generic skills, seven were significantly in favour of the public sector in 2012, but only three favoured the private sector. There is no consistent pattern of change over time.

8.5.2. Discretion and Autonomy

The survey series carries a set of questions which address how much personal influence employees report they have over four specific aspects of their jobs: how hard they work; deciding what tasks they are to do; how the tasks are done; and the quality standards to which they work. The response options range from 'a great deal', 'a fair amount' to 'not much' and 'not much at all'. A task discretion index was derived by awarding scores ranging from 3 to 0 for each of these responses.

Despite earlier evidence that jobs in the public sector require higher qualifications on entry, involve lengthier training time, take longer to learn to do well once in post, and (in many respects) entail higher generic skills, discretion levels differed little between the sectors in 2012. However, in 1997 public sector workers enjoyed significantly higher levels of discretion, but from then onwards discretion levels between the sectors have narrowed significantly and become negligible (see Table 8.2, panel B).

Discretion is related to supervision. Respondents were, therefore, asked: 'How closely are you supervised in your job?' We derive a supervision index from the responses given, ranging from 'not at all closely' (scored as '1') to 'very closely' (scored as '4'). The results using this index mirror the trajectory of change for discretion reported above. Supervision over public sector workers' jobs grew in the 1997–2006 period and discretion fell. However, since then both the supervision and discretion gaps between the sectors have disappeared.

Respondents were also asked: 'Suppose there was going to be some decision made at your place of work that changed the way you do your job. Do you think that you personally would have any say in the decision about the change or not?' Here we report the proportion who said that they would have 'a great deal' of say in the resulting changes. Private sector employees were significantly more likely to report enjoying such a level of job control. This four–eight percentage point advantage was maintained at each of the three data points, with a significant widening of the gap between 2001 and 2012.

Dissatisfaction with such relatively tight—and to some extent tightening—control of the labour process among public sector workers can be seen in the growing desire for more job control relative to their private sector peers. At each of the three data points, around a third of private sector employees reported that they would like to have more say in decisions that affected their work. However, among public sector workers such a desire grew from 40.1 per cent in 2001 to 46.5 per cent eleven years later, with the resulting public–private sector gap growing from 2.3 percentage points to 8.9 points over this period. This represents a significant widening of the public–private sector gap (see Table 8.2, panel B).

Overall, these results suggest that the government's modernization of the public sector agenda—both New Labour and the Conservative/Liberal Democrat Coalition—and the increased emphasis this placed on the marketization of the public sector was having an effect on the quality of work in the public sector. In particular, public sector workers' relative room for autonomy was shrinking and with it resentment levels were rising.

8.5.3. Work Intensity

To capture work intensity overall we use responses given to the question: 'please tell me how much you agree or disagree with the statement: my job requires that I work very hard'. If respondents strongly agreed, we define their job as involving 'hard work'. Such hard-working jobs are more prevalent in the public sector than in the private sector. For example, in 2012 over half (52.8 per cent) of public sector jobs required employees to work very hard compared to around two fifths (41.0 per cent) of those working in the private sector, with significant gaps reported at each data point. Even so, the magnitude of the gap grew by around three percentage points between 1997–2001 and 2006–2012 (cf. Felstead et al., 2013c). However, this widening gap is not statistically significant (see Table 8.2, panel C).

In addition to non-discretionary effort levels respondents were asked about discretionary work effort which they voluntarily give to the organization. Respondents were asked: 'How much effort do you put into your job *beyond* what is required?' A list of options were read out. These were: 'a lot', 'some', 'only a little', or 'none'. We report the percentages saying 'a lot'. The results suggest a similar to pattern to those revealed by the required work effort data; discretionary work effort is higher in the public sector than in the private sector for all of the data points, with statistically significant differences common towards the end of the period. However, the differences between the sectors have not grown significantly.

8.5.4. Insecurity and Anxiety

Given the economic uncertainty and austerity in the public sector which followed the 2008–2009 recession, it is unsurprising that in 2012 respondents in both sectors reported historically high levels of job insecurity—around a quarter thought that they stood a chance of losing their job in the next twelve months (Gallie et al., 2013). However, job insecurity rose more sharply in the public sector, rising significantly by almost twelve percentage points between 2006 and 2012. In contrast, it rose by a more modest (and statistically insignificant, $p>0.1$) four percentage points in the private sector. This is a reversal of the pattern established in previous years. The gap was against the public sector in 2012 and was around four percentage points ($p<0.1$). However, a similar sized gap, but in favour of the public sector (and at higher levels of significance, $p<0.01$), was recorded in 2006. The gap was even more favourable to public sector workers in 2001 when the gap was around seven percentage points. However, there was little sectoral difference in 1997 (see Table 8.2, panel D).

The data also suggest that work reorganization is more prevalent in the public sector than in the private sector. In the former, around two thirds (66.4 per cent) of respondents who were in work with the same employer five, four, and three years ago reported changes to the way work was organized in 2012 compared to approaching three out of five (56.4 per cent) private sector respondents. Furthermore, a greater proportion of public sector respondents rated these as 'major' rather than 'minor changes'; in both 2012 and 2006 the gap was around six to seven percentage points. This suggests a more turbulent workplace environment for those working the public sector.

Despite their relative protection from unfair treatment (Fevre et al., 2009), public sector employees expressed significantly more anxiety about job down-grading in the future than private sector employees. Over a quarter reported feeling 'very' or 'fairly anxious' about being moved to a less interesting job (26.3 per cent) and/or having less ability to use their skills at work (27.9 per cent). Over a third (38.5 per cent) worried that they might have less say in their job in the future and approaching a half (44.8 per cent) were concerned that their pay might be reduced. In all four areas, anxiety levels in the public sector were significantly higher than in the private sector, but the differences with regard to pay and autonomy were especially marked with gaps in double figures (see Table 8.2, panel D).

8.6. PUBLIC SECTOR PAY GAPS, STRUCTURAL VARIATION, AND NON-PAY QUALITY OF WORK DIFFERENCES

In this section we bring together the job quality indicators discussed above and pay data outlined earlier. In so doing, we examine the impact that job quality has on the public sector pay premium. We begin by measuring the raw hourly pay gap between public and private sector employees over time and then proceed to examine how much of it can be explained by differences in individual characteristics (such as sex, age, and education) and employment characteristics (such as workplace size, occupation, and contractual status). Finally, job quality-related controls are also added (where available consist-ently between 1997 and 2012). Consider, for example, job skills requirements. If working in the public sector involves using higher level skills, we might expect public sector wages to be higher to reflect the enhanced demands of the job. Inclusion of a job characteristic can either close or extend the pay gap but, if job quality is related to wages and is differentially distributed by sector, inclusion will provide a more precise measure of any pay premium which is specific to the public sector.

Regression analysis provides the standard method for measuring the public sector wage premium while controlling for the effect of individual, employ-ment, and job characteristics. We assume that we have a list of variables (x_k) that affect earnings and capture the effect of sector by including an indicator variable (PUB_{it}) which shows whether or not the individual is employed in the public sector. We then regress the natural logarithm of earnings on these variables. Thus,

$$\ln E_{it} = \mu_t PUB_{it} + x_{it}\beta_t + \varepsilon_{it} \quad i = 1, .., N_t; t = 1997, .., 2012 \quad (2)$$

where i indexes the ith individual and t the survey year. E is hourly earnings and $x = \{1, x_2 \ldots, x_K\}$ is $1 \times K$ vector of variables, where the first variable is the constant 1 and the remaining variables measure individual, employment, and job characteristics. β is a $1 \times K$ vector of parameters capturing the impact of the corresponding variable on log earnings. ε is the random error term which satisfies the standard OLS assumptions.

The estimate of the coefficient of the public sector variable (μ_t) measures the difference in log earnings for two individuals with exactly the same observable characteristics (values for x_k) but where one works in the public sector (so $PUB_{it}=1$) and the other works in the private sector ($PUB_{it}=0$). It measures the public sector pay premium, that is, the increase in log earnings for an employee working in the public sector compared to those of employees in the private sector matched in terms of measured characteristics. In estimating the public sector premium the model assumes that these characteristics have the same influence on earnings across sectors. For example, the returns to education are constrained to be the same in both the public and private sectors.

We run this regression first with just the public sector identifier and, where the data are pooled across time, a control for survey year to capture trends in nominal earnings. The coefficient on public sector reported in Table 8.3, column 1, row 1 measures the resulting raw unadjusted public sector pay gap. We add further sets of control variables in succession beginning with individual characteristics and report the adjusted public sector premia in columns 2–5. The specification reported in column 2 is broadly equivalent in terms of methodology to that of Emmerson and Jin (2012). A set of controls for employment characteristics is included in column 3. The public sector pay premium here is broadly equivalent in terms of methodology to that estimated by Blackaby et al. (2012) and ONS (2012). Job quality variables, including job skill requirements, measures of autonomy and discretion, work intensity, and job security are included as further controls with the public sector premium reported in column 4. The impact of including the job quality variables without personal and employment characteristics is apparent from column 5. Here, the job quality variables in the SES reduce the public sector pay premium as, if not more, effectively than the more traditional personal and employment-related characteristics. Separate regressions are run for each year (rows 2–5) and for men, women, full-time, and part-time employees (rows 6–9) of Table 8.3. Further regressions are run at the five quantile points of the earnings distribution and are reported in rows 10–14.

Table 8.3. Estimating the Public–Private Sector Pay Gap, 1997–2012

	Unadjusted (1)	Adjusted to include personal characteristics (2)	Adjusted to include personal and employment-related characteristics (3)	Adjusted to include personal, employment-related characteristics and job skill requirements, discretion and autonomy, work intensity, and perceived insecurity (4)	Adjusted to include controls for job skill requirements, discretion and autonomy, work intensity, and perceived insecurity only (5)
1 All employees, all years	0.151***	0.074***	0.030***	0.009	−0.006
2 1997	0.160***	0.074***	0.059***	0.031*	0.020
3 2001	0.134***	0.055***	0.014	0.007	−0.007
4 2006	0.150***	0.079***	0.028***	0.004	−0.014
5 2012	0.172***	0.089***	0.034**	0.013	0.002
6 Men all years	0.134***	0.022**	−0.008	−0.007	0.004
7 Women all years	0.250***	0.111***	0.055***	0.022***	0.042***
8 Full-time all years	0.136***	0.047***	0.015*	0.003	−0.010
9 Part-time all years	0.296***	0.169***	0.070***	0.034***	0.072***
10 10th	0.141***	0.129***	0.081***	0.049***	0.064***
11 25th	0.202***	0.120***	0.065***	0.041***	0.036***
12 50th	0.211***	0.094***	0.051***	0.026***	0.001
13 75th	0.169***	0.029***	0.023**	0.004	−0.042**
14 90th	0.036**	−0.014	−0.032***	−0.033**	−0.059***

Notes: Data are unweighted. *, **, *** indicate statistical significance at the 10 per cent, 5 per cent, and 1 per cent levels, respectively. Column (1) includes controls for survey year in the models which pool data over time. Personal characteristics in (2) include gender (where appropriate), age band (20–29, 30–39, 40–49, 50–59, 60–65), highest educational attainment (NVQ level), marital status, and region of residence. Employment-related characteristics in (3) include occupation (one-digit SOC), workplace size (<25, 25–99, 100–499, 500+), part-time (as appropriate) and temporary employment. Job skill requirements in (4) include indices measuring required education level, pre-job training time, post-entry learning time and a range of generic skill requirements (literacy, numeracy, physical strength, influence, planning, client communication, problem-solving, computer use, and sophisticated computer use). Controls for autonomy and discretion include the task discretion index and supervision index. Controls for work intensity include two dummy variables indicating that the employee strongly agrees that 'my job requires that I work very hard' and that the respondent puts a lot of effort beyond what is required. The control for perceived insecurity is a dummy variable capturing any positive chance of job loss in the next twelve months.

Source: SES

The coefficients indicate the size of the public sector premium. These log points are multiplied by 100 in what follows with percentage mark-ups in parentheses (where log points and percentages differ). The results presented in Table 8.3 are comparable both across columns and down rows. The raw public sector premium across the four surveys is 15.1 log points (or 16.3 per cent) (see Table 8.3, row 1). Looking across the columns of row 1, factoring in personal characteristics such as gender, age, and educational attainment reduces the gap to 7.4 log points (or 7.7 per cent). When employment-related characteristics are also added, the public sector pay gap shrinks further to 3.0 per cent, although the premium remains statistically significant. Importantly, when measures of intrinsic job quality are taken into account at the aggregate level (columns 4 and 5, rows 1–5) the public–private sector pay gap disappears in all specifications except one where it remains weakly significant ($p<0.1$). However, it remains significant for certain groups of employees which we consider below.

The raw unadjusted gap is greater for women (25.0 log points or 28.4 per cent) than for men (13.4 log points or 14.3 per cent). Furthermore, for women the pay gap shrinks to 2.2 per cent in the full model (column 4), but it remains statistically significant, while for men it disappears completely and is negative, although not significant. In so far as the public sector offers a wage premium this seems to be restricted to women and is consistent with a lower gender wage gap within the public sector (see Jones et al., 2014). The pattern for full-time employees is similar to that of male workers and so the public–private sector pay gap disappears when the quality of work indicators are added to the model (see row 8 of Table 8.3). The unadjusted public sector pay gap for part-time employees, who are predominately female, is far higher at 29.6 log points (or 34.4 per cent) and a premium of 3.4 log points (or 3.5 per cent) remains after accounting for the most comprehensive set of controls (column 4). This is greater than the 2.2 per cent premium for all females.

When the regressions are run at different points on the earnings distribution using quantile regressions, the public sector premium is found to decrease as earnings increase. So, in the full model (see column 4, Table 8.3), those who work in the public sector and whose hourly pay is in the bottom 10 per cent of the distribution receive 4.9 log points (or 5.0 per cent) more than an otherwise identically placed private worker. Those in the bottom quartile receive 4.1 log points (or 4.2 per cent) more and median earners 2.6 per cent more. However, in the top half of the pay distribution the advantages of working in the public sector disappear and for the top earners they are reversed. Those in the top decile, for example, earn 3.3 log points (or 3.4 per cent) *less* than equivalent counterparts who work in the private sector (see rows 10–14, column 4, Table 8.3). The pattern of advantage/disadvantage found for public sector workers at the bottom and top ends of the earnings distribution reported here is broadly similar to that found elsewhere for the UK, most notably by

Blackaby et al. (1999 and 2012), Disney and Gosling (1998), and Murphy et al. (2014).

In further specifications estimated separately by gender for each year (results not reported), the unadjusted gap is significant for men throughout the period. The fully adjusted gap is insignificantly different from zero across all years and for part-time or full-time status. In contrast, for females, the unadjusted gap is larger and while the gap tends to narrow as additional controls are included in the model, it remains significant for part-time and full-time workers and is especially pronounced for part timers. Across the distribution, the adjusted differential is insignificantly different from zero for men until the 90th percentile when there is evidence of a public sector pay penalty. While the latter is also evident for women, the public sector premium is most pronounced at the bottom end of the distribution and is significant at points up to and including the median.

8.7. CONCLUSION

It is popularly assumed that public sector workers enjoy better pay and better terms and conditions than their private sector counterparts. Reports of average pay comparisons, for example, frequently generate headlines such as 'You are £86 a week better off if you work in the public sector' (Mail Online, 22 November 2012). Such reports often go on to claim—based on little or no evidence—that public sector workers are advantaged in other ways too, such as working under less pressure, enjoying greater job security, and getting better pensions. The presumption of a 'double premium' has been used to justify public sector pay restraint. This chapter has presented evidence which challenges this notion by first examining sector differences in the qualitative aspects of work and second by showing how differences in these qualitative characteristics can explain the unadjusted public sector pay mark-up on which many of these newspaper headlines are based.

Differences in the quality of work are most pronounced in terms of job skill requirements which are consistently higher in the public sector. For example, public sector jobs are higher skilled in terms of the level of qualification required on entry, the length of prior training for that type of work, and the length of initial post-entry learning needed to get up to speed. However, contrary to the 'double premium' presumption public sector jobs do not offer workers more autonomy. In fact, according to some measures they have far less say at work and the gap between the sectors has been moving against public sector workers. We also find that workers in the public sector work harder and expend more discretionary effort than their private sector counterparts. Furthermore, the growth in perceived levels of job insecurity in the public sector in the period

2001–2012 means job stability is no longer a positive feature of public sector employment, with work reorganization also more prevalent than in the private sector.

Consistent with the earlier literature we find evidence of a raw hourly earnings gap which favours the public sector. This narrows with the inclusion of personal and employment-related characteristics but remains significant (at about 3 per cent). Previous analyses have stopped at this point since data on job quality are not collected in official surveys such as the LFS and ASHE. However, we have taken the analysis a step further by adding in data on features of the intrinsic quality of work which contribute to explaining some of the remaining pay gap. The inclusion of these features reduces the wage premium to insignificantly different from zero overall and reduces the premium for women from 5.7 per cent (i.e. 5.5 log points) to 2.2 per cent. So, in so far as there is a public sector pay premium, it is much smaller than has been suggested and its benefits are confined to women (and may therefore explain the lower gender pay gap in the public sector) and particularly those who are low paid (with positive effects in terms of poverty and equality outcomes).

The policy implications of these findings are twofold. First, Pay Review Bodies which review and recommend the pay of public sector workers need to note how the inclusion of job quality measures almost eliminates the overall pay gap. Their 'market-facing' pay reports have acknowledged how a number of key structural differences between the two sectors may account for a pay gap (e.g. NHS Pay Review Body, 2012, chapter 2). The employment profiles of each sector are very different. For example, professionals with specific service roles and high-level qualifications are over-represented in the public sector, especially within healthcare and education. Indeed, much of the pay gap disappears when these factors are controlled for in wage equations (Blackaby et al., 2012; Emmerson and Jin, 2012). This chapter suggests that using a richer set of variables that control for the quality of work further reduces the pay gap. Far from promoting and sustaining a double premium, the setting of public sector pay appears to have equalized the current reward package between the sectors.

Second, restraining public sector pay can have important implications for recruitment and retention issues in the public sector. Nickell and Quintini (2002), for example, noted that the marked decline in relative public sector pay in the 1980s resulted in a decline in the quality of men entering teaching and public sector general administration in the early 1990s, when measured using ability scores compared to the late 1970s. Clearly, it is important that wage rates in the public sector are high enough to attract and retain individuals with the skills and qualifications to deliver high-quality public services. The long-standing public sector wage penalty observed at the upper tail of the wage distribution (Blackaby et al., 1999 and Murphy et al., 2014) has implications for the delivery of high-quality public services which are also worth scrutiny by the Pay Review Bodies. Furthermore, the tendency for low-paid women to be treated more favourably in the public sector is likely to be weakened if public sector pay is restrained across the board (Cribb and Sibieta, 2013). This will have consequences for the egalitarian tendencies—sometimes prompted by government—which PRBs have successfully followed for a number of years.

The chapter also has lessons for labour market researchers. Foremost among them is the finding that entering the quality of work indicators alone into our wage equations produces similar results to the full model. This suggests that they are powerful indicators alone and are helpful in providing further explanatory power over and above standard individual and employment-related characteristics. They are therefore indicators worth collecting in order to fully understand pay differentials and the extent to which differences in the quality of work are reflected in the extrinsic rewards employees receive.

9

The Employee Experience of High-Involvement Management in Britain

Andy Charlwood

9.1. INTRODUCTION

In the mid-1980s High-Involvement Management (HIM; Lawler, 1986) and the closely related concept of High-Commitment Management (HCM; Walton, 1985) were held up as superior normative models of work design and management practice which offered the possibility of better-performing organizations and higher-quality work. In this chapter, the contribution of these ideas to the development, patterning, and distribution of job quality in Britain are considered and analysed.[1]

At the heart of Lawler's original formulation was the PIRK rubric (Lawler, 1986, 191): that work and jobs should be designed so that employees are empowered (P) to make decisions about how they do their jobs, given opportunities for involvement (I) in deciding how their organization is run, rewarded (R) according to their performance or contribution, and are given extensive opportunities for training and learning on the job (K denoting knowledge).[2] Therefore, the model can be seen as designing key aspects of job quality (higher skill and greater autonomy and voice) into the job.

There have been many refinements and variations of this basic idea since Lawler first proposed it (e.g. Applebaum et al., 2000; Kochan and Osterman, 1994; Pfeffer, 1998) but all share three distinct components. First, enriched job

---

[1] I am grateful to David Angrave for research assistance in preparing and analysing the data for this chapter.

[2] Note that Lawler's use of the term 'knowledge' differs somewhat from its usage in subsequent debates about 'knowledge work' and 'the knowledge economy'. Throughout this chapter 'knowledge' is used in the way that Lawler defined it: giving knowledge to employees so that they can be involved in the organization's performance.

design so that employees are empowered to make decisions about how they do their jobs, so they enjoy a relatively high degree of autonomy, control, and task discretion. Second, organizational-level opportunities for employee involvement through mechanisms like two-way team briefings, town hall meetings, suggestion schemes, and quality circles. Third, supporting human resource policies, including the careful recruitment and selection which prioritizes hiring for the cultural fit between the organization and the individual and the 'soft skills' of teamwork, ability to learn, and general agreeableness; goal and target focused appraisal and performance management systems; contingent pay, which relates pay to the performance of the individual, team, and/or organization; and extensive and structured opportunities for skill development and learning (de Menezes and Wood, 2006; Godard, 2004). Some variants of the model also stress the importance of guaranteeing employment security (e.g. Pfeffer, 1998), although evidence suggests that such guarantees are rare in practice.

HIM, then, is an integrated system of job design and management practice centred around critical aspects of job quality, specifically higher skill and greater autonomy. HIM theory also claims that higher job quality results in a better subjective experience of work for employees. Consequently, this chapter seeks to answer two key questions. First, what factors influence the distribution of jobs where workers experience HIM and how is this distribution changing; is HIM more prevalent among particular groups and sectors? Second, what impact does HIM have on other aspects of job quality (particularly effort) and the subjective experience of work (commitment, job satisfaction, and well-being at work)? In the light of the answers to these questions, the contribution of HIM to the inequalities in job quality in Britain is considered.

The chapter is organized as follows. The first section discusses theory and evidence on HIM, its adoption and effects. Following from this, we investigate the characteristics of jobs and workplaces where employees report being covered by HIM arrangements, focusing particularly on whether HIM is distributed unequally across the workforce so that we can go on to answer the question of 'who benefits from HIM?' if indeed there are benefits for employees. Finally, we investigate the associations between HIM, effort, commitment, and subjective well-being. The analysis is based on the 2001, 2006, and 2012 Skills and Employment Surveys (SES). Because the chapter looks at a particular form of *management practice*, the focus is on employees, i.e. those who are managed, so does not include the self-employed. The chapter begins by reviewing existing theory and evidence on these questions.

9.2. THEORY AND EVIDENCE ON HIM AND ITS EFFECTS

9.2.1. The Incidence of HIM in Britain

The existing evidence on the implementation and effects of HIM in Britain suggests that despite the normative claims made about the superiority of the HIM model made by Lawler, it has been adopted relatively rarely in British workplaces. Using a latent variable approach to analyse data from the 1998 Workplace Employment Relations Survey (WERS), de Menezes and Wood (2006, 132) identify a cluster of management practices which they labelled HIM, used in 24–30 per cent of British workplaces with ten or more employees, that included practices which promote flexible working, skill acquisition, and the capture of employees' suggestions and ideas. However, at a workplace level, the inter-correlation between this cluster of practices and pay linked to employee performance was just 0.14, while the correlation between the HIM cluster and enriched job design was just 0.07, suggesting Lawler's HIM model is rarely adopted. Use of the HIM cluster of practices was more likely in financial services, other business services, and public administration, it was also more common in larger workplaces. The limitations of de Menezes and Wood's study is that it conceptualizes HIM in terms of management practices, and does not investigate how these practices translate into employee experience; are employees experiencing the components of the Lawler HIM model or not? It is possible that if HIM is studied from the perspective of employee experience rather than management practice, we may observe a different pattern of adoption (Yandori and van Jaarsveld, 2014). The critical point here is that the way in which HIM is implemented will condition its effects on employee experience, so employee experience cannot be observed by measuring management practices (Boxall and Macky, 2014). By contrast, if we ask employees about their experiences of work, we can identify the places where HIM is implemented in a way that results in employees experiencing all the components of the Lawler model in their jobs. Therefore, the first research question that this chapter seeks to answer is whether or not data on employees' experience of work as reported in the SES series confirms de Menezes and Wood's findings about the incidence and determinants of HIM use in Britain.

9.2.2. The Effects of HIM on Employees

Lawler specified that HIM leads to superior organizational performance by improving employee commitment and satisfaction, improving decision-making through employee input and enhancing returns to investments in human capital by improving employee retention and greater employee involvement and commitment to knowledge development (Lawler, 1986, 192–3). As job satisfaction is a measure of subjective well-being, this implies that HIM will result in enhanced well-being levels for the employees who experience it. There is support for this contention from several different theoretical perspectives that stress the importance of autonomy and control (the P of PIRK in the Lawler model) for job quality and employee well-being (Gallie, 2007a). However, not all agree with this perspective—key elements of HIM work practices have been described as 'management by stress' (Parker and Slaughter, 1988), with HIM as a form of work intensification, leading therefore to lower levels of employee well-being (Kelly, 1992; Ramsay et al., 2000).

Empirical evidence on the effects of HIM on employees is mixed. Based on analysis of the Employment in Britain Survey (conducted in 1992) Gallie et al. (1998, 79 and 221) found that likely aspects of HIM, specifically greater skill use and task discretion were associated with higher levels of work strain. They also found evidence to suggest that these practices improved employee commitment, but these effects were only found in the private sector because public sector employees were motivated by values rather than management practices (Gallie et al., 1998, 250). By contrast, Wood and de Menezes (2011) found that enriched jobs (including autonomy and control) were associated with higher job satisfaction and employee well-being (greater contentment), but that HIM (as they defined it, i.e. as a cluster of involvement-focused management practices) had no impact on job satisfaction and a negative impact on contentment. Wood et al. (2012) extended this analysis to look at how enriched job design and the HIM variable previously developed by de Menezes and Wood (2006) impacted on job satisfaction, employee well-being, and organizational performance. Their empirical results suggested that enriched job design is positively associated with job satisfaction and employee well-being, but that the effects of HIM are negative. They also investigated whether there were interaction effects where HIM and enriched job design were combined, but they found no relationship between the interaction term and job satisfaction or employee well-being.

Boxall and Macky (2014) investigated the relationship between aspects of HIM and job quality among a sample of employees in New Zealand. Their analysis was based on a survey that asked employees if they experienced aspects of the Lawler HIM model in their jobs. They found that empowerment, contingent rewards, and knowledge acquisition opportunities were all associated with higher job satisfaction and that empowerment, involvement, and information-sharing and contingent rewards were associated with better work–life balance. There were no statistically significant relationships between any of the dimensions of HIM and fatigue or stress. The results on work–life imbalance seem to directly contradict equivalent analysis based on the Employment in Britain and Working in Britain surveys (White et al., 2003), which suggested specific constituent practices of HIM were associated with greater work–life imbalance, particularly for women. The difference in results might be explained by the fact that Boxall and Macky do not split their analyses by gender in the way that White et al. do, but could also be the result of differences in measures of HIM practices and work–life imbalance as well as contextual differences between Britain and New Zealand.

Godard (2010) found evidence that an additive index of 'alternative work practices' (AWPs), which included practices associated with both the P and the I of the Lawler HIM model, were asociated with higher stress levels but also higher job satisfaction in a sample of English employees (results for Canada were more positive, but the positive results were explained by traditional human resources practices rather than AWPs associated with the Lawler model). Finally, using the 2006 wave of the SES, Gallie (2013) found evidence that participation practices that are constituent parts of HIM have positive effects on psychological well-being, contentment-anxiety, and enthusiasm-depression, but that the size of the effects depended on class position, with those in lower social classes getting less positive effects. However, there was no evidence that participation had negative effects on well-being for any groups of employees.

Overall, then, the evidence on the effects of HIM on workers is mixed, some studies find positive results, some no results at all, and others somewhat negative results. However, with the partial exception of Wood et al. (2012), who found that the combination of enriched job design and HIM management practices had no independent effects on employee well-being and job satisfaction over and above those of the constituent packages of practices, these studies have not looked at the effects of HIM when all the constituent components of the Lawler HIM model are present. Therefore, the second set of research questions that this chapter seeks to answer is whether the full Lawler model of HIM has positive or negative effects on commitment, effort, and subjective well-being (including job satisfaction) over and above any effects from individual constituent practices.

9.3. METHODS: CONCEPTUALIZING AND MEASURING HIM

There are both general problems that are likely to be common to any attempt to measure and quantify HIM and specific problems and issues arising from the approach to measuring HIM adopted in this chapter, which the reader needs to be aware of before proceeding further. Note first that there are three broad approaches to investigating HIM and its effects. (1) To ask managers whether their workplaces or organizations have the management practices Lawler argued would result in HIM. The problem here is that management practices, even if in line with those specified by Lawler, may fail to produce HIM, because HIM depends on the way in which the practices are experienced by the employee (Lawler, 1986, 192). (2) To ask employees about their experience of work, to see if they report the components of Lawler HIM model being present in their jobs (e.g. Boxall and Macky, 2014; Godard, 2010). The problem here is that the experience of the Lawler HIM model may be unrelated to the management practices that are supposed to produce them, and employees may not always be fully aware of the management practices that they are subject to. The third approach aims to address these weaknesses by collecting information from management about management practices, and from employees about their experience of work (e.g. Vandenberg et al., 1999). Even here, problems may arise because there is no clear consensus about some of the theoretical constructs underpinning the model should be operationalized, for example, does 'giving knowledge' to employees (Lawler, 1986, 191) involve providing general training opportunities, providing training in specific knowledge intensive skills, or providing structured systems and opportunities for employees to share knowledge and learn from one another? If the researcher decides that it is some combination of these three activities, what is the relative weighting that should be given to each? Decisions about how to measure HIM will in all likelihood influence the results.

With this in mind, the approach taken in this chapter is to ask employees about their experience of work to determine whether they experience the Lawler HIM model in their jobs. This approach is necessary because the SES are surveys of employees and do not contain direct measures of management practices (which employees may not be aware of anyway). Although not specifically designed to measure the Lawler model, there are sufficient measures of it included to be able to operationalize the concept.

Once the components of HIM have been measured, however imperfectly, how do researchers decide whether the management practices and experiences of work they have captured equate to HIM? The most common approach is to identify its use through some form of latent variable analysis, whereby the presence of HIM is inferred from patterns of inter-correlation between variables that seek to represent and measure theoretically important components of the HIM model (e.g. variables that capture empowerment, involvement, contingent reward, and knowledge embedded in jobs), see, for example, de Menezes and Wood (2006), Vandenberg et al. (1999), Wood and de Menezes (2011), Wood et al. (2012). The problem with this approach is that if HIM including all elements of the Lawler HIM model is rare, latent variable analysis will not identify it. Therefore, an alternative approach is to identify variables that are likely to capture theoretically important aspects of HIM and then to define HIM as being present when variables that capture these aspects are all present at the same time. This line of analysis is pursued here.

Given these general and specific issues with quantitative analysis of HIM, it is perhaps better to view the analysis contained within this chapters as 'ficts'— reasonable attempts to quantify and represent a complex social reality, which may nevertheless be subject to error, so that the analysis offers a trace or outline of the HIM in Britain and its effects rather than a detailed and necessarily accurate picture (Olsen and Morgan, 2005, 276).

9.3.1. Operationalizing the Lawler HIM Model

9.3.1.1. Empowerment (P)

The employee experience of enriched job design or empowerment is captured by a four-item scale, where the items are (1) 'my job allows me to take part in making decisions that affect my work'; (2) 'how much influence do you personally have on deciding what tasks you do?' (3) 'how much influence do you personally have on deciding how you do the task?' (4) 'how much choice do you have over the way you do your job?' Responses for each item were on a 0–3 scale, where a high score denotes a greater level of empowerment. From this, a 0–12 scale was created with a Cronbach's alpha scale reliability coefficient of 0.799. A dummy variable was then created with a positive value where the scale score was 10 or higher—this amounted to 34.5 per cent of respondents.

9.3.1.2. Involvement (I)

A dummy variable to measure organizational-level policies to encourage employee involvement was created where respondents answered positively to the following two questions: (1) 'At your workplace, does management organize meetings where you are informed about what is happening in the organization?' (2) At your workplace, does management organize meetings where you can express your views about what is happening in the organization? 70.7 per cent of respondents reported these arrangements at their workplace.

9.3.1.3. Contingent Reward (P)

A dummy variable denoting the use of pay linked to employee performance if respondents answered positively to any of the following questions: (1) 'Do appraisals affect your earnings in any way?' (2) 'Do you receive any incentive payment, bonus, or commission that is linked directly to the performance of yourself or any workgroup you belong to?' (3) 'Do you receive any incentive payment, bonus, or commission that is linked directly to the results achieved by the organization or workplace?' 51.4 per cent of respondents reported receiving contingent pay of some sort.

9.3.1.4. Knowledge (K)

The employee experience of knowledge development and acquisition was captured by the SES job learning demands index (Felstead et al., 2015), a four-item scale that captures the extent to which there is an in-built requirement for workers to learn by spotting problems and faults, seeking solutions to problems, learning new things on the job, and thinking about how their work is done. The items were 'my job requires that I keep learning new things', 'in your job, how important is it to spot problems or faults?', 'how important is it to work out the causes of problems or faults?', and 'how important is thinking of solutions to problems?' Responses to the first item were on a four-point scale with responses to the other three items on five-point scales. The scale reliability coefficient for a summative index of the four items was 0.826. From this index, a dummy variable denoting high knowledge and learning requirements was created when respondents scored 14 or 15 (out of a possible maximum score of 15). 27.3 per cent of respondents were in this category.

A dummy variable was then created when all four components of HIM were present. This operationalization of HIM is necessarily somewhat arbitrary, particularly the cut-off points used to denote high levels of employee involvement and high knowledge requirements. An alternative approach would have been to use an additive index (as per Godard, 2010). However, an index misses the point that Lawler conceived HIM as a binary variable—it is either present or not present; it would be possible to report a moderately high score on an index measure with one part of Lawler's formula being absent. To test the extent to which decisions about how to operationalize HIM affected results, an extensive set of sensitivity analyses, including different methods of operationalizing HIM, was carried out. These analyses are described in more detail in section 9.4.3.

9.3.2. Outcome Measures

The key outcomes of interest are effort, commitment, and measures of subjective well-being (job satisfaction, enthusiasm-depression, and comfort-anxiety). Effort is measured by a five-item latent effort index comprised of the following items: (1) 'How often does your work involve working at very high speed?' (2) 'How often does your work involve working to tight deadlines?' (3) 'My job requires that I work very hard' (respondents were asked the extent they agreed or disagreed with this statement). (4) 'How much effort do you put into your job beyond what is required?' (5) 'I often have to work extra time, over and above the formal hours of my job, to get through the work or to help out'.

Commitment was measured using a six-item scale where respondents were asked to rate the extent that they agreed or disagreed with the following statements: (1) 'I find that my values and the organization's values are quite similar.' (2) 'I feel very little loyalty to this organization.' (3) 'I am proud to be working for this organization.' (4) 'I am willing to work harder than I have to in order to help this organization succeed.' (5) 'I would take almost any job to keep working for this organization.' (6) 'I would turn down another job to stay with this organization.' This commitment index combines evaluative judgements about the employing organization with measures of the balance of positive and negative beliefs and feelings about it. The scale reliability coefficient for a summative scale of responses to these questions was 0.798. A higher score denotes higher levels of commitment. The commitment scale was standardized for use in the regression analysis.

Similarly, job satisfaction as a measure of subjective well-being captures an evaluative judgement about the job, made by combining an imperfect assessment of affect experienced on the job with an assessment of how the job shapes up compared to the respondents' goals and available alternative jobs (Deiner, 1984; Weiss, 2002). Therefore, job satisfaction does not necessarily measure job quality because workers can be satisfied with objectively poor-quality work if they have low expectations of their job. Nevertheless, low job satisfaction is likely to indicate poor-quality work, and may contribute towards poor mental and physical health (Brown et al., 2012). Job satisfaction was measured using a single-item question that asks about overall satisfaction with the job, with responses on a seven-point scale (running 1–7, with 7 denoting high satisfaction). The measure was standardized for use in the regression analysis. Evidence suggests that single-item measures of job satisfaction have an acceptable level of reliability compared to multi-item index measures (Wanous et al., 1997).

Affective aspects of subjective well-being at work were measured using well-tested and validated scales developed by Warr (1990). Anxiety-contentment is measured using the questions 'thinking of the past few weeks, how much of the time has your job made you feel...' with the following six emotions specified: 'calm', 'contented', 'relaxed', 'tense', 'uneasy', and 'worried'. A positive score denotes contentment. Enthusiasm-depression was measured in the same way, substituting 'depressed', 'gloomy', 'miserable', 'cheerful', and 'optimistic' for the emotions used to measure anxiety-contentment. The resulting scale variables were standardized for use in the regression analysis.

Regression analysis was used to investigate the relationship between HIM and these outcome measures. The control variables included in these analyses are described in the next section.

9.3.3. Control Variables

The general principle when selecting control variables to include in the empirical analysis was to identify job, individual, and workplace characteristics that could be systematically related to adoption or non-adoption of HIM and to the outcome variables under investigation. By including these control variables, we are able to estimate whether the HIM–outcome relationship is in fact explained by these other characteristics rather than by HIM.

Job characteristics: dummy variables to denote whether the respondent usually works fewer than thirty hours, forty to forty-eight hours, or more than forty-eight hours a week; the natural logarithm of hourly pay; whether the respondent's employment contract is temporary or fixed term in nature; whether the respondent has managerial or supervisory responsibilities; whether the respondent's job is done wholly or primarily by men or by women (compared to jobs done equally by men and women); dummy variables indicating if job tenure is less than one year or more than five years; dummy variables for occupational group based on the seven-class model of the National Statistics Socioeconomic Classification (NS-SEC). A measure interacting the complexity and importance of computer use within the job was also included as a proxy for the role of advanced technology in the job.

Workplace characteristics: whether or not the workplace is owned by a company based overseas; whether the workplace is in the non-trading sector; whether the workplace is in the public sector; whether the respondent thinks that their workplace faces a very high or high degree of product market competition; whether or not unions or staff associations are present at the workplace; dummy variables for broad industry measured using the SIC92 classification.

Individual characteristics: the gender and age of the respondent; whether or not the respondent is from an ethnic minority; the highest educational qualification of the respondent; dummy variables that indicate the region in which the respondent lives.

Respondents with missing values on any of the variables used in the analysis were discarded. Following standard assumptions, item non-response should be a random process and so should not bias results. The mean values of the variables used in the regression analyses are reported in Table 9.A1.

9.4. RESULTS

9.4.1. The Incidence of HIM

Table 9.1 reports the incidence of HIM and its component elements over the 2001–2012 period, while Table 9.2 reports the inter-correlations between the

Table 9.1. Incidence of HIM

	% reporting empowerment	% reporting employee involvement	% reporting contingent reward	% reporting knowledge requirements	% of employees reporting HIM
2001	34.1	70.3	50.5	27.5	6.1
2006	35.7	71.1	52.6	27.8	7.4
2012	32.4	72.3	50.1	25.9	5.7
All	34.5	70.7	51.4	27.3	6.6

Note: Weighted base: 11,920.

Source: 2001, 2006, and 2012 SES

Table 9.2. Correlations between Components of HIM

	Empowerment (P)	Employee involvement (I)	Contingent reward (R)	Knowledge (K)
Empowerment	1.00			
Employee Involvement	0.13	1.00		
Contingent reward	0.08	0.21	1.00	
Knowledge	0.16	0.10	0.08	1.00

Note: Weighted base: 11,920.

Source: 2001, 2006, and 2012 SES

variables measuring empowerment, involvement policies, variable pay, and knowledge work. Results are not directly comparable to the results of de Menezes and Wood (2006, 132) because of different sampling frames and methods for measuring HIM, but they are broadly comparable in that they suggest that managerial practices to encourage employee involvement (I) and enriched job design or empowerment (P) are not well correlated, and that pay related to performance is not particularly highly correlated with any of the other three aspects of Lawler's formulation. Given this pattern of inter-correlation, it is unsurprising that just 6.6 per cent of SES respondents reported all four elements of Lawler's HIM model being present in their jobs. An examination of the incidence of HIM and its components over time, from 2001 to 2012, shows that there has been little or no aggregate change in its use as the differences between years were not statistically significant.

What explains the limited take-up of HIM in Britain? Why have the prescriptions of Lawler and others not been followed? One answer to this question focuses on the perceived failures of management vision and skill (Kochan and Osterman, 1994). A second attributes blame to the neo-liberal political economy and the dominance of finance-driven m-form organizations, which has resulted in economic and management systems where management are unable to build trust or genuinely empower employees because they are compelled to cut costs at employees' expense (Thompson, 2003). A third, related answer stresses the contingent nature of management practice, which means the one-size-fits-all approach to management of Lawler and related theorists will not work in many industries, contexts, or national systems of employment regulation (Boxall and Purcell, 2008). For example, systems of total quality management reduce discretion and control over the way that individual employees do their jobs while requiring them to participate in quality circles that rigorously test ideas for cutting cost and improving quality. Developments in computer-controlled machinery and robots have reduced the knowledge and skill requirements of many skilled but routine jobs even as the educational credentials required to secure them has increased (Sennett, 1998). As a result, employers have been able to increase quality and flexibility at the same time as controlling labour costs by investing in technology that deskills jobs and reduces autonomy, discretion, and control (Hopkins 2009).

In the context of this generally low level of take-up for HIM, which groups of workers experience it? Table 9.3 provides some answers to this question. It shows that HIM was more common in higher-skill and higher-status occupations and in manufacturing, electricity, gas, and water, and business services industry groups. Men, those who work longer hours and the more highly educated, were more likely to experience it than women, part-time workers, and those with few or no qualifications. Regression analysis of the determinants of HIM also suggested that those covered by HIM were higher paid and did work where use of complex IT systems is an important part of the job. Further analysis (not reported for reasons of space) suggested that there was general stability in the incidence of HIM within the groups reported in Table 9.3 between 2001 and 2012. One exception to this stability was among workers in manual occupations and with lower levels of educational qualification, for whom the coverage of HIM had declined by small but statistically significant amounts through the recession years between 2006 and 2012. In short, if HIM does result in higher-quality work, there are significant inequalities of class, gender, and education in terms of who benefits, and these inequalities have got slightly worse since 2006. Next, we investigate whether HIM does in fact result in higher-quality jobs for those who experience it.

9.4.2. How Does HIM Affect Employee Effort, Commitment, and Well-Being?

The approach taken in all of the analyses reported below was to first estimate a regression model with the dependent variable (effort or commitment, etc.) and the binary HIM measure only. The full set of controls described above was

Table 9.3. The Incidence of HIM by Job, Personal, and Workplace Characteristics

	% covered by HIM
ALL	6.6
Occupation/contract type	
Higher managerial, administrative, and professional occupations	13.0***
Lower professional and higher technical occupations	10.4***
Intermediate occupations	3.9***
Lower supervisory occupations	6.6
Semi-routine occupations	2.3***
Routine occupations	1.6***
Temporary or fixed-term contract	1.4***
Works less than 35 hours a week	2.1***
Works more than 44 hours a week	12.0***
Personal characteristics	
Female	4.5***
Male	8.7***
Ethnic minority	6.5
No educational qualification	
Educated to NVQ Level 1 or equivalent	4.0**
Educated to NVQ Level 2 or equivalent	4.6***
Educated to NVQ Level 3 or equivalent	6.2
Educated to NVQ Level 4 or 5 or equivalent	9.7***
Educated to degree level or equivalent	9.5***
Workplace characteristics	
No trade union at the workplace	7.3*
Trade union at the workplace	6.3
Public/voluntary sector workplace	3.9***
Private sector workplace	8.2***
Workplace faces very high product market competition	10.3***
Workplace faces high product market competition	5.7*
Workplace is part of a foreign-owned organization	11.4***
Industry group (SIC2003), 2006, and 2012 only	
Agriculture, forestry, fishing	5.3
Mining, quarrying, and extraction	20.2**
Manufacturing and recycling	9.0***
Electricity, gas, water	13.5*
Construction	6.7
Wholesale and retail trades	6.2
Hotels and restaurants	4.2*
Transport and communications	7.6
Financial intermediation	9.5
Other business services	11.5***
Public administration and defence	4.1**
Education	4.0**
Health and social work	5.3*
Other community services	4.2*

Notes: Weighted base: 9,080. *** statistically significant at the 0.01 level, ** statistically significant at the 0.05 level, * statistically significant at the 0.1 level.

Source: 2001, 2006, and 2012 SES

then added to look at the relationship between HIM and the dependent variable, other things being equal. Next, to investigate the extent to which there was a relationship between HIM and the outcome variable over and above that which resulted from the components of Lawler's model on their own, these models were estimated again with further measures of the individual elements of Lawler's HIM model.

9.4.2.1. Effort

Table 9.4 examines the associations between HIM and employee effort, based on weighted least squares (WLS) regression analysis. Columns 1 and 2 show that there was a significant positive relationship between HIM and effort. In the model with controls, SES respondents covered by HIM reported effort levels that are on average 0.37 of a standard deviation higher than those reported by respondents without HIM. However, once the effects of the constituent components of Lawler's HIM model are controlled for (columns 3 and 4), the effects of HIM as an integrated package of measures became small and statistically insignificant. The largest effects on effort come from high knowledge requirements, with effort also being higher where there was a high degree of autonomy and control, and employee-involvement practices. This provides some evidence to suggest that the constituent management practices of HIM contribute to work intensification through higher effort levels.

9.4.2.2. Commitment

The relationship between HIM and commitment is explored in Table 9.5. Once again, the results of WLS analysis suggest that there was a positive and statistically significant relationship between HIM and commitment. Once again this relationship becomes statistically and quantitatively insignificant once measures of the constituent parts of the Lawler HIM model were included. Here, high levels of autonomy and control, and employee-involvement practices explain the HIM–commitment relationship. Recall that Gallie et al. (1998, 250) found evidence to suggest that the effect of HIM practices on commitment was greater in the private sector than the public sector. To test for whether this was still the case, the sample was split according to public/ private sector, and the analyses were repeated on these separate samples. Results (not reported for reasons of space) suggested that the key results were similarly positive in both sectors. Overall, then, these results suggest that HIM is associated with more committed employees, but this is related to employee involvement and empowerment rather than being dependent on the full HIM model.

Table 9.4. Is HIM Associated with Higher Effort Levels? WLS Regression Results

	(1) HIM-only model	(2) HIM and controls	(3) HIM and components of HIM	(4) HIM, components, and controls
HIM	0.369***	0.166***	−0.029	−0.035
	(0.026)	(0.025)	(0.032)	(0.029)
High knowledge			0.265***	0.200***
			(0.018)	(0.017)
High empowerment			0.039***	0.018***
			(0.003)	(0.003)
Employee-involvement practices			0.069***	0.035***
			(0.010)	(0.010)
Contingent reward			0.055***	0.022
			(0.016)	(0.017)
Constant	−0.030***	−0.103	−0.520***	−0.240*
	(0.008)	(0.141)	(0.030)	(0.139)
R^2	0.020	0.201	0.095	0.222
N	9,636	9,636	9,636	9,636

Notes: Effort is measured through the standardized latent effort index. Key independent variables: *HIM*: binary variable with a value of 1 if all four components of HIM present. *High knowledge*: a binary variable where a respondent scored 14 or 15 on the fifteen-point job learning demands index. *High empowerment*: a binary variable with the value of 1 where a respondent scored 10 or more out of 12 on the empowerment scale. *Employee-involvement practices*: a binary variable if a respondent reported that managers organize information-sharing meetings where employees can put across their views. *Contingent reward*: a binary variable with the value of 1 where a respondent reports any form of contingent pay element to their remuneration.

Control variables: *Job characteristics*: working less than thirty, forty–forty-seven, or forty-nine+ hours a week; log of hourly pay; temporary/fixed-term contract; managerial or supervisory role; job done mainly by men or women; importance of computer use; complexity of computer use; job tenure; occupation. *Workplace characteristics*: overseas ownership; non-trading sector; public sector; product market competition; union presence; one-digit SIC92 classification. *Individual characteristics*: region; gender; age; ethnic minority; highest educational qualification.

*** statistically significant at the 0.01 level, ** statistically significant at the 0.05 level, * statistically significant at the 0.1 level.

Source: 2001, 2006, and 2012 SES

9.4.2.3. Job Satisfaction

Table 9.6 shows the key results for analysis of the HIM–job satisfaction relationship. Results suggest that after controls are added, job satisfaction was just under one fifth of a standard deviation higher where HIM was present, and that this relationship is statistically significant. However, there was no relationship between HIM and job satisfaction over and above that derived from the constituent parts of the Lawler HIM model. Of the separate elements of HIM, involvement and empowerment had positive relationships with job satisfaction.

Table 9.5. Is HIM Associated with Higher Organizational Commitment Levels? WLS Regression Results

	(1) HIM-only model	(2) HIM and controls	(3) HIM and components of HIM	(4) HIM, components, and controls
HIM	0.488***	0.369***	0.038	0.004
	(0.046)	(0.047)	(0.053)	(0.052)
High knowledge			0.077***	0.121***
			(0.027)	(0.028)
High empowerment			0.104***	0.097***
			(0.005)	(0.005)
Employee-involvement practices			0.139***	0.175***
			(0.015)	(0.016)
Contingent reward			−0.035	0.021
			(0.023)	(0.026)
Constant	−0.064***	−0.017	−1.083***	−0.734***
	(0.012)	(0.257)	(0.042)	(0.242)
R^2	0.016	0.098	0.126	0.179
N	9,190	9,190	9,190	9,190

Notes: Commitment is measured through the standardized commitment index. Key independent variables: *HIM*: binary variable with a value of 1 if all four components of HIM present. *High knowledge*: a binary variable where a respondent scored 14 or 15 on the fifteen-point job learning demands index. *High empowerment*: a binary variable with the value of 1 where a respondent scored 10 or more out of 12 on the empowerment scale. *Employee-involvement practices*: a binary variable if a respondent reported that managers organize information-sharing meetings where employees can put across their views. *Contingent reward*: a binary variable with the value of 1 where a respondent reports any form of contingent pay element to their remuneration.

Control variables: *Job characteristics*: working less than thirty, forty–forty-seven, or forty-nine+ hours a week; log of hourly pay; temporary/fixed-term contract; managerial or supervisory role; job done mainly by men or women; importance of computer use; complexity of computer use; job tenure; occupation. *Workplace characteristics*: overseas ownership; non-trading sector; public sector; product market competition; union presence; one-digit SIC92 classification. *Individual characteristics*: region; gender; age; ethnic minority; highest educational qualification.

*** statistically significant at the 0.01 level, ** statistically significant at the 0.05 level, * statistically significant at the 0.1 level.

Source: 2001, 2006, and 2012 SES

9.4.2.4. Subjective Well-Being: Enthusiasm–Depression

Table 9.7 summarizes the results of analyses of the relationships between enthusiasm–depression and contentment–anxiety dimensions of subjective well-being and HIM. Columns 1–4 investigate the associations between HIM and enthusiasm–depression. Column 1 results show that where HIM was present, responses to the enthusiasm–depression scale were almost one half of a standard deviation higher. This relationship remained statistically significant after the addition of measures of the individual components of the

Table 9.6. The Determinants of Job Satisfaction, WLS Regression Results

	Job satisfaction			
	(1) HIM	(2) HIM and controls	(3) HIM and components	(4) HIM, components, and controls
HIM	0.413***	0.174***	0.050	0.001
	(0.037)	(0.037)	(0.044)	(0.043)
High knowledge			0.064**	0.039
			(0.030)	(0.027)
High empowerment			0.107***	0.068***
			(0.005)	(0.005)
Employee-involvement practices			0.146***	0.083***
			(0.0178)	(0.0163)
Contingent reward			−0.109***	−0.020
			(0.0264)	(0.0255)
Commitment		0.589***		0.534***
		(0.013)		(0.013)
Effort index		−0.033		−0.054***
		(0.020)		(0.020)
Constant	−0.147***	−0.113	−1.160***	−0.561**
	(0.014)	(0.242)	(0.0505)	(0.244)
R^2	0.010	0.339	0.113	0.365
N	9080	9080	9080	9080

Notes: Job satisfaction is measured by a standardized single-item question on overall job satisfaction. Key independent variables: *HIM*: binary variable with a value of 1 if all four components of HIM present. *High knowledge*: a binary variable where a respondent scored 14 or 15 on the fifteen-point job learning demands index. *High empowerment*: a binary variable with the value of 1 where a respondent scored 10 or more out of 12 on the empowerment scale. *Employee-involvement practices*: a binary variable if a respondent reported that managers organize information-sharing meetings where employees can put across their views. *Contingent reward*: a binary variable with the value of 1 where a respondent reports any form of contingent pay element to their remuneration.

Control variables: *Job characteristics*: working less than thirty, forty–forty-seven, or forty-nine+ hours a week; log of hourly pay; temporary/fixed-term contract; managerial or supervisory role; job done mainly by men or women; importance of computer use; complexity of computer use; job tenure; occupation. *Workplace characteristics*: overseas ownership; non-trading sector; public sector; product market competition; union presence; one-digit SIC92 classification. *Individual characteristics*: region; gender; age; ethnic minority; highest educational qualification.

*** statistically significant at the 0.01 level, ** statistically significant at the 0.05 level, * statistically significant at the 0.1 level.

Results are broadly consistent with those obtained from an ordered logit model.

Source: 2001, 2006, and 2012 SES

Lawler HIM model, effort, commitment, and other controls, although it diminished in absolute terms. Of course, it is not necessarily the case that HIM causes employees to experience more enthusiastic and positive emotions; more enthusiastic and positive people might be more likely to be selected into HIM jobs.

Table 9.7. The Determinants of Subjective Well-Being, WLS Regression Results

	Enthusiasm–depression				Contentment–anxiety			
	(1) HIM	(2) HIM and controls	(3) HIM and components	(4) HIM, components, and controls	(1) HIM	(2) HIM and controls	(3) HIM and components	(4) HIM, components, and controls
HIM	0.463***	0.268***	0.171***	0.139***	0.107***	0.212***	0.054	0.116***
	(0.032)	(0.034)	(0.038)	(0.037)	(0.033)	(0.035)	(0.040)	(0.039)
High knowledge			0.055**	0.053**			−0.116***	−0.017
			(0.027)	(0.026)			(0.027)	(0.027)
High empowerment			0.086***	0.056***			0.039***	0.047***
			(0.005)	(0.005)			(0.005)	(0.005)
Employee-involvement practices			0.115***	0.066***			0.012	0.052***
			(0.016)	(0.016)			(0.015)	(0.016)
Contingent reward			−0.143***	−0.047*			−0.103***	−0.052*
			(0.0250)	(0.0264)			(0.026)	(0.027)
Commitment		0.447***		0.403***		0.320***		0.285***
		(0.013)		(0.013)		(0.013)		(0.013)
Effort		−0.062***		−0.080***		−0.368***		−0.377***
		(0.020)		(0.020)		(0.012)		(0.020)
Constant	−0.112***	−0.316	−0.875***	−0.667***	−0.075***	0.377*	−0.314***	0.0858
	(0.013)	(0.213)	(0.046)	(0.215)	(0.0127)	(0.22)	(0.046)	(0.21)
R²	0.023	0.242	0.093	0.261	0.001	0.186	0.016	0.200
N	9076	9076	9076	9076	9080	9080	9080	9080

Notes: Enthusiasm–depression and contentment–anxiety are measured through standardized indexes. Key independent variables: *HIM*: binary variable with a value of 1 if all four components of HIM present. *High knowledge*: a binary variable where a respondent scored 14 or 15 on the fifteen-point job learning demands index. *High empowerment*: a binary variable with the value of 1 where a respondent scored 10 or more out of 12 on the empowerment scale. *Employee-involvement practices*: a binary variable if a respondent reported that managers organize information-sharing meetings where employees can put across their views. *Contingent reward*: a binary variable with the value of 1 where a respondent reports any form of contingent pay element to their remuneration.

Control variables: *Job characteristics*: working less than thirty, forty–forty-seven, or forty-nine+ hours a week; log of hourly pay; temporary/fixed-term contract; managerial or supervisory role; job done mainly by men or women; importance of computer use; complexity of computer use; job tenure; two-digit SOC classification. *Workplace characteristics*: overseas ownership; non-trading sector; public sector; product market competition; union presence; one-digit SIC92 classification. *Individual characteristics*: region; gender; age; ethnic minority; highest educational qualification.

*** statistically significant at the 0.01 level, ** statistically significant at the 0.05 level, * statistically significant at the 0.1 level.

Source: 2001, 2006, and 2012 SES

9.4.2.5. Contentment–Anxiety

Columns 5–8 show the key results of analyses of the relationship between contentment–anxiety and HIM. Once again, the results suggest a statistically significant relationship between HIM and greater contentment which was robust to the inclusion of control variables and measures of the constituent parts of the Lawler HIM model. After all controls and measures of the HIM components had been added, scores on the contentment—anxiety scale were around one tenth of a standard deviation higher when HIM was present. It is also interesting to note that there was a negative relationship between contingent reward and both contentment–anxiety and enthusiasm–depression.

Recall that Gallie (2013) found evidence that the relationship between participation practices (the involvement of Lawler's model) and contentment–anxiety and enthusiasm–depression depended on class position, with the magnitude of the relationship greater for those in higher-status occupations. To investigate whether this was the case for our HIM variable, a further set of models was estimated, where the sample was split according to the NS-SEC 3 class model. This three-class model comprises: the service class, consisting of occupations typically employed on a long-term service type employment contract; the working class, composed of occupations where the employment relationship is typically based around a short-term exchange of money for effort; and an intermediate class consisting of occupations with elements of both types of employment relation. Results (not reported in full for reasons of space) suggested that there were quantitative and statistically significant relationships between the well-being measures and HIM for all three classes, but that the magnitude of the relationship was greater for service-class occupations.

9.4.2.6. Discussion

Overall, then, these results suggest that HIM is associated with higher effort, a finding compatible with the idea that it results in work intensification, but HIM is also associated with more positive evaluations of the employing organization and the job, and higher levels of work-related subjective well-being. However, only the relationships between the measures of work-related subjective well-being and HIM are statistically and quantitatively significant once the impact of the constituent parts of the Lawler HIM model is taken into account. Knowledge demands, employee involvement, and empowerment were the more important determinants of commitment and job satisfaction. These results are broadly in line with the Wood et al. (2012) and Wood and de Menezes (2011) studies (based on employer-provided data on management practices) in finding that the positive relationships between HIM, job satisfaction, and work-related subjective well-being are related to higher levels of empowerment and enriched job design. Although Wood and his colleagues (2012) found no interaction effects between employee-involvement practices and enriched job design, the results reported here suggest that where all four components of the Lawler model are present, there is a positive association with subjective well-being measures over and above the effects of the individual components. On balance, then, these results support the idea that HIM is associated with higher-quality work (although an alternative explanation might be that organizations that utilize HIM select employees with more positive attitudes about work), however, the benefits are not without costs in terms of higher expected effort levels.

Finally, note that while theory predicts that it is HIM that causes higher job quality, the type of analysis reported above does not demonstrate this causal relationship. It is possible that other, unmeasured factors associated with HIM are responsible, or that there is an alternative chain of causality at work (for example, employees are more positive about their work when the organization they work for is successful, and successful organizations are more likely to implement HIM-related policies).

9.4.3. Sensitivity Analyses

The possibility that results are an artefact of potentially arbitrary choices about how to operationalize HIM has already been noted. To investigate this possibility, the analyses reported above were repeated with a number of alternative approaches to operationalizing HIM. First, an alternative operationalization of 'knowledge' was used, which included measures of the importance of specialist knowledge within the job and the extent to which helping co-workers learn was part of the job. The resulting scale had a lower scale reliability coefficient than the preferred knowledge measure reported above. Results for different measures of HIM using each knowledge measure were broadly similar (the only significant difference was in the results for anxiety-contentment, which were noticeably stronger using the preferred measure). Second, more expansive definitions of high knowledge and high empowerment were tried. Again, results were broadly similar, in terms of the direction of relationships and indicators of statistical significance, to those reported above, although the magnitude of the results diminished, a finding compatible with the idea that the more expansive definitions introduced measurement error, so biasing results downwards. Third, the high-knowledge variable was dropped from the definition of HIM, allowing data from the 1992 Employment in Britain Survey to be included in the analysis without the knowledge variable. Once again, results were broadly similar to those reported above. Further, key results were robust to changes to the model specification and associated changes in sample size (i.e. removing or adding control variables in a stepwise manner did not alter the substantive results). Fourth, results from the single-item job satisfaction variable were compared to equivalent analysis based on an index measure of job satisfaction (from 2006 and 2012 only) and they were broadly similar. Finally, all results reported above were run on weighted data but the addition or removal of weights did not substantially alter the results.

9.5. CONCLUSION

This chapter has investigated the incidence and effects of high-involvement management in Britain from 2001 to 2012. It has sought to operationalize Lawler's model of HIM by investigating whether employees report experiencing empowerment (autonomy and control), employee-involvement policies, contingent reward and high knowledge demands in their work. The SES is well suited to this topic because, in contrast to the WERS series, which Wood and his colleagues have used to investigate HIM, it asks questions that allow us to observe whether the components of Lawler's model are present in employees' jobs, rather than asking about the use of management practices that ought to be associated with it, but will not necessarily result in the experience of HIM if implemented poorly.

The key results reported in this chapter support the conclusions of previous studies that have investigated HIM through surveys of management practices collected from employers (e.g. de Menezes and Wood, 2006): HIM is rare in Britain, covering just 6.6 per cent of employees on the measure used in this study. This finding supports both those who have argued that the political economy of Britain is inimical to high-trust management systems like HIM (Thompson, 2003) and those who have argued that the universalist nature of Lawler's prescriptions are unrealistic given the multiple contingencies faced by management (Boxall and Purcell, 2008).

Lawler argued that HIM resulted in better-performing organizations and a better experience of work for the worker. In contrast, critics (e.g. Parker and Slaughter, 1988) argued that HIM represents work intensification and management by stress. The results reported in this chapter go some way to supporting Lawler's claims, while also providing some evidence that the criticisms were not entirely unfounded. Workers subject to HIM report working harder and work longer hours, findings compatible with the work-intensification hypothesis. However, they also report high job satisfaction and greater levels of commitment to their employer. Furthermore, they report more positive feelings (greater enthusiasm and contentment) while at work. Involvement practices, enriched job design, and higher knowledge demands all appear to contribute to higher commitment, job satisfaction, and subjective well-being. There is also a positive relationship between HIM and the subjective well-being measures over and above that which results from involvement practices, enriched job design, and greater knowledge requirements on their own. The finding that HIM is more likely to be found in organizations facing very high levels of product market competition also suggests that it is a tool for competitive advantage.

Overall, then, the results and analysis presented in this chapter suggest that HIM is an idea that holds out significant benefits for employees, in terms of higher job quality and a better subjective experience of work, but that the contextual and environmental constraints (limited managerial capacity, the dominance of the finance function, and capital markets) have limited its appeal to management. To the extent that HIM is practised in Britain, those more likely to experience it could be characterized as being at the more privileged end of the labour market: men who work longer hours, who are higher paid, better educated, and in higher status occupations that typically offer more secure employment. Further, this concentration of HIM use among those at the top of the occupational hierarchy became more pronounced between 2006 and 2012. Therefore, HIM (and its limited adoption) can be seen as factors which contribute to class and gender inequalities in the employee experience of work.

Finally, it is important to keep in mind the limitations of this study, particularly the lack of detailed measures of management practices related to involvement and participation. In the future, it would be desirable to re-examine the questions studied here using data that include measures of managerial practices related to the Lawler HIM model alongside measures of the employee experience which show whether or not these practices have the desired effects. Therefore, these results present a necessarily provisional approximation of HIM use and effects in Britain, albeit one which is broadly in line with other studies in the same field.

APPENDIX

Table 9.A1. Mean Values of Variables Used in the Analysis

	Weighted mean (standard deviation)	Standard error
Dependent variables		
Enthusiasm/depression (unstandardized)	25.5 (4.97)	0.078
Contentment/anxiety (unstandardized)	21.4 (4.78)	0.074
Job satisfaction (unstandardized)	4.3 (1.02)	0.020
Effort index	0.01	0.010
Commitment (unstandardized)	10.12 (3.26)	0.051
Job characteristics		
Importance of computer use; complexity of computer use	6.252	0.075
Works less than 30 hours a week	0.209	0.005
Works 30–40 hours a week	0.5	0.005
Works 41–49 hours a week	0.152	0.005
Works 50 or more hours a week	0.139	0.004
Fixed-term or temporary employment contract	0.055	0.008
Supervisory responsibilities	0.450	0.008
Job is done wholly or mainly by men	0.347	0.008
Job is done wholly or mainly by women	0.203	0.007
Job is done by both men and women	0.316	0.006
Job tenure less than 1 year	0.135	0.006
Job tenure 1–5 years	0.407	0.007
Job tenure more than 5 years	0.458	0.008
Occupation		
Higher managerial, administrative, and professional occupations	0.112	0.004
Lower professional and higher technical occupations	0.328	0.006
Intermediate occupations	0.158	0.004
Lower supervisory and technical occupations	0.100	0.004
Semi-routine occupations	0.179	0.005
Routine occupations	0.106	0.004
Geographical location		
North of England	0.259	0.007
Midlands of England	0.286	0.007
Wales and the Southwest of England	0.135	0.005
Scotland	0.084	0.003
London, the South and East of England	0.236	0.007
Workplace characteristics		
Owned by a company based overseas	0.124	0.006
Organization is in the non-trading sector	0.147	0.006
Organization faces very high product market competition	0.376	0.008
Organization faces high product market competition	0.286	0.007
Organization does not face high/very high product market competition	0.191	0.006
Union presence at the workplace	0.559	0.008
Industry (one-digit SIC 92)		

(*continued*)

Table 9.A1. Continued

	Weighted mean (standard deviation)	Standard error
Agriculture, hunting, forestry, and fishing	0.011	0.002
Mining and quarrying	0.002	0.001
Manufacturing	0.150	0.006
Electricity, gas, and water supply	0.008	0.001
Construction	0.042	0.003
Wholesale, retail, and repair of motor vehicles	0.132	0.006
Hotels and restaurants	0.038	0.004
Transport, storage, and communications	0.057	0.004
Financial intermediation	0.042	0.003
Real estate and business service	0.124	0.006
Public administration and defence	0.094	0.005
Education	0.110	0.005
Health and social services	0.149	0.005
Other community, social, and personal services	0.040	0.003
Personal characteristics		
Female	0.485	0.008
Age	39.3	0.186
Ethnic minority	0.075	0.005
Married	0.718	0.007
Educated to NVQ Level 1 or equivalent	0.089	0.005
Educated to NVQ Level 2 or equivalent	0.197	0.006
Educated to NVQ Level 3 or equivalent	0.233	0.007
Educated to NVQ Level 4 or 5 or equivalent	0.405	0.008
Educated to degree level or equivalent	0.267	0.007

Notes: Weighted base 9,076 (as per the enthusiasm–depression analysis sample, results are near identical when based on alternative regression samples).

10

Policies for Intrinsic Job Quality

Alan Felstead, Duncan Gallie, and Francis Green

10.1. INTRODUCTION

Job quality matters because it has substantial effects on general well-being. There is, therefore, a strong case for trying to improve job quality at all levels.[1] A good job can be the platform for working people to gain some fulfilment in their lives. Conversely, as an increasing body of research has shown over the last twenty years, poor-quality jobs adversely affect both mental and physical health. Insecurity, job strain (combining high work intensity with low levels of job control), a poor work–life balance, bad leadership, and a lack of social support have all been shown to be deleterious for health and well-being. These effects can also have an impact on individuals' non-working lives and their families. The practical consequences include lower productivity, increases in absenteeism, and quitting, bringing retirement forward, and, closely related, expanding the numbers of the long-term sick who cannot return to work.[2]

This book has presented many analyses of how the level and distribution of job quality has evolved over the last quarter century. We have adopted a broad perspective on job quality, to include both pay and important non-pay domains covering the intrinsic quality of jobs. While wage inequality has risen significantly in the UK since the late 1970s, the dispersion of non-pay aspects of work has not changed so dramatically. In certain aspects there has been convergence between groups, yet the problem of differentiation in all forms of job quality remains, and this inequality is reflected in substantial portions of the workforce experiencing poor job quality in one or more domain.

---

[1] We would like to thank Agnès Parent-Thirion for her helpful comments on a draft of this chapter and David Walters for pointing us in the direction of additional material.
[2] See Warr (2007) for a review of this expanding literature and Niedhammer et al. (2014) for recent evidence on the effects of poor job quality for health and the implications for public policy.

In this final chapter we develop the case for stronger policy attention on the need to improve the *intrinsic* quality of work. We ask: what, if anything, could policy interventions do to improve intrinsic job quality, and/or make it more equal? While growing inequalities in pay have been the subject of much public discussion and policy development, inequalities in the intrinsic quality of work have received rather less attention. There is, however, an increasing recognition of their importance for employee well-being (O'Donnell et al., 2014; Sweeney, 2014). We argue that this oversight should be tackled and that policy-makers should adopt a more egalitarian approach to tackling inequalities not only in pay but also in the non-pay aspects of job quality. This approach means, not that job quality should be equalized, but that all workers should be provided with adequate opportunities for self-validation and for self-development, as well as for meeting their material needs.

The chapter draws on a variety of sources including the evidence presented in this book. It does so by first arguing why, contrary to neo-liberal thinking, more policy focus is needed. It outlines four principles on which the case can be made for policies intended to raise the floor for conditions of work, compress inequalities, and provide the basis for more egalitarianism at work. The second part of the chapter proceeds to map out seven policy levers which have the potential to make a difference by driving up the quality of work and reducing some of the inequalities identified in previous chapters. This discussion is based on a review of what can be learnt from overseas as well as consideration of policy levers in the UK which could be modified to produce a new set of policies for improving intrinsic job quality and reversing patterns of inequality. The chapter ends by summarizing the case for intervention and the most likely routes an enlightened government could take to tackle the issues of unequal Britain at work.

10.2. WHAT'S THE PROBLEM AND SHOULD GOVERNMENT TRY TO FIX IT?

The need for improvement in intrinsic job quality has been underlined by evidence that employer policies in recent decades, accentuated by the economic crisis of 2008–2009, have led to a deterioration in key aspects of job quality. In particular, the SES have shown a marked decline in the discretion that employees can exercise in their jobs since the early 1990s, together with a sharp rise in levels of work intensity (Felstead et al., 2013c; Inanc et al., 2013). There is now substantial evidence that the combination of low control with high work demands is a source both of psychological and physical ill-health (Chandola, 2010). It seems likely that this has been an important factor underlying the rising levels of work-related mental illness. Such problems are particularly concentrated among those in lower positions in the occupational hierarchy, thereby exacerbating problems of inequality at work. A concern to improve the intrinsic quality of work needs, then, to focus primarily upon ways in which employers can be encouraged to adopt forms of work design that reduce the risks of psychological ill-health, in particular by enhancing the capacity of employees to exercise initiative and discretion in the way they carry out their tasks.

The prevalence of neo-liberal thinking in recent decades has discouraged governments from seeking to take action to address these issues. Neo-liberals would neither recognize that there is a problem nor would they countenance intervention in the free workings of the market. For them, wealth creation and a rising standard of living for all rests on the unfettered activities of private property owners, businesses, and multinational corporations. Employees, in this perspective, can choose between jobs with different employers, and so all aspects of job quality are driven up through the impersonal forces of labour market competition. Belief in these ideas grew in the 1970s and culminated politically in the election of Margaret Thatcher's government in 1979. Her governments—as well as those which have followed—have confronted trade union power, dismantled or rolled back the welfare state, privatized public enterprises, reduced taxation, and deregulated labour markets in order to give employers greater freedom to manage.

According to neo-liberal theory, the less government taxes the rich and defends workers through regulating the labour market, the greater the prosperity for all. This process has been termed 'trickle-down' economics. It is based on the idea that tax cuts given to higher earners and businesses will raise the employment prospects, pay, and quality of work of those they employ. The employment relation is seen, moreover, as a private domain, where government should not intervene. All attempts to reduce inequality or to regulate work are expected by neo-liberals to damage this process and to hinder the tendency for a 'rising tide to lift all boats'.

However, a prolonged period of growing income inequality has failed to provide solid foundations for future economic growth. Increasing inequality is evident in national pay data. For example, the annual average income of the top decile was around £55,000 in 2008, almost twelve times higher than those in the bottom decile, who had an average income of £4,700. In 1985 the gap was narrower, when the ratio was eight to one. Changes in taxation have served to widen the gap further with the top marginal income tax rate falling from 60 per cent in the 1980s to 40 per cent in the 2000s, before rising to 50 per cent in 2010 (as an emergency measure) and then falling back to 45 per cent in 2013 (OECD, 2011). Instead of strengthening the UK economy, as predicted by neo-liberals, the rising level of inequality tends to do the reverse. This is because the rich have a lower propensity to spend their (growing) income, while the poor are more likely to supplement their (declining) income with debt. So, few of the benefits enjoyed by higher earners tend to trickle down (Burgess and Propper, 1999; Danziger and Gottschalk, 1993; Muriel and Sibieta, 2009).

Nevertheless, while *neo-liberals* are emphatically against market intervention on ideological grounds, it is possible to argue for intervention to improve the quality of work from within the *neo-classical* economic paradigm. The economic case for market intervention is that, while it may be economically rational for employers to take a given action, this can incur costs for others. These externalities are not included in the employer's original decision-making calculus. So, in the case of Britain, if employers design work arrangements which result in workers taking prolonged periods of time off work because of work-related stress, or leave the workforce altogether because of disability, the majority of these rehabilitation costs will be borne by the National Health Service and not the employer. As has been mentioned, increased work-related stress is strongly related to work designs which drive workers hard in the context of low levels of job control. Around a third of all self-reported health complaints are reportedly caused or made worse by work (Chandola, 2010). Hence, the market price for products and services produced in these work environments will not incorporate the full opportunity cost to society of their production.

Neo-classical economics can also accept that rational decisions may be made on the basis of incomplete information. So, employers may not always be aware of best practice management techniques which enhance the quality of work while also maximizing business benefits. Indeed, there is a wealth of evidence that British management is poorly educated and less knowledgeable than managers operating overseas (Bloom et al., 2011; Totterdill, 2009, 2013). Even where there is the knowledge, enlightened managers often face substantial difficulties in bringing about the changes in organizational culture that are needed to improve job design. Nevertheless, in this perspective managers, rather than being constrained by some technological imperative, can be seen to have some scope to make the working lives of those they manage and the quality of their own jobs better (Child, 1972; Felstead et al., 2009; Grugulis et al., 2011; Lambert and Henly, 2012). This is confirmed by the considerable difference in job quality between different countries of Europe at comparable levels of technological development (Gallie, 2007a, 2013).

In addition to the economic case for intervention, governments have a duty of care to protect all citizens, thereby placing a social rather than a market value on their protection. In the work context, this is underpinned by a statutory undertaking. Under the Health and Safety at Work Act (HSWA) 1974, employers have a duty under law to ensure, as far as is reasonably practical, the health and safety of their employees at work. Since individual workers are ill-placed to acquire full information about an employers' health and safety record and calculate the risks associated with the work, the Health and Safety Executive (HSE) was set up to do so on workers' behalf. When originally conceived, the 'duty of care' undertaking was drafted with the physical well-being of the worker in mind. However, increasing recognition of the deleterious impact of stress on employees has widened the meaning of 'health' to include both physical and mental well-being.

This shift in emphasis was based on mounting evidence that the mental dangers of work were becoming more prevalent, while the physical dangers of non-fatal and fatal accidents were on the decline. 'High-strain' jobs—defined as those where work effort is high yet job control is low—have increased in prevalence over the last twenty years, rising from 23 per cent in 1992 to 35 per cent in 2012 (Felstead et al., 2013c). In numerical terms, estimates from the Quarterly Labour Force Survey show that around two fifths of work-related illnesses can be classified as cases of stress, with the highest prevalence in the predominantly public sector industries of health and social work, education, and public administration. The main activities reported as causing or aggravating work-related stress are work pressures and lack of managerial support, as well as violence and bullying at work (HSE, 2013b). A poor work–life balance has also been shown to have a strong association with low mental health (e.g. Lunau et al., 2014). In 2011–2012 over 10 million working days were lost due to work-related stress at an estimated cost of £6.4 billion to the economy. A typical person suffering from this condition took twenty-four days off work, one of the highest averages recorded for work-related health complaints. Non-fatal physical injuries, on the other hand, resulted in shorter periods of absence and have been declining in frequency by around a third since the turn of the millennium (HSE, 2013a).

In addition to fulfilling their duty-of-care commitments, governments can intervene to improve the quality of work on grounds of equity. Workplace anti-discrimination legislation, for example, is framed with this equity principle in mind. The equity principle already underpins the provision of minimum standards for some aspects of job quality and so provides a safety net for all workers including the most vulnerable. The introduction of the National Minimum Wage (NMW) in April 1999 is a case in point. Prior to that time, no national minimum applied in the UK. There was a variety of systems of wage control focused on specific industries but most of these had been abolished by the late 1990s (see Chapter 1). Part of the reason for the introduction of the NMW was the decline of trade union membership and a weakening of employees' bargaining power, as well as a recognition that the employees most vulnerable to low pay worked in services which had a weak history of unionization. On both grounds, the case was made for an NMW, echoing debates a century earlier when minimum wages were first introduced in the 'sweated trades' (Deakin and Green, 2009). Nevertheless, it has been argued that the rate-setting procedure is a balancing act between the desire for social justice for those in work and the welfare of the unemployed. The Low Pay

Commission is responsible for advising government on the most appropriate rate to 'help as many low-paid workers as possible without any significant adverse impact on employment or the economy' (Low Pay Commission, 2014; Mantouvalou, 2011). This trade-off continues to be a matter of controversy.

10.3. WHAT POLICIES ARE THERE AND HOW MIGHT THEY WORK?

Making and winning the case for government intervention to improve the quality of work is one thing, but outlining a realistic and achievable set of policies to deliver these improvements is another. This section of the chapter focuses on the latter. Seven types of possible government action are discussed: (1) following the Scandinavian model; (2) building on European labour market regulation; (3) enhancing employee voice; (4) strengthening the HSE's Management Standards approach; (5) providing better legal redress; (6) using public sector procurement; and (7) celebrating best practice and providing greater transparency.

10.3.1. Following the Scandinavian Model

It is commonly assumed that Britain's market-driven skills system tends to generate a lower and more unequal level of skills than the coordinated systems of Northern Europe, especially those in Scandinavia (e.g. Olsen et al., 2010; Soskice, 1999). As a result, wages are more dispersed and, faced with weaker regulation, British employers are more likely to compete on the basis of price, hence putting downward pressure on the non-pay features of work. While recent evidence has cast some doubt on the strength of this characterization, it still remains the case that on many indicators the quality of work in the UK falls short of levels reached in Scandinavian countries, especially in terms of the skills use and discretion levels exercised at work (Gallie, 2003, 2007b; Green et al., 2013). Similarly, employees in the Scandinavian countries have better jobs in terms of the variety of work, the opportunities for skill development, and the level of organizational participation, reflected in their ability to influence decisions about changes in work organization and the prevalence of meetings in which they can express their views (Gallie, 2013; Hartikainen et al., 2010).

   The emergence of the 'Scandinavian' model from the late 1970s onwards (Gustavsen, 2007) shows that government intervention can make a difference to the quality of employees' working lives. This model has a number of characteristics, but two are of particular relevance. These are typified by developments in Sweden in the mid-1970s. First, the 1977 Co-Determination at Work Act extended collective bargaining into areas of organizational and technical change in an attempt to give unions a real say over working conditions before any final decisions are taken. Although the employer retained ultimate control, unions also acquired important rights to information on issues like production, finance, and human resource strategy (Cressey, 1992). Second, the Work Environment Act 1977 stipulated that all employees

> shall be given the opportunity of participating in the design of his (sic) own working situation and in processes of change and development affecting his (sic) own work. Technology, work organisation and job content shall be designed in such a way that the employee is not subjected to physical or mental strains which can lead to ill-health or accidents . . . Closely controlled or restricted work shall be avoided or limited.
>
> (quoted in CEC, 2011, 79)

The intention, therefore, was to minimize risks to health caused by excessive work controls and limited job control (cf. Karasek, 1979).

Similar developments took place in Denmark, with a shift from external inspection to internal monitoring of the causes and elimination of work stress as a result of amendments to the Working Environment Act of 1975. From that point on, it became compulsory for employers to establish a safe and sound working environment for staff, and to provide proof of doing so by carrying out a risk assessment of work-related stress among employees and to take corrective action to minimize its occurrence (Egger and Sengenberger, 2003). Some of the earliest psychosocial questionnaires were developed for application in the work setting as a result. The Copenhagen Psychosocial Questionnaire was first developed in Denmark in 1977, and has subsequently been developed, modified, and used in many countries (Moncada et al., 2014).

However, the policy impetus for improving work quality through legislative regulation has cooled in Denmark and Sweden since the 1970s and 1980s when these policies were first enacted. In Sweden this partly reflected the decline in the hegemony of the Swedish Social Democrats and the electoral victory in 2006 of the centre-right after twelve years of Social Democratic rule. Indeed, the new government even closed the Swedish National Institute for Working Life, originally set up in the 1960s to study and advise government on enhancing the quality of work (Westerholm, 2007).

At all events, in the UK effective policies for achieving higher job quality cannot directly follow the Scandinavian model. Much of the leverage of the Swedish and Danish initiatives, for example, was based on the traditional role of the social partners in regulating the work environment. As a result, initiatives involving trade unions covered in one fell swoop a large number of workplaces and affected the working lives of many workers. Trade union density in Sweden, for example, is around 71 per cent compared to a figure of around 27 per cent in the UK (BIS, 2013; Coats, 2013, annex 1). UK trade unions, therefore, provide a relatively weak basis on which to effect change.

Nevertheless, softer forms of intervention have also been pioneered in Scandinavia which may have more traction in the UK context. These interventions are designed to spread best practice and provide employers with better information on which to base their decisions, hence nudging them to improve the quality of work (see section 10.3.7 below). In 1996 in Finland, for example, the Workplace Development Programme (TYKE) was set up to improve both productivity and the quality of working life. Between 1996 and 2010, more than 1,800 projects were funded through various versions of the programme. The programme touched the lives of nearly 350,000 workers, which equates to around 10 per cent of the working population (Alasoini, 2013). The programme was refreshed, refocused, and rebranded in 2012, but it is still based on the idea of providing expert advice and support to businesses to improve both productivity and the quality of working life. It forms part of a wider government strategy of making 'working life in Finland the best in Europe by 2020' (Ministry of Employment and the Economy, 2012, 3). A similar government vision for the quality of work is absent in the UK, but its presence would usefully serve to focus the minds of policy-makers on the types of policy solutions available to lever change (see section 10.4).

10.3.2. Pursuing European Labour Market Regulation

Another avenue to improve job quality and tackle growing inequality is to use the institutional tools of the EU to equalize standards and set a common threshold across Europe. This would prevent a race to the bottom in terms of the quality of work and prevent further widening of the inequalities between countries which already exist (Green et al., 2013). A key feature of the European Commission's agenda is 'delivering stronger, lasting growth and creating more and better jobs' (CEC, 2005, 7). This commitment was first enshrined in the 2000 Lisbon Strategy for economic, employment, and social development. It remains a key element of the revised European Employment Strategy launched in 2005, although its prominence has diminished with the increased emphasis placed on competitiveness (see Dieckhoff and Gallie, 2007). Nevertheless, it still remains a basis on which to seek improved labour market regulation.

There have been a number of European Union directives on job quality which require member states to enact its provisions in national legislation. When taken out on grounds of health and safety, directives can be issued if a majority of member states agree. However, opt outs are possible. For example, employees in the UK are able to work longer than the forty-eight-hour working week maximum stipulated by the Working Time Directive if they wish. This directive also gives EU workers the right to a minimum number of holidays each year, rest breaks, and rest of at least eleven hours in any twenty-four hours; as well as restricting excessive night work. The stated purpose of the directive is to protect people's health and safety and excessive working time is cited as a major cause of stress, depression, and illness. Other directives seek to protect those working for temporary work agencies, those on fixed-term contracts and those working part time from unfair treatment in terms of pay and terms and conditions of employment. These are referred to as 'daughter' directives since they were enacted under the umbrella of protecting the health and safety of workers across the EU (Leka et al., 2010).

However, since the turn of the millennium there has been a policy shift in terms of EU governance from detailed top-down imposition through the use of directives to a greater reliance on social dialogue among partners leading to voluntary agreements (i.e. 'softer' regulation) (Branch, 2005). This comprises discussions, consultations, negotiations, and joint actions by European-level peak federations of management and labour. The voluntary nature of these agreements gives employers the power of veto and therefore provides a route through which they can promote their preferred mode of intervention, namely self-regulation (Dundon et al., 2014).

Under this mechanism the European social partners signed a framework agreement on work-related stress in 2004. It defines work-related stress as 'a state, which is accompanied by physical, psychological or social complaints or dysfunctions and which results from individuals feeling unable to bridge a gap with the requirements or expectations placed upon them' (European Social Partners, 2008, 43). This general description is broad and imprecise as it conflates the requirements of the job with the individual's expectations and obligations at as well as outside of work. However, it was the product of a compromise between workers' organizations that were keen to emphasize work-related aspects of stress and employers who favoured definitions which focused on individual circumstances (Ertel et al., 2010). The agreement led to the development of 'soft' instruments such as guidelines and recommendations of the sort embodied in the HSE's Management Standards (see section 10.3.4).

Future European-level regulation is, therefore, likely to be limited, but still worthwhile as a means of improving the quality of work and thereby providing a brake on the tendency for inequalities at work to widen. In the words of a former general secretary of the European Trade Union Confederation, 'if it's a choice between legislation that may not come in for years, or agreements that are implemented and improved by the social partners, then as politics stands: I would opt for the latter (André, 2007 quoted in Ertel et al., 2010, 177). We would also add that the option exists to revise European labour market regulation by modifying the original directive or framework agreement and/ or amend the way in which the EU regulation is translated into national law/

voluntary agreements (see section 10.3.3). While the prospects for tackling inequalities in the intrinsic quality of work by either following the Scandinavian model or responding to a reinvigorated set of European Union directives look remote, other policy levers offer greater hope. The remainder of this section focuses on five which have the greatest potential.

10.3.3. Enhancing Employee Voice

An effective system of employee voice in the wider workplace—whether through indirect representation or direct participation—is likely to be a precondition of successful local policies for addressing the factors that aggravate work stress (Westgaard and Winkel, 2011). However well-motivated the intentions of employers, it is employees that experience the pressures of work and the restrictions of their work roles and have the knowledge that is essential for devising viable solutions.

Until the 1980s trade unions provided the major channel for employee voice in the UK. They have traditionally acted as a 'sword of justice' in those workplaces where they were recognized. The late 1970s were the high point in trade union influence: union membership was at an all-time high and the reach of union influence through collective bargaining was at its most extensive. However, since that time union membership levels have plummeted from around 13 million in 1979 to about 10 million in 1989 and have since continued to fall (Brownlie, 2012, table 1.1; Chapter 7). Falling trade union membership is not unique to the UK and has occurred across many parts of Europe. However, trade union influence has fallen faster in the UK than elsewhere, partly because employers in many other parts of Europe have continued to adhere to collective agreements and partly because governments have required employers to follow the terms of the collective agreements which cover their sector or industry, irrespective of whether or not they are signatories to the original agreement (Coats, 2013, annex 1).

As Chapter 7 demonstrates, unions continue to have an influence with respect to pay by securing *ceteris paribus* higher wages for their members and reducing pay differentials. Even in this respect declining trade union power has weakened union influence: the union wage premium has declined and the wage compression effect has been restricted to those in the top half of the distribution. But the influence of trade union membership with respect to protection against deterioration of non-pay aspects of the quality of work appears to have been minimal. Effort levels have risen in unionized jobs, discretion levels have been reduced, and job insecurity has risen.

However, greater employee involvement—not necessarily through trade unions—has been shown to ameliorate some of the negative features of work associated with 'bad jobs'. Results from the SES, for example, suggest that those who had higher levels of involvement at work were less worried that they might lose their employment with the organization, they were less anxious about unfair treatment, and they were less concerned about a risk of job-status loss (Gallie et al., 2013).

A quick revival of trade union membership is unlikely, however sympathetic the legislative environment. Membership levels and influence have been declining since the late 1970s. This means that most employers and many employees, especially younger ones, have no experience of unions and the benefits they may provide. Trade unions need a long-term strategy that helps them recover strength in union-free private sector employers, increasing the scope of collective organization and eventually securing collective bargaining rights (Coats, 2005). Involvement in Information and Consultation (I&C) bodies may provide an opportunity for them to take the first step in this process. However, the regulations which underpin such consultative bodies need reform (BIS, 2006).

The UK is notably different from many other countries in Europe in that works councils are not part of the industrial relations landscape. As a result, employers in the UK communicate directly with employees, if they do so at all, about non-pay issues such as the management of workplace change and reorganization. However, it is very different elsewhere in Europe where works councils play a pivotal role in giving employees voice. The German works council system is regarded as the most developed. According to German law, a works council can be established in any enterprise if at least five employees make a request for one. All employees have the right to vote to elect representatives to the council who may or may not be backed by a trade union. Councillors can call on expert advice when necessary and are allowed time off to conduct their activities. The number of councillors is stipulated by law in accordance with the size of the establishment and meetings with the employer have to take place at least once a month. Works councils are not allowed to bargain over pay nor can they organize strikes or other forms of industrial action—these activities are reserved for trade unions. However, they are to be consulted on workforce planning, training, job regrading, redeployment, work reorganization, and job redesign. While the reality of works council prevalence and influence in Germany may fall short of the picture provided by the formal provisions, it is a system that, potentially at least, provides significant protection for the job quality at least of more skilled employees in larger establishments.

Given its lack of any comparable institutional provisions, the 2002 EU Directive on Employee Information and Consultation could be seen to be of particular significance for the UK. However, transposing this directive into the Information and Consultation of Employees (ICE) Regulations 2004 weakened many of the original directive's features and diluted its impact (Dundon et al., 2014). Notably, the statutory trigger threshold to initiate the establishment of I&C bodies (or works councils) was set much higher than in the German system.

According to the regulations, UK employers do not have to act unless at least 10 per cent of their employees make such a request or, if 'pre-existing agreements' already exist, when 40 per cent and a majority of those voting support the setting up of an I&C body in preference to arrangements already in place.

Yet the ICE regulations were meant to provide a mechanism for creating representative structures through which employers could inform and consult their employees about significant changes, as in the German system of works councils. The regulations came into effect in stages according to organization size, but by April 2008 they applied to all organizations with at least fifty employees. However, in quantitative terms 'the impact of the ICE Regulations in promoting the expansion of workplace JCCs [Joint Consultative Commit-tees] has been very limited' (van Wanrooy et al., 2013, 61). In 2011, 8 per cent of workplaces had a JCC on site compared to 9 per cent in 2004. In qualitative terms, too, the regulations appear to have had 'only limited significance for I&C practice' (Hall et al., 2013, 376) and, in particular, encouraging employers to become 'active consulters' as opposed to 'communicators' of management decisions.

Based on this evidence, we suggest that three reforms need to be made to the ICE regulations in order to enhance employee voice. First, the threshold to trigger the formation of I&C bodies needs to be lowered to the German level with the intention of raising the incidence of works council-style bodies in UK workplaces. Second, we suggest that pre-existing agreements should only be allowed to deflect requests to set new arrangements when existing agreements cover the issues specified in the regulations. Third, we suggest that statutory rights should be given to employee representatives to hold pre-meetings without the presence of management, to undertake training for the role and are able to use office facilities in furtherance of I&C activities.

10.3.4. Strengthening the HSE's Management Standards Approach

While enhanced I&C bodies may have a key role in reducing work-related stress, they are most likely to be effective if they can relate local experience to wider knowledge about the forms of work organization that help mitigate excessive work pressures. It was this concern that prompted the HSE—the government agency responsible for health and safety at work—to attempt to improve job quality through developing a system of 'management standards'. In the 1990s, it commissioned several research studies to explore these issues, culminating in a consultation process in 1999 about the type of policy that should be implemented.

Three options were considered. The first was enforceable legislation (of the type adopted in Sweden and Denmark in the 1970s). This option has to be initiated by the Health and Safety Commission (HSC) and then translated into law after approval by parliament. The second option considered was the adoption of an Approved Code of Practice (ACoP). Such codes provide practical examples of good practice. They also have a special legal status. If employers are prosecuted for a breach of health and safety law, and it is proved that they have not followed the relevant provisions of the code, a court can find them at fault unless they can show that they have complied with the law in some other way. The third option involved the lightest touch intervention of all in that it does little more than guide employers through their obligations under the HSWA. Following this guidance is not compulsory and employers are free to take other action if they wish. However, if they do follow the guidance issued they will normally be doing enough to comply with the law and therefore avoid prosecution.

During the consultation period, equal proportions of employers and employees favoured a code of practice, but there was no clear consensus. Of those calling for something else, employees preferred stronger action (i.e. regulation), while employers favoured weaker action in the form of guidance (Cousins et al., 2004). It was decided to develop clear, agreed standards of good management practice designed to reduce a number of stress-generating working conditions with the option of developing an approved code of practice at a later date.

Uncertainties about the means of enforcement and measurement had prevented the HSC from proposing an ACoP (Mackay et al., 2004). In response, the HSE commissioned research as a first step in making the stressors at work visible. Six stressors were identified: (1) demands, including workload, work patterns, and the working environment; (2) control, such as how much say the person has in the way they do their work; (3) support, which includes the encouragement, sponsorship, and resources provided by the organization, line management, and colleagues; (4) relationships at work, such as mechanisms to promote positive working practices to avoid conflict and handle unacceptable behaviour; (5) role, including whether people understand their role within the organization and do not experience conflicting duties; and (6) change, which includes how organizational change is managed and communicated to staff.

A thirty-five item questionnaire was developed in the light of this research. Known as the Management Standards Indicator Tool, employers are encouraged to use these questions in pre-existing staff surveys or carry out a standalone survey. They are then advised to use the results to explore the issues raised with employees in more detail—through, for example, focus groups—and subsequently to make changes to work organization in order to minimize the causes of stress at source. In order to help benchmark organizations, the HSE commissioned an annual survey of its own for six years from 2004, although the series was stopped in 2010 (HSE, 2012).

In keeping with the UK's non-interventionist stance on labour market issues, following these Management Standards is voluntary. As a result, it has not been easy to determine how effective they have been in prompting change (Kompier, 2004; Mustard, 2004). The evidence on trends in work quality from the SES, however, would suggest that their impact has been very limited indeed with respect to improvements in work demands, job control, and the management of change. Given the weak leverage provided by the standards, there are grounds for revisiting the need for a tougher regulatory framework with the aim of making substantive, and verifiable, improvements to the quality of work. Were this policy option to be taken up, the HSE would need to be strengthened to ensure employer compliance; this would, of course, require some additional resource.

10.3.5. Providing Better Evidence for Legal Redress

Problems of very low intrinsic job quality are more likely to be addressed if employees have a channel for challenging cases of seriously bad practice. At around the same time as the health and safety authorities were considering how to respond to rising levels of work-related stress, the first case taken against an employer came to court. The case was a social worker who claimed that his employer was in breach of their common law duty of care in relation to the design and management of his workload, which led to two nervous breakdowns during his employment with the council between 1970 and 1987. *Walker* v. *Northumberland County Council* [1995] 1 All ER 737 became a landmark case in that it established that employers had the same duty of care under the HSWA towards employees' mental as well as their physical health.

Since then, there has been an increase in the number of people claiming compensation for work-related stress illnesses, but few have succeeded. Subsequent case law has made it difficult for work-related stress claims to be upheld. Following *Hatton* v. *Sutherland and Others* [2002] 2 All ER 1, a series of propositions have to be met in order to demonstrate employer liability. In short, they place emphasis on the employee reporting the stress to the employer or proving that the employer knew of the employee's condition and that the work-related illness was foreseeable. However, many stressed employees are reluctant to report such problems, for fear of dismissal, demotion, or prejudice, and there is no duty on employers to enquire about employees' health in the first place.

Nevertheless, successful compensation cases do arise when employees can show that these conditions have been met (Hamilton, 2010). In 2008, for example, the telecommunications company, O2, was ordered to pay damages of £110,000 by the Court of Appeal to an accountant who suffered ill-health due to excessive working hours and a demanding workload. The employee had warned her managers that she could not cope and was 'at the end of her tether'. The court heard that the employee had been a conscientious, hard-working, and reliable employee who had mentioned difficulties over a period of time—both informally and formally in appraisals—'yet managers did nothing of substance about it'. Managers had not referred her to occupational health for specialist advice or done anything to alleviate the pressure. The court ordered O2 to pay £110,000 in damages (*Dickins* v. *O2 Plc* [2008] EWCA Civ 1144).

Proving forseeability, however, may become a little easier following recent revisions to the reporting procedures for statutory sick pay. After seven days of self-certification, employees have to provide a medical certificate which indicates the nature of the illness or the condition in order to qualify for statutory sick pay. Until 2010 'sick notes' were issued by a doctor which simply stated whether a person should be off sick or was able to return to work. However, these 'sick notes' were replaced by 'fit notes' in March 2010. The 'fit note' has two options: (1) that the patient is 'not fit for work'; (2) that the patient 'may be fit for work taking account of the following advice'. There are four types of alterations listed which the GP can tick. These are: a phased return to work (i.e. a gradual increase in work duties or hours); altered hours (i.e. changing work times and total hours); amended duties (i.e. changes to work roles, tasks, and duties); and workplace adaptations (i.e. changing aspects of the work environment). These are advisory, non-binding suggestions, but the 'fit note' remains the property of the employee (DWP, 2013; Taylor et al., 2010).

Information taken from 'fit notes' may therefore be subsequently used as evidence of employers' knowledge of work-related ill-health issues and suggested ways of mitigating them in cases where employees are seeking legal redress from the employer. However, much depends, of course, on how the new 'fit notes' are completed by GPs. Since their introduction GPs have been cautious about providing detailed information or advice on the 'fit note', either because of lack of appointment time with their patients or because they take the view that it is not their job to provide occupational health advice to employers (Fylan et al., 2012; Lalani et al., 2012). When GPs decide to provide no or little information on the 'fit note', the statement is of little use to employment lawyers. Where they do, however, the courts may regard non-binding advice on a GP 'fit note' as a trigger for employers to take action. In these circumstances, requiring GPs to complete 'fit notes' more thoroughly may strengthen the pressures on employers to provide better-quality work.

However, recent legislative change to legal aid means that all personal injury cases—which include work-related stress—are no longer eligible for financial help to cover the costs of taking legal action. Furthermore, even if the case is successful the claimant has to pay a success fee which can be quite high and will therefore significantly erode any damages received. So, in order to ensure that legal redress and access to justice is available to employees, access to legal aid for work-related stress needs to be reinstated.

10.3.6. Using Public Sector Procurement

A lever that has already proved its effectiveness in securing better working conditions and that could be extended to issues relating to the intrinsic quality of work is the use of public procurement to require acceptable standards as a condition of awarding contracts.

In the past, the public sector has been used to spreading good practice to the private sector through means such as the Fair Wages Resolution which was first enacted in 1891 and then revised in 1909 and 1945. This obliged contractors carrying out work for the public sector to abide by the wage rates of the equivalent public sector worker. It was repealed in 1983. Without this safety net and as a result of other changes, the pay and non-pay quality of work among those who carry out work for, but are not employed by, the public sector has fallen. In the 1980s and 1990s, for example, local authorities were required to procure particular services, such as refuse collection and catering, through a competitive tendering process. In-house providers could, and often did, take part in the competition, but to compete with private sector providers costs had to be cut and terms and conditions of employment reduced. This process—known as Compulsory Competitive Tendering—took place at fixed intervals according to nationally specified guidelines. It was superseded in 1999 by Best Value principles, which dropped the requirement to put certain services out to tender and instead required local authorities to evaluate the delivery of services on the basis of value for money rather than the lowest unit price (Roper et al., 2005). However, despite these changes, contracting out services still has 'an inherent tendency to intensify work and drive down terms and conditions, while engaging workers in tightly prescribed tasks' (Cunningham and James, 2009, 372).

Extending the conditions that contractors have to meet before being considered eligible to hold a public sector contract would provide some protection against such tendencies. To safeguard and improve the quality of work, these could include evidence of carrying out and acting upon the results of employee surveys of the type currently promoted by the HSE, demonstrating employee involvement in decision-making and/or being recognized as a best practice employer by an external agency (see section 10.3.7).

These principles could be extended to public procurement in general; that is, the process whereby public sector organizations acquire goods, services, and works from third parties. This includes much that supports the work of government and ranges from routine items (e.g. stationery, temporary office staff, furniture, or printed forms) to complex spend areas (e.g. construction, private finance initiative projects, aircraft carriers, or support to major change initiatives). The public sector spends over £150 billion a year on the goods and services needed to deliver public services (Office of Government Commerce, 2008).

Including employment-related conditions in the pre-qualification requirements of the procurement process has been successfully applied in a number of large construction projects, such as the construction of the London 2012 Olympic Park and the building of Terminal 5 at Heathrow. In both cases, contractors were required to modify their traditional employment practices in order to improve the quality of work (Deakin and Koukiadaki, 2009; Drucker and White, 2013; Walters et al., 2012). The former required the use of direct labour, adherence to nationally agreed collective agreements and the payment of the London Living Wage. The latter was designed primarily to avoid risk-shifting behaviour and the claim and counterclaim culture typical of construction projects such as the construction of Wembley in 2007, the extension of the Jubilee Line in 1999, and the construction of the Thames Barrier in the 1970s (Bishop et al., 2009). With these experiences in mind, all contractors on Terminal 5 had to agree to a number of principles. These included: the negotiation of local agreements no less favourable than existing national and sectoral agreements; the use of direct labour in preference to other forms of employment; limits on overtime working; the establishment of clear structures for basic wage rates and for productivity-related bonuses and allowances; the 'cascading' of agreed terms and conditions and employment quality standards to second-tier subcontractors and suppliers, coupled with arrangements for the monitoring of their performance; setting and meeting exemplary levels of health and safety protection; and a proactive approach to diversity and equality issues. Such examples suggest that it would also be possible to use public sector procurement procedures to drive up those aspects of the quality of work that underlie work stress by requiring contractors to meet certain labour standards while delivering projects on time and to budget.

More directly, as an employer of around a fifth of the UK workforce, the government could lead the way by providing workers it employs with high-quality work. It has not done this very well in recent years. The evidence presented in this book (see Chapter 8) suggests that workers in the public sector are in jobs which are better than those in the private sector in some respects, but worse in others. Once compositional differences are taken into account the pay gap between the sectors is relatively low. If public sector job quality was to deteriorate further this would undermine the integrity of the traditional model of the public sector as a progressive norm-setter of employment standards.

10.3.7. Celebrating Best Practice and Providing Greater Transparency

Improving legal redress and using the levers available through public procurement conditions involve strategies based upon heightening the constraints on employers. But a rather different approach to improving the quality of work is to celebrate those employers who provide employees with good-quality jobs. There are a range of schemes and awards which aim to raise standards in other areas. For example, to ensure that food hygiene standards are met and improved, the Food Standards Agency requires all establishments serving prepared food to be inspected and given a Food Hygiene Standards Rating by local authority inspectors. An online list of ratings is available for consumers to consult and, in some parts of the UK, stickers have to be prominently displayed so that consumers can make an informed decision about purchasing food from the premises or not. The scheme was introduced in 2010 and is mandatory (Gibbens and Spencer, 2013).

Voluntary schemes also exist. For example, goods marked as 'Fair Trade', such as coffee, tea, and various fruits, are now commonplace. These are products which have been certified as providing farmers with a fair price for their goods as well as ensuring that minimum social, economic, and environmental standards are met elsewhere in the supply chain.

Similar voluntary certification schemes exist for the quality of work provided to UK workers. One such scheme is the list compiled by the *Sunday Times* which began in 2001. It lists in rank order the top 100 companies in Britain according to a number of factors, including employees' commitment to the organization, the quality of the training they receive, their level of job security, and their prospects of promotion. The list is based on the results of an employee survey. This is carried out by a private company which asks a random sample of an employer's workforce to complete a fifty-four question survey either online or by post. Sampling fractions are applied according to the number employed. So, while all those who work for an employer with up to 250 staff are surveyed, only 10 per cent of those working for an employer with over 5,000 employees are asked for their views. In order to compete to become a top-100 employer, minimum response rates have to be met. These, too, vary according to employer size from 40 per cent for small employers to 30 per cent for those employing over 5,000 (Bradon, 2008).

Employers pay to take part in the process for which they are entered into the *Sunday Times* competition, receive feedback on their performance with reference to the overall averages, and can apply for grading according to a 'Michelin-style' star rating system. In 2013, 896 employers applied for 'Star Status' and 240,000 employees were surveyed in that year alone. The starring system is based on meeting certain criteria rather than out-competing other employers, although the criteria used are unclear and the precise wording of the survey questions are not publicly available. The *Great Place to Work* list operates on similar principles, is well established and is publicized through association with the *Guardian* and the *Daily Telegraph*. However, rank order on this list is not wholly based on employee surveys, the protocols used to collect data are not publicized and the wording of the fifty-eight statements that comprise its survey are not publicly available (Great Place to Work Institute, 2013, 2014).

Both lists celebrate best practice and have some similarities with Investors in People (IIP), a government-backed voluntary award scheme designed to celebrate excellence in people management. One way to improve the quality of work would be to develop a similar government-backed award for the quality of work by expanding the remit of IIP to incorporate the issues covered and methods used by such lists and/or the HSE's Management Standards. This could then be used as evidence of adherence to quality of work standards which could be made a condition of holding contracts procured by public sector organizations (see section 10.3.6).

Best practice studies could also be used to demonstrate the value of organizing work in such a way as to make the most of the creative potential of employees. Previous research has shown the economic benefits to management, for example, of involving workers in operational decisions about how they carry out their jobs as well as strategic decisions about the direction of the business. These high-involvement work organizations often do better than organizations which do not involve their employees in these ways. This holds according to a number of business performance measures, including profitability, productivity, sales per employee, and inventory levels (e.g. Applebaum et al., 2000; Batt, 1999; MacDuffie, 1995; UKCES, 2010). These forms of work organization also hold out benefits for employees in terms of higher levels of job-related well-being (see Chapter 9).

The Partnership Fund created in 1999 by the then Department of Trade and Industry was intended to demonstrate the economic value of employee involvement with high-profile examples of best practice. It provided support for small-scale projects set up to change working practices through employees and management collaborating to improve the quality of work while also delivering business benefits. In the first three years of its operation eighty-six projects were supported with funding of up to £50,000 each. The fund supported a range of workplace changes, including the introduction of team-working, the development of continuous process improvement, the roll-out of flexible working, and an enhancement of employee training. The changes made and benefits gained were disseminated to other employers of examples of good (and rewarding) practice. However, despite the fund receiving a positive evaluation, its funding was cut in 2004 (Terry and Smith, 2003) and even at its height it was a relatively small programme compared to similar initiatives in Finland (see section 10.3.1).

More generally, a duty could be placed on employers to provide a transparent account in company reports of the quality of employees' working conditions using agreed instruments (such as those identified above). This should encourage employers to give serious consideration to improvements in work quality because of its potential implications for their capacity to recruit the best employees. Currently, narrative disclosures of this sort are rare in the UK since—unlike financial reporting—they are voluntary for most companies. These disclosures relate to non-financial matters (such as environmental, social, and community-related information) of relevance to understanding the performance of the business. However, such narrative disclosures are mandatory for those listed on the stock exchange, although 'many organisations disclose the bare minimum or simply state that it is not considered sufficiently important' (ACCA, 2009, quoted in Scraggs et al., 2013). Under company law, this could be widened further by requiring all businesses to disclose information on the quality of the working environment using, for example, the HSE's thirty-five item questionnaire or revamped versions of the 'best companies to work for' lists (see section 10.3.4). This would require amendments to the Companies Act 2006 to ensure that reported results are based on independently collected data collected by reputable organizations using the same instrument, and hence providing both verifiable and comparable accounts of job quality.

10.4. CONCLUSION

While the pay of many workers in Britain is regulated through collective bargaining, the recommendations of Pay Review Bodies, and the National Minimum Wage, intervention in the non-pay features of work is more circumscribed. There are controls to prevent unsafe working arrangements, limit hours of work, and, in certain circumstances, provide the means through which employees can make their views heard. However, these are limited forms of regulation, predominantly associated with the UK's membership of the European Union (see section 10.3.2). The intrinsic features of work normally have relatively low visibility and are the product of private decisions made by employers about how work is organized.

Yet for some workers, coping with poor intrinsic job quality is an everyday experience with individual responses to issues such as high work intensity and lack of input into work design. Trade unions may be able to push back some of these pressures, but their power to do so has fallen as membership levels have declined and bargaining coverage has shrunk. Operational managers enjoy some discretionary space in how work is organized at the workplace level. Senior managers can have more of an impact, though their actions are often constrained, not only by the markets in which they are trading, but also by the difficulties of altering an organizational culture. The problem is that many managers lack the resources to bring about desired change. The issues facing them are rarely simple and, even if the general principles of high-involvement management can be set out, the appropriate strategy varies in complex ways according to each organization's situation.

In this chapter we have proposed that the state has considerable scope and power to intervene to raise the intrinsic quality of work for its citizens. In opposition to the neo-liberal argument, there are four principles on which government intervention can be justified. First, there is the economic case that poor-quality work can lead to costs for society as a result of the need to treat illness resulting from work-related stress such as work-related anxiety and depression, workplace accidents, and cardiovascular disease. Second, employers may make decisions regarding the organization of work without a full understanding of their implications for employee well-being. Informed government agencies can act to plug this information gap, thereby enhancing the efficiency of market-based decisions. Third, the government has a duty of care to ensure that, as far as is reasonably practical, the health and safety of employees is protected through workplace inspections, enforcement notices, fines, and even the imprisonment of offenders. Government intervention can be justified to prevent the quality of work causing unreasonable harm to workers. Fourth, government intervention can be justified on grounds of equity since poor-quality work tends to affect the most vulnerable disproportionately, given the asymmetries of power in the labour market.

We have outlined seven types of policy action that might lead to significant improvements in work quality, drawing on practice and experience to date. We have identified five of these in particular as the potential foundation of a viable strategy for driving improvements in the quality of work in the UK, as well as reducing inequality at work:

1. There is a need to strengthen the ICE regulations to give employees—whether union members or not—a greater say in how their work is organized.

2. The HSE's Management Standards procedures should be reinforced, so that employers can be found at fault if the standards have not been followed and a worker suffers psychological or physical ill-health as a result.

3. The implementation of 'fit note' procedures could be enhanced by providing more adequate training to GPs. This would increase pressure on employers to raise the quality of work for their staff, by establishing that they had been alerted to the existence of conditions detrimental to employee health and facilitating legal redress if no corrective actions were taken.

4. Public procurement could be used to drive up the quality of work by including employment-related conditions in the tendering process. This has already been done on several high-profile construction projects.

5. The transparency of work quality in companies could be improved partly through an expanded IIP system and partly by requiring companies to formally report on the quality of employees' working conditions using an agreed instrument as part of reforms to company reporting procedures.

In making these proposals, we remain aware that there are limits to the extent to which the quality of jobs can be raised and equality in job quality achieved. It must be accepted that for the foreseeable future every society will have some relatively low-skilled jobs which are difficult to restructure in ways that will provide adequate scope for self-direction and personal development. Moreover, in the context of a capitalist society, improvements in work conditions must necessarily be introduced in a way that is compatible with the objective of economic efficiency and the improvement (or at least maintenance) of profitability. Projects will fail if they build on a hope for harmonious shared values, rather than a realistic appraisal of power relationships and conflicts of interest in society. Nevertheless, consistent with the idea that there are varieties of capitalism, we reject the position that the constraints of global capitalism close down all options for alternative paths. Similarly, we do not subscribe to the view that no change is conceivable without a radical alteration of the prevailing system of economic ownership.

We believe there is a strong economic and social case for government intervention within the constraints of modern capitalism to ameliorate the worst aspects of low-quality jobs. While preceding chapters have documented the contours of an unequal Britain at work, the measures we have highlighted could be expected to contribute significantly to greater equality. Given the very substantial costs to society of poor intrinsic job quality, which recent research has uncovered, it is essential that these issues gain a more central place on the public agenda and become the subject of sustained dialogue between the social partners.

Our final proposal, therefore, is that progress be instituted in a new centre for the intrinsic quality of work, whose vision would be to lead and encourage the needed changes in British businesses. Its remit would be to engage with employers (including the government itself as employer) to promote and assist in better job design, to build on social dialogue between the social partners on matters relating to intrinsic job quality, to monitor the level and pattern of change, and to promote and evaluate job quality policies.[3] One way of operationalizing such a centre might be within the UK Commission for

---

[3] This proposal has similarities with, but is more narrowly focused than, the idea for a 'Forum for the Workplace of the Future' proposed by Totterdill (2013).

Employment and Skills (UKCES) (which already has responsibility for promoting training through IIP). The centre could complement the Low Pay Commission's responsibility for recommending and setting minimum rates of pay. However, whatever its precise institutional form, the presence of such a centre would signal the policy importance of tackling the problems of intrinsic job quality which have, for too long, been a neglected feature of UK labour market policy.

The Skills and Employment Survey Series

A1.1. Introduction

In this technical appendix we briefly describe how each of the surveys which make up the Skills and Employment Survey (SES) series were designed and executed. The series comprises six cross-sectional surveys of working life in Britain. These have been carried out over a period of more than a quarter of a century and have enough in common to constitute a series which allows trends in job quality to be examined and analysed. The aim of this appendix is to outline the common features of the surveys as well as to highlight some of the subtle differences to be borne in mind when reading research based on the series—such as the chapters in this book—and/or analysing the data series first hand. More detail on each of the individual surveys can be found in source books and other material published elsewhere (Ashton et al., 1999; Felstead et al., 2002, 2007, 2014; Gallie et al., 1993, 1996, 1998; Penn et al., 1994).

A1.2. Overview of the Series

Although the series consists of six separate surveys, it was not originally conceived of as a series but rather, it developed into one. Hence, the surveys in 1986 and 1992 were branded rather differently. Since then, however, the importance of comparability between surveys has grown and with it name changes have become relatively rare and quite modest—the Skills Survey was the label used in 1997, 2001, and 2006, and only in 2012 was it slightly modified to the Skills and Employment Survey in recognition of the broader nature of its content (see Table A1.1).

A key commonality of all six constituent surveys is that they are nationally representative sample surveys of individuals in employment aged 20–60 years old (although the 2006 and 2012 surveys additionally sampled those aged 61–65 and the 2006 survey included Northern Ireland and the Highlands and Islands). As a result, each comprises a large number of respondents (with adjustments required to ensure comparability, see section A1.5): 4,047 in the Social Change and Economic Life Initiative (SCELI) 1986 survey; 3,855 in the Employment in Britain (EIB) 1992 survey; 2,467 in the Skills Survey 1997 (SS97); 4,470 in the Skills Survey 2001 (SS01); 7,787 individuals in the Skills Survey 2006 (SS06); and 3,200 workers in the Skills and Employment Survey 2012 (SES 2012). In addition, a number of questions in the Working in Britain survey which was carried out in 2000 were also asked of respondents to the 1992 and/or 2012 surveys (although the degree of overlap is minimal, hence that survey is not considered part of the SES series) (McGovern et al., 2007).

Funding for the surveys has come from a mixture of sources, with no single funder involved in even part funding all six. Nevertheless, the Economic and Social Research Council (ESRC) has been involved in funding four surveys—wholly funding the SCELI survey in 1986 and the Skills Survey in 1997, and partly funding the surveys in 2006

Table A1.1. Skills and Employment Survey Series: Constituent Surveys, Fieldwork Details, and Sample Sizes

Date	Title	Fieldwork period	Response rate[†]	Sample size of respondents in paid work, aged 20–60, and living in Britain
1986	Social Change and Economic Life Initiative	June–November 1986	76.3[‡]	4,047
1992	Employment in Britain	April–August 1992	71.5	3,855
1997	Skills Survey	January–May 1997	67.1	2,467
2001	Skills Survey	February–June 2001	68.9	4,470
2006	Skills Survey	March 2006–March 2007	61.8	6,369 (aged 20–65, UK: 7,787)
2012	Skills and Employment Survey	January–November 2012	48.7	2,949 (aged 20–65: 3,200)

Notes:

† We report gross responses in this table as given in the source documentation for each survey. The gross response rate is the achieved number of interviews as a proportion of successfully screened households which contain an adult aged twenty to sixty (sixty-five in the case of 2006 and 2012) who was in paid work in the week prior to interview (across the UK in the case of 2012 and across Britain in all other surveys).

‡ Here we report the gross response rate for interviews completed among adults aged twenty–sixty regardless of their economic status.

and 2012. Various government departments and agencies have helped to fund five of the six surveys and in 2001 a single government department—the then Department for Education and Skills (DfES)—was the sole funder. In three out of six occasions (1992, 2006, and 2012) funds have come from a variety of sources. More recently, the ESRC has provided around half of the funds with the remainder coming from a variety of government departments. The 2012 survey, for example, was funded by the ESRC and the UK Commission for Employment and Skills (UKCES) under a Strategic Partnership.[1] In addition, the Wales Institute of Social and Economic Research, Data and Methods (WISERD)[2] funded a boost to the sample in Wales. The 1992 survey was also funded by a variety of sources. In this case, the Leverhulme Trust, the Employment Department, and the Employment Service were the largest contributors with additional funds coming from an industrial consortium of twenty-seven funders, including Tesco, Boots, Thomas Cook, and W. H. Smith (Gallie and White, 1993, ii).

The Skills Survey 2006 also had a complex funding structure with financial support for the survey coming from the ESRC along with funds from a variety of government departments and agencies, many of which no longer exist in the same form. These funders included the Department for Education and Skills, the Department for Trade and Industry, the Learning and Skills Council, and the Sector Skills Development Agency. This was supplemented by funding for area boosts secured from Futureskills Wales, the East Midlands Development Agency, Scottish Enterprise, and Highlands

---

[1] ESRC project number: RES-241-25-0001 (<http://www.cardiff.ac.uk/socsi/ses2012>).

[2] WISERD is a research centre initially funded by the ESRC and the Higher Education Funding Council for Wales (<http://www.wiserd.ac.uk>). A separate Welsh report is available (Felstead et al., 2013a).

and Islands Enterprise. This permitted boosts to the sample sizes in Wales, the East Midlands, and Scotland, where sample sizes were doubled, almost tripled, and more than tripled, respectively. Furthermore, the survey was extended to cover the Highlands and Islands for the first time. Frequently this area of Britain is largely excluded from the coverage of many surveys since for market research purposes the border of Britain lies south of the Caledonian Canal, hence excluding *most* of the Highlands and Islands from coverage. In 2006, then, 2,000 respondents out of the 7,787 respondents were living in Scotland, the boost funding adding significantly to the numbers of interviews and providing robust results for Scotland as a whole and areas within it (including the Highlands and Islands). Furthermore, many surveys focus on Britain and hence do not cover Northern Ireland. A boost to the 2006 Skills Survey extended the reach of the survey to this part of the UK for the first time (separate reports for each boost area are available, see Felstead and Green, 2008a, 2008b, 2008c, and 2008d). Taken together, these boosts added 2,987 respondents to the main sample of 4,800.

A1.3. Sample Design

While the data contained in the SES series are from those in paid employment, two of the six surveys were designed to collect data on a wider group of respondents, sometimes consisting of more than one survey as well as follow-up studies. SCELI, for example, collected data on the widest of all since it collected data on individuals aged 20–60 years old regardless of their economic status. This survey then provided the sampling frame for subsequent follow-ups directed at respondents' partners and their employers. As a result, many themes were covered in the first survey that were then picked up in follow-up studies. Data were therefore collected on a range of issues, including the work histories of respondents, their experiences of and attitudes to work, their views on trade unions, their motivation to work, and other aspects of life, what sociopolitical values they held, and the financial position of the household in which they lived. The SCELI data in the SES series, then, are a subset of the material collected by SCELI and provided by 4,047 employed respondents.

The EIB 1992 survey is focused more tightly on issues relating to the quality of work and employment. It consists of two samples: one containing data on those employed and one comprising data on the unemployed. Again, for comparability in the SES series we use only the first type of data provided by 3,855 employed respondents.

The four surveys carried out in 1997, 2001, 2006, and 2012 were largely repeat cross-sectional surveys, thereby allowing comparisons to be made over time. All followed the tradition of measuring job quality through the eyes of workers pioneered by SCELI and EIB. In so doing, they also repeated some of the survey questions used in 1986 and 1992. However, these latest surveys have focused on collecting data on skills used at work and have developed new ways of collecting such data.

All the surveys have used sampling frames considered to be the best available and most up to date at the time. In all cases, except the 1986 survey when the electoral register was used, this meant that addresses have been drawn from the Postal Address File (PAF). This is a computerized database of all addresses held by the Post Office and used to aid delivery of the mail to over 29 million addresses.

In five out of six of the surveys postal sectors (that is, small geographical areas) were selected according to the principles of stratified random probability. This meant that postcode sectors or combinations of postcode sectors acted as the primary sampling units (PSUs) for each survey. Each such area contains around 3,000 addresses and is denoted by the area, district, and sector components of postcodes (such as CF10 3). The convention amongst most PAF-based probability sample designs is for sample points to be stratified prior to selection by one or more stratifiers that correlate or are expected to correlate with key survey variables, since stratification generally improves the precision of survey representativeness. In this case, stratifiers included sub-region and its occupational make-up and unemployment profile.

However, whereas five of the six surveys selected sampling points from across Britain, the SCELI 1986 survey sampled areas comprising six contrasting travel-to-work areas (TTWAs)—Aberdeen, Coventry, Kirkcaldy, Northampton, Rochdale, and Swindon. Technically speaking, then, SCELI is not a random national sample of British workers. That said, subsequent analyses—such as those contained in this book—treat it as a nationally representative survey of working life in Britain in 1986 when weights are applied (see section A1.5). It was shown, for example, to have 'a social class distribution which closely matched the national profile' (Gallie et al., 1998, 317) and for that reason it provides the earliest national baseline used in some of the chapters contained in this book.

In all six surveys one person per household was interviewed provided they met the selection criteria. In all surveys, with the exception of SCELI which had a remit to interview respondents whatever their labour market status, all those aged twenty–sixty inclusive (in 2006 and 2012 the upper limit was raised to sixty-five) and in employment (that is, in paid working at least one hour in the previous week) were eligible. If only one person was eligible at the address, an interview was sought with that person. When the interviewer was faced with a choice about selection, a Kish Grid was used to determine selection. This is a table of randomly generated numbers individually prepared for each address. It was also used to select the dwelling unit where the postal delivery point contains more than one, such as houses partitioned into separate flats, and to select a single household in multi-household dwellings. The effect of using such a procedure is to give each eligible person an equal chance of selection in line with probability principles. This procedure was used in all six surveys in the series.

A1.4. Data Collection and Fieldwork Outcomes

All households sampled for each of the surveys were sent a letter about the survey in advance of the interviewer calling. The letter provided information about the survey, who was managing the survey, the survey sponsors, and the fieldwork agency. Since 1997 a dedicated freephone number and email address were also included in the letter in order to facilitate communication with the fieldwork agency. The letters bore the logos of the sponsors as well as the fieldwork agency.

Given that the PAF was used as the sample frame for surveys since 1992 (and the electoral register for six TTWAs in 1986), the initial letter was anonymously addressed to 'The Householder'. However, a personally addressed letter to introduce the survey to the selected respondent was left by the interviewer when the selected person was not present and where the interviewer felt that it would be of some benefit. The aim of the letter was to reinforce the importance of taking part in the survey to the person selected in the absence of the interviewer and to avoid the purpose of the interview not being explained adequately by other household members.

Around two-thirds of the way through the fieldwork for the 2006 survey and for all the fieldwork carried out in 2012, respondents were given a financial incentive to take part as recognition of the time involved. All those completing a full interview were offered high street vouchers (in 2006 this was £5 and in 2012 it was raised to £10). This conditional incentive was mentioned in advance communications in approaching households and eligible respondents for interview.

All the surveys in the series data were collected through face-to-face interviews with respondents, sometimes containing self-completion components. The 1986 and 1992 surveys in the series were carried out using pen and paper questionnaires, but since then the data have been collected using Computer Assisted Personal Interviewing (CAPI) techniques. In these circumstances, interviewers are equipped with a laptop containing the electronic questionnaire. They read the questions from a screen and enter the responses given using a keyboard. When used all aspects of the CAPI script, including questionnaire content, question wording, routing, internal consistency checks, and text substitution, were systematically checked on several occasions to minimize errors.

The four surveys from 1997 onwards also partly used Computer Assisted Self-Interviewing (CASI). This is the electronic equivalent of self-completion questionnaires and occurs when respondents are asked in the course of the interview to complete sections of the survey themselves. Two sections of the 1997, 2001, 2006, and 2012 surveys were completed in this way. Interviews lasted, on average, just less than an hour. In 2012, for example, they lasted an average of fifty-nine minutes and around the same in 2006.

In line with other social surveys, the SES series has suffered from declining response rates over time, although measures have been put in place to try to arrest this decline. These measures included: ensuring the survey design reduced respondent burden through clear communication and incentives (i.e. information leaflets, advance letters, and high street vouchers for each interview completed); ensuring interviewers and the fieldwork process were managed properly; and reissuing addresses which failed to deliver a productive outcome when first issued to another, more experienced interviewer (this was used in the 2006 and 2012 surveys). Despite these efforts, response rates have fallen fairly consistently over time, from 76.3 per cent in 1986 to 48.7 per cent in 2012 (cf. Table A1.1). While disappointing, this is in line with other surveys, such as the Labour Force Survey (LFS), which have seen response rates decline by twenty-one percentage points between 1993 and 2008 (Barnes et al., 2008).

A key design feature of the questionnaires for each of the surveys was the inclusion, where possible, of questions that had been tried and tested on other surveys. As a result, the 1992 survey included many of the questions asked of respondents to the 1986 survey. Some of these questions were also included in the four surveys which followed. However, more interview time was spent in these surveys on collecting data on the skills used at work.

Whenever questions were used from previous surveys strict principles applied so that the same question wording, points of emphasis, and response sets were used to maximize comparability. Nevertheless, each survey also developed new lines of enquiry or revisited themes pursued in earlier surveys. When completely new questions were introduced, cognitive testing was used to provide insights into the thought processes a respondent goes through in understanding and answering a survey question. The aim is not to test questionnaire length or flow, but rather, to see whether the respondent understands the question in the intended manner. As such it is a valuable tool in fine-tuning the wording of new questions and response items. It was used in 2001, 2006, and 2012 on around a dozen survey questions each time.

A1.5. Weighting

For each survey, weights were computed to take into account the differential probabilities of sample selection according to the number of dwelling units at each issued address, the number of eligible interview respondents, the over-sampling of the boost areas (if appropriate), and the slight under-representation of certain groups. To do so, we compared survey distributions across a number of socioeconomic indicators with the distributions produced by the LFS for the relevant year (the most up-to-date Office for National Statistics' (ONS) weights were used). The weights issued with the dataset, therefore, correct for non-response rates by sex, age, and occupational group for all of the surveys in the series. For these reasons, the data reported using these newer weights will differ slightly from publications which are based on the older weights supplied with the original datasets in the UK Data Archive.

We took the decision to compute new weights for all six surveys for three reasons. First, in 2011 the ONS reweighted the LFS to reflect more up-to-date population estimates. We thought it prudent to follow ONS's lead and to recalculate our survey weights accordingly. Second, we wanted to be certain that exactly the same weighting procedures were used for all the surveys in the series and for a transparent account to be provided to other users. Third, since 2006 the LFS has been released on a calendar basis and only updated historic versions of the calendar dataset are now available. Weights for surveys in the series before 2006, however, were calculated using now-redundant (and non-updated) seasonal versions of the LFS. This section will, therefore, outline the design effects and non-response rate protocols used to derive the new weights used in the chapters in this book and contained in the publicly available series dataset (see section A1.6).

A1.5.1. Design Weights

The data files for all of the surveys are supplied with design weights. These are provided by the market research companies responsible for the fieldwork. They ensure that the data are representative of the target population by correcting for differential probabilities of selection. Unequal selection probabilities can occur at three points in the design process, the selection of:

- one dwelling per address;
- one household per selected dwelling;
- one eligible adult per (selected) household.

In many datasets these are referred to as 'Kish weights'. Where there are no boosts to the sample sizes (this was the case for all but the 2006 and 2012 surveys), we use the Kish weights to produce the sample distributions. However, in the case of the 2006 and 2012 surveys, we additionally weight the samples inversely proportional to the LFS estimates for the boost areas. So, Wales was over-sampled in both surveys given additional funding to boost the Welsh sample size. To take this into account, Welsh respondents are given a weight of less than one (that is, the LFS estimate divided by the

Kish-weighted sample estimate). Similar adjustments are made for other over-sampled areas. For completeness, this applies to the following:

- East Midlands over-sampling in 2006;
- Scotland over-sampling in 2006;
- Highlands and Islands sampling in 2006 (only applies to UK estimates, weights not supplied in the dataset);
- Northern Ireland sampling in 2006 (only applies to UK estimates, weights not supplied in the dataset);
- Wales over-sampling in 2006 and 2012.

A1.5.2. Non-Response Rates

Although the samples were designed to ensure that they were representative of workers in Britain at the time of the survey, we first checked whether the sample was broadly representative. We classified the data against some standard socioeconomic variables and compared each of the six surveys against the spring LFS for that year. Since the LFS has a substantially larger sample size, and since it gleans information from every member of households, it can be argued that the LFS sample is likely to be closely representative of the employed workforce.

We compare the representation of the Kish-weighted survey results (adjusted for boosts, where necessary) against the results given by the LFS for the second quarter of that year.[3] We compare the results by sex, age, and occupation (see Felstead et al., 2014b for details). These results are then used to produce sex, age, and occupational weights which when applied adjust for the under-representation of men, the young, and certain occupational groups. To make occupational comparisons, we use the classification system in place at the time:

- for the 1986 survey we use the Registrar General's Social Class system;
- for 1992 and 1997 we use the 1990 Standard Occupational Classification (SOC90) system;
- for 2000, 2001, and 2006 we use SOC2000;
- for 2012 we use SOC2010.

A1.5.3 Weights in Dataset

The following weights take all of the above considerations into account and have been used in analysis contained in each of the chapters in this book.[4] Other researchers should do likewise when analysing data contained in the SES series:

- 'weight0612' = applies to the 2006 and 2012 surveys, Britain, 20–65-year-olds;
- 'weightall' = applies to all surveys in series, Britain, 20–60-year-olds.

---

[3] Previous weights derived for the 2001, 2000, 1997, and 1992 surveys used the Spring LFS (March–May). The LFS data were switched to calendar quarters in 2006. The LFS became quarterly in 1992, so for 1986 the annual release of the LFS continues to be used.

[4] In May 2014, a number of coding errors were identified in the four-digit SOC variable for the 2012 survey. Their correction resulted in changes to the one-digit coding of SOC on which the weights were based. Hence, revised datasets were deposited in the Data Archive with updated weights and corrected SOC codes.

A1.6. Accessing the Data

The SES data series, as well as the original six cross-sectional surveys, can be accessed via the UK Data Archive (<http://www.data-archive.ac.uk>). In addition, documentation such as the questionnaires used can be freely accessed without the need to download data. The Study Numbers are as follows:

- SN 7467—Skills and Employment Survey Series, 1986, 1992, 1997, 2001, 2006, and 2012;
- SN 7466—Skills and Employment Survey 2012;
- SN 6004—Skills Survey 2006;
- SN 4972—Skills Survey 2001;
- SN 3993—Skills Survey 1997;
- SN 5368—Employment in Britain 1992;
- SN 2788—Social Change and Economic Life Initiative 1986.

References

Acemoglu, O. and D. Autor (2011). 'Skills, Tasks and Technologies: Implications for Employment and Earnings'. In O. Ashenfelter and D. E. Card (eds), *Handbook of Labor Economics* (Volume 4), pp. 1043–172. Amsterdam: Elsevier.

Ajayi-Obe, O. and S. Parker (2005). 'The Changing Nature of Work among the Self-Employed in the 1990s: Evidence from Britain'. *Journal of Labor Research*, 26(3): 501–17.

Alasoini, T. (2013). 'Two Decades of Programme-Based Workplace Development in Finland: Past Experiences and Future Challenges'. Paper Presented to the International Helix Conference, 12–14 June, Linköping, Sweden.

Algan, Y., P. Cahuc, and A. Zylberberg (2002). 'Public Employment: Does It Increase Unemployment?' *Economic Policy*, 17: 7–66.

Anxo, D., C. Fagan, M. Smith, M. T. Letablier, and C. Perraudin (2007). *Part-Time Work in European Companies: Establishment Survey on Working Time 2004–2005*. Dublin: European Foundation for the Improvement of Living and Working Conditions.

Applebaum, E. (1992). 'Structural Change and the Growth of Part-Time and Temporary Employment'. In V. L. DuRivage (ed.), *New Policies for the Part-time and Contingent Workforce*, pp. 1–14. New York/London: ME Sharpe Inc.

Applebaum, E., T. Bailey, P. Berg, and A. Kalleberg (2000). *Manufacturing Advantage: Why High Performance Work Systems Pay Off*. Ithaca, NY: Cornell University Press.

Ashton, D., B. Davies, A. Felstead, and F. Green (1999). *Work Skills in Britain*. Oxford: ESRC Centre on Skills, Knowledge and Organisational Performance.

Atkinson, J. (1987). 'Flexibility or Fragmentation? The UK Labour Market in the Eighties'. *Labour and Society*, 12(1): 87–105.

Autor, D. H., F. Levy, and R. J. Murnane (2003). 'The Skill Content of Recent Technological Change: An Empirical Exploration'. *Quarterly Journal of Economics*, 118(4): 1279–333.

Bach, S., R. K. Givan, and J. Forth (2009). 'The Public Sector in Transition'. In W. Brown, A. Bryson, J. Forth, and K. Whitfield (eds), *The Evolution of the Modern Workplace*. Cambridge: Cambridge University Press.

Barnes, W., G. Bright, and C. Hewat (2008). 'Making Sense of Labour Force Survey Response Rates'. *Economic and Labour Market Review*, 2 (12): 32–42.

Barron, R. and G. Norris (1976). 'Sexual Divisions and the Dual Labour Market'. In D. Barker and S. Allen (eds), *Dependence and Exploitation in Work and Marriage*. London: Longman.

Batt, R. (1999). 'Work Organization, Technology, and Performance in Customer Service and Sales'. *Industrial and Labor Relations Review*, 52(4, July): 539–64.

Beaumont, P. (1981). *Government as Employer—Setting an Example*. London: Royal Institute of Public Administration.

Becker, G. (1985). 'A Theory of the Allocation of Time'. *Economic Journal*, 75: 493–517 (first published in 1965).

Beechey, V. (1978). 'Women and Production: A Critical Analysis of Some Sociological Theories of Women's Work'. In A. Kuhn and A. M. Wolpe (eds), *Feminism and Materialism: Women and Modes of Production*, pp. 155–97. London: Routledge and Kegan Paul.

Beechey, V. and T. Perkins (1987). *A Matter of Hours: Women, Part-Time Work and the Labour Market*. Cambridge: Polity Press.

Beer, M., B. Spector, P. Lawrence, D. Mills, and R. Walton (1984). *Managing Human Assets*. New York: Free Press.

Beham, B. and S. Drobnič (2011). 'Job Demands and Work–Home Interference: Empirical Evidence from Service Sector Employees in Eight European Countries'. In S. Drobnič and A. M. Guillén (eds), *Work–Life Balance in Europe: The Role of Job Quality*, pp. 95–119. Houndmills: Palgrave Macmillan.

Bell, D. and D. Blanchflower (2011). 'Young People and the Great Recession'. *Oxford Review of Economic Policy*, 27(2): 241–67.

Bell, D. and D. Blanchflower (2013). 'Underemployment in the UK Revisited'. *National Institute Economic Review*, 224: F8–22.

Bellante, D. and J. Long (1981). 'The Political Economy of the Rent-Seeking Society: The Case of Public Employees and Their Unions'. *Journal of Labor Research*, 2: 1–14.

Bennett, J. T. and B. E. Kaufman (eds) (2007). *What Do Unions Do? A Twenty-Year Perspective*. New Brunswick, NJ and London: Transaction Publishers.

Benz, M. and B. Frey (2008). 'Being Independent Is a Great Thing: Subjective Evaluations of Self-Employment and Hierarchy'. *Economica*, 75(298): 362–83.

Binder, M. and A. Coad (2013). 'Life Satisfaction and Self-Employment: A Matching Approach'. *Small Business Economics*, 40(4): 1009–33.

BIS (2006). *The Information and Consultation of Employees Regulations 2004: DTI Guidance (January 2006)*. London: Department for Business, Innovation and Skills (BIS).

BIS (2011). *Agency Worker Regulations: Guidance*. London: BIS.

BIS (2013). *Trade Union Membership 2012: Statistical Bulletin*. London: BIS.

Bishop, D., A. Felstead, A. Fuller, N. Jewson, L. Unwin and K. Kakavelakis (2009). 'Constructing Learning: Adversarial and Collaborative Working in the British Construction Industry'. *Journal of Education and Work*, 22(4): 243–60.

Black, C. (2008). *Working for a Healthier Tomorrow: Dame Carol Black's Review of the Health of the Working Age Population*. London: TSO.

Blackaby, D., P. Murphy, and N. O'Leary (1999). 'The Payment of Public Sector Workers in the UK: Reconciliation with North-American Findings'. *Economics Letters*, 65(2): 239–43.

Blackaby, D., P. Murphy, N. O'Leary, and A. Staneva (2012). 'An Investigation of the IFS Public–Private Sector Pay Differential: A Robustness Check'. Department of Economics Discussion Paper Series, University of Swansea.

Blanchflower, D. (2004). 'Self-Employment: More May Not Be Better'. *Swedish Economic Policy Review*, 11(2): 15–73.

Blanchflower, D. and A. Bryson (2007). 'What Effect Do Unions Have on Wages Now and Would "What Do Unions Do?" Be Surprised'. In J. T. Bennett and B. E. Kaufman (eds), *What Do Unions Do?: A Twenty-Year Perspective*, pp. 79–113, New Brunswick, NJ and London: Transaction Publishers.

Blanchflower, D. G. and A. Bryson (2009). 'Trade union decline and the economics of the workplace', Chapter 3 in W. Brown, A. Bryson, J. Forth and K. Whitfield (eds.), *The Evolution of the Modern Workplace*, pp. 48–73, Cambridge University Press.

Blanchflower, D. G. and A. Bryson (2010). 'The Wage Impact of Trade Unions in the UK Public and Private Sectors'. *Economica*, 77(305): 92–109.

Blau, F. and L. M. Kahn (1997). 'Swimming Upstream: Trends in the Gender Wage Differential in the 1980s'. *Journal of Labor Economics*, 15(1): 1–42.

Blauner, R. (1964). *Alienation and Freedom: The Factory Worker and His Industry*. Chicago, IL: University of Chicago Press.

Bloom, N., R. Lemos, M. Qi, R. Sadun, and J. Van Reenen (2011). 'Constraints on Developing UK Management Practices'. *BIS Research Paper*, 58. London: Department for Business, Innovation and Skills.

Boeri, T. (2011). 'Institutional Reforms and Dualism in European Labor Markets'. In O. Ashenfelter and D. Card North (eds), *Handbook of Labor Economics*, pp. 1173–236. Amsterdam: Elsevier.

Booth, A. (1995). *The Economics of the Trade Union*. Cambridge: Cambridge University Press.

Booth, A. L., M. Francesconi, and J. Frank (2002). 'Temporary Jobs: Stepping Stones or Dead Ends'. *Economic Journal*, 112: F189–213.

Boxall, P. and K. Macky (2014). 'High-Involvement Work Processes, Work Intensification and Employee Well-Being'. *Work, Employment and Society*, 28: 963–84.

Boxall, P. and J. Purcell (2008). *Strategy and Human Resource Management* (2nd Edition). Basingstoke: Palgrave Macmillan.

Bradon, P. (2008). *Best Companies: Methodology*. Wrexham: Best Companies.

Branch, A. (2005). 'The Evolution of the European Social Dialogue towards Greater Autonomy: Challenges and Potential Benefits'. *International Journal of Comparative Law and Industrial Relations*, 21(2): 321–46.

Braverman, H. (1974). *Labor and Monopoly Capital: The Degradation of Work in the Twentieth Century*. New York: Monthly Review Press.

Brown, A., A. Charlwood, C. Forde, and D. A. Spencer (2007). 'Job Quality and the Economics of New Labour: A Critical Appraisal Using Subjective Survey Data'. *Cambridge Journal of Economics*, 31: 941–71.

Brown, A., A. Charlwood, and D. A. Spencer (2012). 'Not All that It Might Seem: Why Job Satisfaction Is Worth Studying despite It Being a Poor Summary Measure of Job Quality'. *Work Employment and Society*, 26(6): 1007–18.

Brown, C. (1980). 'Equalizing Differences in the Labor Market'. *Quarterly Journal of Economics*, 94: 113–34.

Brown, W., A. Bryson, and J. Forth (2009). 'Competition and the Retreat from Collective Bargaining'. In W. Brown, A. Bryson, J. Forth, and K. Whitfield (eds), *The Evolution of the Modern Workplace*, pp. 22–47. Cambridge: Cambridge University Press.

Brownlie, N. (2012). *Trade Union Membership 2011*. London: BIS.

Bruce, D. and H. Schuetze (2004). 'The Labor Market Consequences of Experience in Self-Employment'. *Labour Economics*, 11(5): 575–98.

Bryson, A. (2004). 'Unions and Employment Growth in British Workplaces during the 1990s: A Panel Analysis'. *Scottish Journal of Political Economy*, 51(4): 477–506.

Bryson, A. (2014). 'Union Wage Effects'. *IZA World of Labor*, 35.

Bryson, A. and J. Forth (2011). 'Trade Unions'. In P. Gregg and J. Wadsworth (eds), *The Labour Market in Winter: The State of Working Britain*, pp. 255–71. Oxford: Oxford University Press.

Bryson, A. and R. B. Freeman (2013). 'Employee Perceptions of Working Conditions and the Desire for Worker Representation in Britain and the US'. *Journal of Labor Research*, 34(1): 1–29.

Bryson, A. and M. White (1997). *Moving in and out of Self-Employment*. PSI Report no. 826. London: Policy Studies Institute.

Bryson, A. and M. White (2013). 'Not So Dissatisfied after All? The Impact of Union Coverage on Job Satisfaction', *NIESR Discussion Paper*, 412.

Bryson, A., H. Dale-Olsen, and E. Barth (2013). 'The Effects of Organizational Change on Worker Wellbeing and the Moderating Role of Trade Unions'. *Industrial and Labor Relations Review*, 66(4): 989–1011.

Burchell, B. and J. Rubery (1992). 'Categorising Self-Employment: Some Evidence from the Social Change and Economic Life Initiative in the UK'. In P. Leighton and A. Felstead (eds), *The New Entrepreneurs: Self-Employment and Small Business in Europe*, pp. 101–22. London: Kogan Page.

Burchell, B., A. Dale, and H. Joshi (1997). 'Part-Time Work among British Women'. In H. P. Blossfeld and C. Hakim (eds), *Between Equalization and Marginalization: Women Working Part-Time in Europe and the United States of America*, pp. 210–46. Oxford: Oxford University Press.

Burgess, S. and C. Propper (1999). 'Poverty in Britain'. In P. Gregg and J. Wadsworth (eds), *The State of Working Britain*. Manchester: Manchester University Press.

Cam, S., J. Purcell, and S. Tailby (2003). 'Contingent Employment in the UK'. In O. Bergström and D. Storrie (eds), *Contingent Employment in Europe and the United States*, pp. 52–78. Cheltenham: Edward Edgar.

Campbell, M. and M. Daly (1992). 'Self-Employment: Into the 1990s'. *Employment Gazette*, 100(6): 269–92.

Card, D., T. Lemieux, and W. C. Riddell (2004). 'Unions and Wage Inequality'. *Journal of Labor Research*, 25: 519–59.

Carmichael, L. and B. MacLeod (2000). 'Worker Cooperation and the Ratchet Effect'. *Journal of Labor Economics*, 18(1): 1–19.

Casey, B. (1991). 'Survey Evidence on Trends in "Non-Standard" Employment'. In A. Pollert (ed.), *Farewell to Flexibility?*, pp. 179–99. Oxford: Blackwell.

CEC (2005). *Working Together for Growth and Jobs: A New Start for the Lisbon Strategy*, COM 24. Brussels: Commission of the European Communities.

CEC (2011). *Report on the Implementation of the European Partners' Framework Agreement on Work-Related Stress*, SEC(2011) 241. Brussels: Commission of the European Communities.

Cegarra-Leiva, D., M. E. Sánchez-Vidal, and J. G. Cegarra-Navarro (2012). 'Understanding the Link between Work–Life Balance Practices and Organisational Outcomes in SMEs: The Mediating Effect of a Supportive Culture'. *Personnel Review*, 41: 359–79.

Chandola, T. (2010). *Stress at Work*. London: British Academy.

Chatterji, M., K. Mumford, and P. Smith (2011). 'The Public–Private Sector Gender Wage Differential: Evidence from Matched Employee-Workplace Data'. *Applied Economics*, 43(26): 3919–4833.

Child, J. (1972). 'Organisational Structure, Environment and Performance: The Role of Strategic Choice'. *Sociology*, 6(1): 1–22.

Chung, H. (2011).'Work–Family Conflict across 28 European Countries: A Multi-Level Approach'. In S. Drobnič and A. M. Guillén (eds), *Work–Life Balance in Europe: The Role of Job Quality*, pp. 42–68. Houndmills: Palgrave Macmillan.

CIPD (2012). *The Rise in Self-Employment*. Work Audit, January. London: Chartered Institute of Personnel and Development. Available online at: <http://www.cipd.co.uk/publicpolicy/policy-reports/rise-self-employment.aspx>.

Coats, D. (2005). *Raising Lazarus: The Future of Organised Labour*. London: Fabian Society.

Coats, D. (2013). *Just Deserts? Poverty and Income Inequality: Can Workplace Democracy Make a Difference?* London: Smith Institute.

Connolly, M. and M. Gregory (2008a). 'Moving Down: Women's Part-Time Work and Occupational Change in Britain 1991–2001'. *Economic Journal*, 118(February): F52–76.

Connolly, M. and M. Gregory (2008b). 'The Part-Time Pay Penalty: Earnings Trajectories of British Women'. *Oxford Economic Papers*, 1–22.

Cooper, C., S. Lewis, J. Smithson, and J. Dyer (2001). *Flexible Futures: Flexible Working and Work–Life Integration. Summary Findings from Stage One of the Research.* London: Institute of Chartered Accountants in England and Wales.

Cousins, R., C. J. Mackay, S. D. Clarke, C. Kelly, P. J. Kelly, and R. H McCaig (2004). '"Management Standards" and Work-Related Stress in the UK: Practical Development'. *Work and Stress*, 18(2): 113–36.

Cowling, M. and P. Mitchell (1997). 'The Evolution of UK Self-Employment: A Study of Government Policy and the Role of the Macroeconomy'. *Manchester School*, LXV(4): 427–42.

Cressey, P. (1992). 'Worker Participation: What Can We Learn from the Swedish Experience?' *European Participation Monitor*, 3: 3–7.

Cribb J. and L. Sibieta (2013). *Hard Choices Ahead for Government Cutting Public Sector Employment and Pay*. December. London: Institute of Fiscal Studies.

Crompton, R. and G. Jones (1984). *White-Collar Proletariat*. London: Macmillan.

Crompton, R. and C. Lyonette (2007). 'Are We All Working Too Hard? Women, Men, and Changing Attitudes to Paid Employment'. In A. Park, J. Curtice, K. Thomson, M. Phillips, and M. Johnson (eds), *British Social Attitudes: The 23rd Report. Perspectives on a Changing Society*, pp. 55–70. London: Sage.

Crompton, R. and Lyonette, C. (2010). 'Family, Class and Gender "Strategies" in Maternal Employment and Childcare. In J. Scott, R. Crompton and C. Lyonette (eds.) *Gender Inequalities in the 21st Century*. Cheltenham: Edward Elgar.

Cunningham, I. and P. James (2009). 'The Outsourcing of Social Care in Britain: What Does It Mean for Voluntary Sector Workers?' *Work, Employment and Society*, 23(2): 363–75.

Damant, A. and J. Jenkins (2011). 'Estimating Differences in Public and Private Sector Pay'. Newport: Office for National Statistics. Available online at: http://www.nomisweb.co.uk/articles/ref/stories/8/public_private_sector_pay_july2011.pdf.

Danzer, A. M. and P. Dolton (2012). 'Total Reward and Pensions in the UK in the Public and Private Sectors'. *Labour Economics*, 19(4): 584–94.

Danziger, S. and P. Gottschalk (1993). 'Introduction'. In S. Danziger and P. Gottschalk (eds), *Uneven Tides: Rising Inequality in America*. New York: Russell Sage Foundation.

D'Arcy, C. and L. Gardiner (2014). *Just the Job—or a Working Compromise? The Changing Nature of Self-Employment in the UK*. London: Resolution Foundation.

Darton, D. and K. Hurrell (2005). *People Working Part-Time below Their Potential*. September. Manchester: EOC.

Davies, S. (2012). *The Public Service Ethos and Union Mobilisation: A Case Study of the Public Service Library*. Unpublished PhD thesis, Cardiff University.

de Menezes, L. and S. J. Wood (2006). 'The Reality of Flexible Work Systems in Britain'. *International Journal of Human Resource Management*, 17(1): 106–38.

Deakin, S. and F. Green (2009). 'One Hundred Years of British Minimum Wage Legislation'. *British Journal of Industrial Relations*, 47(2): 205–13.

Deakin, S. and A. Koukiadaki (2009). 'Governance Processes, Labour-Management Partnership and Employee Voice in the Construction of Heathrow Terminal 5'. *Industrial Law Journal*, 38(4): 365–89.

Deiner, E. (1984). 'Subjective Well-Being'. *Psychological Bulletin*, 95(3): 542–75.

Dellot, B. (2014). *Salavation in a Start-up? The Origins and Nature of the Self-Employment Boom*. London: RSA.

Department for Business, Innovation and Skills (2013). 'Trade Union Membership 2012: Statistical Bulletin'. London: ONS.

Department for Communities and Local Government (2006). *Government Action Plan: Implementing the Women and Work Commission Recommendations*. London: Department for Communities and Local Government.

Dickens, L. and M. Hall (2009). 'Legal Regulation and the Changing Workplace'. In W. Brown, A. Bryson, J. Forth, and K. Whitfield (eds), *The Evolution of the Modern Workplace*, pp. 332–51. Cambridge: Cambridge University Press.

Dickens, R., S. Machin, and A. Manning (1999). 'The Effects of Minimum Wages on Employment: Theory and Evidence from Britain'. *Journal of Labor Economics*, 17(1): 1–22.

Dickerson, A. and F. Green (2009). 'Fears and Realisations of Employment Insecurity'. *Labour Economics*, 19(2): 198–210.

Dieckhoff, M. and D. Gallie (2007). 'The Renewed Lisbon Strategy and Social Exclusion Policy'. *Industrial Relations Journal*, 38(6): 480–502.

DiMaggio, P. J. and W.W. Powell (1983). 'The Iron Cage Revisited: Institutional Isomorphism and Collective Rationality in Organizational Fields'. *American Sociological Review*, 48: 147–60.

DiNardo, J., N. Fortin, and T. Lemieux (1996). 'Labor Market Institutions and the Distribution of Wages, 1973–1993: A Semi-Parametric Approach'. *Econometrica*, 64(5): 1001–45.

Disney, R. and A. Gosling (1998). 'Does It Pay to Work in the Public Sector?' *Fiscal Studies*, 19(4): 347–74.

Doeringer, P. B. and M. J. Piore (1971). *Internal Labour Markets and Manpower Analysis*. Lexington, MA: D. C. Heath.

Dolton, P. and G. Makepeace (2011). 'Public and Private Sector Labour Markets'. In P. Gregg and J. Wadsworth (eds), *The Labour Market in Winter: The State of Britain*, pp. 272–88. Oxford: Oxford University Press.

Doucouliagos, C. and P. Laroche (2003). 'What Do Unions Do to Productivity? A Meta-Analysis'. *Industrial Relations*, 42(4): 650–91.

Drucker, J. and G. White (2013). 'Employment Relations on Major Construction Projects: The London 2012 Olympic Construction Site'. *Industrial Relations Journal*, 44(5–6): 566–83.

Duncan, G. and B. Holmlund (1983). 'Was Adam Smith Right After All? Another Test of the Theory of Compensating Wage Differentials'. *Journal of Labor Economics*, 1(4): 366–79.

Dundon, T., T. Dobbins, N. Cullinane, E. Hickland, and J. Donaghey (2014). 'Employer Occupation of Regulatory Space of the Employee Information and Consultation (I&C) Directive in Liberal Market Economies'. *Work, Employment and Society*, 28(1): 21–39.

Durbin, S. and J. Tomlinson (2010). 'Female Part-Time Managers: Networks and Career Mobility'. *Work, Employment and Society*, 24(4): 621–40.

Dustmann, C., J. Ludsteck, and U. Schonberg (2009). 'Revisiting the German Wage Structure'. *Quarterly Journal of Economics*, 124(2): 843–81.

DWP (2013). *The Fit Note: A Guide for Patients and Employees*. London: Department for Work and Pensions.

Edwards, C. and O. Robinson (2004). 'Evaluating the Business Case for Part-Time Working amongst Qualified Nurses'. *British Journal of Industrial Relations*, 42(1): 167–83.

Edwards, P. and J. Wajcman (2005). *The Politics of Working Life*. Oxford: Oxford University Press.

Edwards, R. C. (1979). *Contested Terrain: The Transformation of the Workforce in the Twentieth Century*. New York: Basic Books.

Egger, P. and W. Sengenberger (eds) (2003). *Decent Work in Denmark: Employment, Social Efficiency and Economic Security*. Geneva: International Labour Office.

Emmerson, C. and W. Jin (2012). 'Public Sector Pay and Pensions'. In C. Emmerson, P. Johnson, and H. Miller (eds), *IFS Green Budget: February 2012*. London: Institute for Fiscal Studies. Available online at: <http://www.ifs.org.uk/publications/6003>.

Ertel, M., U. Stilijanow, S. Lavicoli, E. Natali, A. Jain, and S. Leka (2010). 'European Social Dialogue on Psychosocial Risks at Work: Benefits and Challenges'. *European Journal of Industrial Relations*, 16(2): 169–83.

European Commission (1998). *Equal Opportunities for Women and Men in Europe? Eurobarometer 44.3: Results of an Opinion Survey*. Luxembourg: Office for Official Publications of the European Communities, available online at: <http://ec.europa.eu/public_opinion/archives/ebs/ebs_097_en.pdf>.

European Commission (2010). *European Employment Observatory Review: Self-Employment in Europe 2010*. Luxembourg: Publications Office of the European Union.

European Social Partners (2008). *Implementation of the European Autonomous Framework Agreement on Work-Related Stress*. Brussels: ETUC European Resource Centre.

Fagan, C. (2001). 'Time, Money and the Gender Order: Work Orientations and Worktime Preferences in Britain'. *Gender, Work and Organisation*, 8(3): 239–66.

Fagan, C. and J. Rubery (1996). 'The Salience of the Part-Time Divide in the European Union'. *European Sociological Review*, 12(3): 227–50.

Faggio, G. and H. Overman (2012). 'The Effect of Public Sector Employment on Local Labour Markets'. *SERC Discussion Paper 111*. London: London School of Economics.

Felstead, A. (1991). 'The Social Organization of the Franchise: A Case of "Controlled Self-Employment"'. *Work, Employment and Society*, 5(1): 37–57.

Felstead, A. (1992). 'Franchising, Self-Employment and the "Enterprise Culture": A UK Perspective'. In P. Leighton and A. Felstead (eds), *The New Entrepreneurs: Self-Employment and Small Business in Europe*, pp. 237–65. London: Kogan Page.

Felstead, A. (2009). 'Are Jobs in Wales High Skilled and High Quality? Baselining the *One Wales* Vision and Tracking Recent Trends'. *Contemporary Wales*, 22: 36–61.

Felstead, A. (2011). 'Patterns of Under-Utilization in the Recession'. *Skills in Focus*, December. Glasgow: Skills Development Scotland.

Felstead, A. and D. Gallie (2004). 'For Better or Worse? Non-Standard Jobs and High Involvement Work Systems'. *International Journal of Human Resource Management*, 15(7): 1293–316.

Felstead, A. and F. Green (2008a). *Skills at Work in Northern Ireland, 2006*. Belfast: Department for Employment and Learning Northern Ireland.

Felstead, A. and F. Green (2008b). *Skills at Work in Scotland, 1997 to 2006: Evidence from the Skills Surveys*. Glasgow: Scottish Enterprise.

Felstead, A. and F. Green (2008c). *Skills at Work in the East Midlands, 1997 to 2006*. Nottingham: East Midlands Development Agency.

Felstead, A. and F. Green (2008d). *Skills at Work in the Highlands and Islands, 2006*. Inverness: Highlands and Islands Enterprise.

Felstead, A., D. Ashton, and F. Green, F. (2000). 'Are Britain's Workplace Skills Becoming More Unequal?' *Cambridge Journal of Economics*, 24(6): 709–27.

Felstead, A., D. Ashton, and F. Green (2001). 'Paying the Price for Flexibility? Training, Skills and Non-Standard Jobs in Britain'. *International Journal of Employment Studies*, 9(1): 25–60.

Felstead, A., D. Gallie, and F. Green (2002). *Work Skills in Britain, 1986–2001*. London: Department for Education and Skills.

Felstead, A., D. Gallie, F. Green, and Y. Zhou (2007). *Skills at Work in Britain, 1986 to 2006*. Oxford: ESRC Centre on Skills, Knowledge and Organisational Performance.

Felstead, A., A. Fuller, N. Jewson, and L. Unwin (2009). *Improving Working as Learning*. London: Routledge.

Felstead, A., R. Davies, and S. Jones (2013a). *Skills and the Quality of Work in Wales, 2006–2012: Main Results*. Cardiff: Wales Institute for Social and Economic Research, Data, and Methods.

Felstead, A., D. Gallie, F. Green, and H. Inanc (2013b). *Skills at Work in Britain: First Findings from the Skills and Employment Survey 2012*. London: Centre for Learning and Life Chances in Knowledge Economies and Societies, Institute of Education.

Felstead, A., D. Gallie, F. Green, and H. Inanc (2013c). *Work Intensification in Britain: First Findings from the Skills and Employment Survey 2012*. London: Centre for

Learning and Life Chances in Knowledge Economies and Societies, Institute of Education.

Felstead, A., D. Gallie, F. Green, and H. Inanc (2015). 'Fits, Misfits and Interactions: Learning at Work, Job Satisfaction and Job-Related Well-Being'. *Human Resource Management Journal*, forthcoming.

Felstead, A., D. Gallie, F. Green, and H. Inanc (2014). *Skills and Employment Survey 2012: Technical Briefing*. London: Centre for Learning and Life Chances in Knowledge Economies and Societies, Institute of Education.

Fernandez-Macias, E. (2012). 'Job Polarization in Europe? Changes in the Employment Structure and Job Quality, 1995–2007'. *Work and Occupations*, 39(2): 157–82.

Fevre, R., T. Nichols, G. Prior, and I. Rutherford (2009). 'Fair Treatment at Work Report: Findings from the 2008 Survey'. *Employment Relations Research Series, 103*. London: Department for Business, Innovation and Skills.

Forde, C. (2001). 'Temporary Arrangements: The Activities of Employment Agencies in the UK'. *Work, Employment and Society*, 15(3), 631–44.

Forth, J. and N. Millward (2000). 'The Determinants of Pay Levels and Fringe Benefit Provision in Britain'. NIESR Discussion Paper, 171.

Forth, J. and N. Millward (2002). 'Union Effects on Pay Levels in Britain'. *Labour Economics*, 9(4): 547–61.

Frandsen, B. R. (2012). *Why Unions Still Matter: The Effects of Unionization on the Distribution of Employee Earnings*. Cambridge, MA: MIT.

Freeman, R. B. and J. L. Medoff (1984). *What Do Unions Do?* New York: Basic Books.

Friedmann, G. (1946). *Problemes humains du machinisme industriel*. Paris: Gallimard.

Fylan, F., Fylan Gwynn, B. and Caveney, L. (2012). 'GPs' perceptions of potential services to help employees on sick leave return to work', *Department of Work and Pensions Research Report 820*, London: Department for Work and Pensions.

Gallie, D. (1983). *Social Inequality and Class Radicalism in France and Britain*. Cambridge: Cambridge University Press.

Gallie, D. (2003). 'The Quality of Working Life: Is Scandinavia Different?' *European Sociological Review*, 19(1): 61–79.

Gallie, D. (2005). 'Work Pressure in Europe 1996–2001'. *British Journal of Industrial Relations*, 43(3): 351–75.

Gallie, D. (2007a). *Employment Regimes and the Quality of Work*. Oxford: Oxford University Press.

Gallie, D. (2007b). 'Production Regimes, Employment Regimes, and the Quality of Work'. In D. Gallie (ed.), *Employment Regimes and the Quality of Work*, pp. 1–34. Oxford: Oxford University Press.

Gallie, D. (2013). 'Direct Participation and the Quality of Work'. *Human Relations*, 66(4): 453–73.

Gallie, D. and M. White (1993). *Employee Commitment and the Skills Revolution: First Findings from the Employment in Britain Survey*. London: Policy Studies Institute.

Gallie, D. and Y. Zhou (2011). 'The Changing Job Skills of Female Part-Time Workers in Britain'. *Human Resource Management Journal*, 21(1): 28–44.

Gallie, D. and Y. Zhou (2013). 'Job Control, Work Intensity and Work Stress'. In D. Gallie (ed.), *Economic Crisis, Quality of Work, and Social Integration*, pp. 115–41. Oxford: Oxford University Press.

Gallie, D., C. Marsh, and C. E. Vogler (1993). *Social Change and the Experience of Unemployment*. Oxford: Oxford University Press.

Gallie, D., R. Penn, and M. E. Rose (1996). *Trade Unionism in Recession*. Oxford: Oxford University Press.

Gallie, D., M. White, Y. Cheng, and M. Tomlinson (1998). *Restructuring the Employment Relationship*. Oxford: Clarendon Press.

Gallie, D., A. Felstead, and F. Green (2004). 'Changing Patterns of Task Discretion in Britain'. *Work Employment and Society*, 18(2): 243–66.

Gallie, D., Y. Zhou, A. Felstead, and F. Green (2012). 'Teamwork, Skill Development and Employee Welfare'. *British Journal of Industrial Relations*, 50(1): 23–46.

Gallie, D., A. Felstead, F. Green, and H. Inanc (2013). *Fear at Work: First Findings from the Skills and Employment Survey 2012*. London: Centre for Learning and Life Chances in Knowledge, Economies and Societies, Institute of Education.

Gash, V., A. Mertens, and L. R. Gordo (2012). 'The Influence of Changing Hours of Work on Women's Life Satisfaction'. *Manchester School*, 80(1): 51–74.

Gibbens, S. and S. Spencer (2013). 'Business Display of Food Hygiene Ratings in England, Wales and Northern Ireland'. *Report Prepared for the Food Standards Agency*. London: GfK NOP.

Ginn, J., S. Arber, J. Brannen, A. Dale, S. Dex, P. Elias, P. Moss, J. Pahl, C. Roberts, and J. Rubery (1996). 'Feminist Fallacies: A Reply to Hakim on Women's Employment'. *British Journal of Sociology*, 47(10): 167–74.

Godard, J. (2004). 'A Critical Assessment of the High-Performance Paradigm'. *British Journal of Industrial Relations*, 42(2): 349–78.

Godard, J. (2010). 'What Is Best for Workers? The Implications of Workplace and Human Resource Management Practices Revisited'. *Industrial Relations*, 49(3): 466–88.

Goldthorpe, J. H. (2000). 'Social Class and the Differentiation of Employment Contracts'. In J. H. Goldthorpe, *On Sociology. Numbers, Narratives and the Integration of Research and Theory*, pp. 206–29. Oxford: Oxford University Press.

Gonäs, L. and J. C. Karlsson (eds) (2006). *Gender Segregation: Divisions of Work in Post-Industrialist Welfare States*. Farnham: Ashgate.

Goos, M. and A. Manning (2007). 'Lousy and Lovely Jobs: The Rising Polarization of Work in Britain'. *Review of Economics and Statistics*, 89: 118–33.

Gordon, I., K. Scanlon, T. Travers, and C. Whitehead (2009). *Economic Impact on the London and UK Economy of an Earned Regularisation of Irregular Migrants to the UK*. London: Greater London Authority.

Gorman, E. and J. Kmec (2007). 'We (Have to) Try Harder: Gender and Required Work Effort in Britain and the United States'. *Gender and Society*, 21(6).

Gosling, A. and S. Machin (1995). 'Trade Unions and the Dispersion of Earnings in British Establishments, 1980–90'. *Oxford Bulletin of Economics and Statistics*, 57(2): 167–84.

Grant, L., S. Yeandle, and L. Buckner (2005). *Working below Potential: Women and Part-Time Work*. EOC Working Paper Series, 40. Manchester: Equal Opportunities Commission.

Great Place to Work Institute (2013). *The 100 Best Workplaces in Europe 2013*. London: Redactive Publishing.

Great Place to Work Institute (2014). *Great Workplaces: Special Report 2014*. London: Redactive Publishing.

Green, F. (ed.) (1989). *The Restructuring of the UK Economy*. London: Harvester Wheatsheaf.

Green, F. (2001). 'It's Been a Hard Day's Night: The Concentration and Intensification of Work in Late 20th Century Britain'. *British Journal of Industrial Relations*, 39(1): 53–80.

Green, F. (2006). *Demanding Work: The Paradox of Job Quality in the Affluent Economy*. Princeton, NJ: Princeton University Press.

Green, F. (2008). 'Leeway for the Loyal: A Model of Employee Discretion'. *British Journal of Industrial Relations*, 46(1): 1–32.

Green, F. (2009). 'Subjective Employment Insecurity around the World'. *Cambridge Journal of Regions, Economy and Society*, 2(3): 343–63.

Green, F. (2011). 'Job Quality in Britain under the Labour Government'. In P. Gregg and J. Wadsworth (eds), *The Labour Market in Winter: The State of Working Britain*, pp. 111–27. Oxford: Oxford University Press.

Green, F. (2012). 'Employee Involvement, Technology and Evolution in Job Skills: A Task-Based Analysis'. *Industrial and Labor Relations Review*, 65(1): 35–66.

Green, F. (2013). *Is Britain Such a Bad Place to Work? The Level and Dispersion of Job Quality in Comparative European Perspective*. London: LLAKES Centre, Institute of Education.

Green, F. and T. Mostafa (2012). *Trends in Job Quality in Europe: A Report Based on the Fifth European Working Conditions Survey*. Dublin: Eurofound.

Green, F. and M. J. Potepan (1988). 'Vacation Time and Unionism in the United States and Europe'. *Industrial Relations*, 27(2): 180–94.

Green, F. and K. Whitfield (2009). 'Employees' Experience of Work'. In W. Brown, A. Bryson, J. Forth, and K. Whitfield (eds), *The Evolution of the Modern Workplace*, pp. 201–29. Cambridge: Cambridge University Press.

Green, F., B. Burchell, and A. Felstead (2000). 'Job Insecurity and the Difficulty of Regaining Employment: An Empirical Study of Unemployment Expectations'. *Oxford Bulletin of Economics and Statistics*, 62(December): 855–84.

Green, F., T. Mostafa, A. Parent-Thirion, G. Vermeylen, G. van Houten, I. Billetta, and M. Lyly-Yrjanainen (2013). 'Is Job Quality Becoming More Unequal?' *Industrial and Labor Relations Review*, 66(4): 753–84.

Greenhalgh, L. and Z. Rosenblatt (1984). 'Job Insecurity: Toward Conceptual Clarity'. *Academy of Management Review*, 9(3): 443–8.

Gregg, P., S. Machin, and M. Fernández-Salgado (2014). 'The Squeeze on Real Wages – and What It Might Take to End It'. *National Institute Economic Review*, 228: R3–16.

Grimshaw, D. and A. Rafferty (2013). 'Social Impact of the Crisis in the United Kingdom: Focus on Gender and Age Inequalities.' In D. Vaughan-Whitehead (ed.), *Work Inequalities in the Crisis: Evidence from Europe*, pp. 525–70. Cheltenham: Edward Elgar.

Grugulis, I., Ö. Bozkurt, and J. Clegg (2011). '"No Place to Hide": The Realities of Leadership in UK Supermarkets.' In I. Grugulis and Ö. Bozkurt (eds), *Retail Work*. Basingstoke: Macmillan.

Gustavsen, B. (2007). 'Work Organization and the "Scandinavian Model"'. *Economic and Industrial Democracy*, 28(4): 650–71.

Hakim, C. (2000). *Work-Lifestyle Choices in the 21st Century: Preference Theory.* Oxford: Oxford University Press.

Hall, M., S. Hutchinson, J. Purcell, M. Terry and J. Parker (2013). 'Promoting Effective Consultation? Assessing the Impact of the ICE Regulations'. *British Journal of Industrial Relations*, 51(2): 355–81.

Hamilton, J. (2010). *Work-Related Stress: What the Law Says.* London: Chartered Institute of Personnel and Development.

Hammer, T. H. and A. Avgar (2007). 'The Impact of Unions on Job Satisfaction, Organizational Commitment and Turnover'. In J. T. Bennett and B. E. Kaufman (eds), *What Do Unions Do? A Twenty-Year Perspective*, pp. 346–72. New Brunswick, NJ and London: Transaction Publishers.

Harkness, S. (1996). 'The Gender Earnings Gap: Evidence from the UK'. *Fiscal Studies*, 17(2): 1–36.

Hartikainen, A., T. Anttila, T. Oinas, and J. Nätti (2010). 'Is Finland Different? Quality of Work among Finnish and European Employees'. *Research on Finnish Society*, 3: 29–41.

Heather, P., J. Rick, J. Atkinson, and S. Morris (1996). 'Employers' use of Temporary Workers'. *Labour Market Trends*, September: 403–12.

Heery, E. and J. Salmon (2000). *The Insecure Workforce.* London: Routledge.

Henrekson, M. and D. Johansson (2010). 'Gazelles as Job Creators: A Survey and Interpretation of the Evidence'. *Small Business Economics*, 35: 227–44.

Hildreth, A. (1999). 'What Has Happened to the Union Wage Differential in Britain in the 1990s?' *Oxford Bulletin of Economics and Statistics*, 61(1): 5–31.

HM Treasury and HM Revenue and Customs (2009). *False Self-Employment in Construction: Taxation of Workers.* July. London: HM Treasury. http://webarchive.nationalarchives.gov.uk/20100407204417/http://www.hm-treasury.gov.uk/d/consult_falseselfemploymentconstruction_200709.pdf

Holman, D. (2013a). 'An Explanation of Cross-National Variation in Call Centre Job Quality Using Institutional Theory'. *Work Employment and Society*, 27(1): 21–38.

Holman, D. (2013b). 'Job Types and Job Quality in Europe'. *Human Relations*, 66(4): 475–502.

Holmes, E. and M. Oakley (2011). 'Public and Private Sector Terms, Conditions and Fairness'. *Policy Exchange Research Note*, May. London: Policy Exchange.

Holmes, E. and M. Oakley (2012). *Local Pay, Local Growth: Reforming Pay Setting in the Public Sector.* London: Policy Exchange.

Home Office (2013). *Implementing a Police Pay Review Body: The Government's Response.* London: Home Office.

Hopkins, B. (2009). 'Inequality Street? Working Life in a British Chocolate Factory'. In S.C. Bolton and M. Houlihan (eds), *Work Matters: Critical Reflections on Contemporary Work*, pp. 129–44. Basingstoke: Palgrave Macmillan.

Hoque, K. and N. Bacon (2014). 'Union Joint Regulation and Workplace Equality Policy and Practice in Britain: Evidence from the 2004 Workplace Employment Relations Survey'. *Work Employment and Society*, 28(2): 265–84.

Hoque, K. and I. Kirkpatrick (2003). 'Non-Standard Employment in the Management and Professional Workforce: Training, Consultation and Gender Implications'. *Work, Employment and Society*, 17(4): 667–90.

Hoque, K. and M. Noon (2004). 'Equal Opportunities Policy and Practice in Britain: Evaluating the "Empty Shell" Hypothesis'. *Work, Employment and Society*, 18(3): 481–506.

Horrell, S. (1994). 'Household Time Allocation and Women's Labour Force Participation'. In M. Anderson, F. Bechhofer, and J. Gershuny (eds), *The Social and Political Economy of the Household*. Oxford University Press.

Horton, S. (2006). 'The Public Service Ethos in the British Civil Service: An Historical Institutional Analysis'. *Public Policy and Administration*, 21(1): 32–48.

HSE (2012). *Psychosocial Working Conditions in Britain in 2010*. Bootle: Health and Safety Executive.

HSE (2013a). *Health and Safety Executive Annual Statistics Report for Great Britain*. Bootle: Health and Safety Executive.

HSE (2013b). *Stress and Psychological Disorders in Great Britain 2013*. Bootle: Health and Safety Executive.

Inanc, H., D. Gallie, A. Felstead, and F. Green (2013). *Job Control in Britain*. London: Centre for Learning and Life Chances in Knowledge, Economies and Societies, Institute of Education.

Incomes Data Services (2011). 'Public and Private Sector Earnings: Fact and Fiction'. *IDS Pay Report No. 1075*. London: Incomes Data Services.

Jones, M. K., P. L. Latreille, and P. J. Sloane (2007). 'Crossing the Tracks? Trends in the Training of Male and Female Workers in Great Britain'. *British Journal of Industrial Relations*, 46(2): 268–82.

Jones, M., G. Makepeace, and V. Wass (2014). 'The Gender Pay Gap 1998–2012: What Is the Role of the Public Sector?' Working Paper, Mimeo.

Kalleberg, A. L. (2011). *Good Jobs, Bad Jobs*. New York: Russell Sage Foundation.

Karasek, R. A. (1979). 'Job Demands, Job Decision Latitude, and Mental Strain: Implications for Job Redesign'. *Administrative Science Quarterly*, 24: 285–308.

Karasek, R. and T. Theorell (1992). *Healthy Work: Stress, Productivity, and the Reconstruction of Working Life*. New York: Basic Books.

Kelly, J. (1992). 'Does Job Re-Design Theory Explain Job Re-Design Outcomes?' *Human Relations*, 42(8): 753–74.

Kern, H. and M. Schumann (1987). 'Limits of the Division of Labour: New Production and Employment Concepts in West German Industry'. *Economic and Industrial Democracy*, 8: 151–70.

Kern, H. and M. Schumann (1992). 'New Concepts of Production and the Emergence of the Systems Controller'. In P. S. Adler (ed.), *Technology and the Future of Work*, pp. 111–48. New York: Oxford University Press.

Kerr, C., J. T. Dunlop, F. Harbison, and C. A. Myers (1960). *Industrialism and Industrial Man*. Cambridge, MA: Harvard University Press.

Kersley, B., C. Alpin, J. Forth, A. Bryson, H. Bewley, G. Dix, and S. Oxenbridge (2006). *Inside the Workplace: First Findings from the 2004 Workplace Employment Relations Survey*. London: Routledge.

Kochan, T. and P. Osterman (1994). *The Mutual Gains Enterprise*. Boston, MA: Harvard University Press.

Kompier, M. (2004). 'Does the "Management Standards" Approach Meet the Standard?' *Work and Stress*, 18(2): 137–9.

Körner, T., K. Puch, and C. Wingerter (2011). *Quality of Employment: Earning Money and What Else Counts*. Wiesbaden: Statistisches Bundesamt (Federal Statistical Office).

Lalani, M., P. Meadows, H. Metcalf, and H. Rolfe (2012). 'Evaluation of the Statement of Fitness for Work: Qualitative Research with Employers and Employees'. *Department of Work and Pensions Research Report Number 797*. London: Department for Work and Pensions.

Lambert, R. (2010). 'The Labour Market and Employment Relations beyond the Recession'. *Warwick Papers in Industrial Relations*, 93, April. Coventry: University of Warwick.

Lambert, S. J. and J. R. Henly (2012). 'Frontline Managers Matter: Labour Flexibility Practices and Sustained Employment in US Retail Jobs'. In C. Warhurst, F. Carré, P. Findlay, and C. Tilly (eds), *Are Bad Jobs Inevitable? Trends, Determinants, and Responses to Job Quality in the Twenty-First Century*. Basingstoke: Palgrave.

Lawler, E. (1986). *High Involvement Management*. San Francisco, CA: Jossey-Bass.

Lawler, E., S. A. Mohrman, and G. E. Ledford (1995). *Creating High Performance Organizations*. San Francisco, CA: Jossey-Bass.

le Roux, S., P. Lucchino, and D. Wilkinson (2013). 'An Investigation into the Extent of Non-Compliance with the National Minimum Wage'. Report to the Low Pay Commission, February.

Leka, S., A. Jain, G. Zwetsloot, and T. Cox (2010). 'Policy-Level Interventions and Work-Related Psychosocial Risk Management in the European Union'. *Work and Stress*, 24(3): 298–307.

Leslie, D. (2008). 'Pay Comparability for the Defence Medical Services and the National Health Service Using a TR Approach'. Mimeo.

Leslie, D. and Y. H. Pu (1995). 'Unions and the Rise in Wage Inequality in Britain'. *Applied Economics Letters*, 2(8): 266–70.

Levy, S. (2013). *Changes in Real Earnings in the UK and London, 2002 to 2012*. February. London: Office for National Statistics. Available online at: <http://www.ons.gov.uk/ons/dcp171766_299377.pdf>.

Lewis, J. and S. Giullari (2005) 'The Adult Worker Model Family, Gender Equality and Care: The Search for New Policy Principles and the Possibilities and Problems of a Capabilities Approach'. *Economy and Society*, 34(1): 76–104.

Lewis, S. and R. Rapoport (2009). *Work and Family in the Recession: Tomorrow's World. Perspectives on Work and Family Life in the Future*. London: Working Families.

Lindley, J. and S. Machin (2012). 'The Quest for More and More Education'. *Fiscal Studies*, 33(2): 265–86.

Lindley, J. and S. Machin (2013). 'Wage Inequality in the Labour Years'. *Oxford Review of Economic Policy*, 29(1): 165–77.

Low Pay Commission (2014). 'Terms of Reference'. Available online at: <http://www.gov.uk/government/organisations/low-pay-commission/about/terms-of-reference>, accessed 28 January 2014.

Lucifora, C. and D. Meurs (2006). 'The Public Sector Pay Gap in France, Great Britain, and Italy'. *Review of Income and Wealth*, 52(1): 43–59.

Lunau, T., C. Bambra, T. Eikemo, K. van der Wel, and N. Dragano (2014). 'A Balancing Act? Work–Life Balance, Health and Well-Being in European Welfare States'. *European Journal of Public Health*, 24(3): 422–7.

Lyonette, C., B. Baldauf, H. and Behle (2010). *'Quality' Part-Time Work: A Review of the Evidence*. London: Government Equalities Office.

MacDuffie, J. P. (1995). 'Human Resource Bundles and Manufacturing Performance: Organizational Logic and Flexible Production Systems in the World Auto Industry'. *Industrial and Labor Relations Review*, 48(2, January): 197–221.

Machin, S. (1997). 'The Decline of Labour Market Institutions and the Rise in Wage Inequality in Britain'. *European Economic Review*, 41(3–5): 647–57.

Machin, S. (2000). 'Union Decline in Britain'. *British Journal of Industrial Relations*, 30(4): 631–45.

Machin, S. (2011). 'Changes in UK Wage Inequality over the Last Forty Years'. In P. Gregg and J. Wadsworth (eds), *The Labour Market in Winter*, pp. 155–69. Oxford: Oxford University Press.

Machin, S. and P. Puhani (2003). 'Subject of Degree and the Gender Wage Differential: Evidence from the UK and Germany'. *Economic Letters*, 79: 393–400.

McGinnity, F. and H. Russell (2013). 'Work–Family Conflict and Economic Change'. In D. Gallie (ed.), *Economic Crisis, Quality of Work, and Social Integration*, pp. 169–94. Oxford: Oxford University Press.

McGovern, P, S. Hill, C. Mills, and P. White (2007). *Market, Class, and Employment*. Oxford: Oxford University Press.

Mackay, C. J., R. Cousins, P. J. Kelly, S. Lee, and R. H. McCaig (2004). '"Management Standards" and Work-Related Stress in the UK: Policy Background and Science'. *Work and Stress*, 18(2): 91–112.

McKnight, A. and F. Cowell (2014). 'Social Impacts: Health, Housing, and Inter-Generational Mobility'. In W. Salverda, B. Nolan, D. Checchi, I. Marx, A. McKnight, I. G. Tóth, and H. van de. Werfhorst (eds), *Changing Inequalities in Rich Countries*, pp. 169–94. Oxford: Oxford University Press.

McRae, S. (2003). 'Constraints and Choices in Mothers' Employment Careers: A Consideration of Hakim's Preference Theory'. *British Journal of Sociology*, 54(3): 317–38.

Mallon, M. and J. Duberley (2000). 'Managers and Professionals in the Contingent Workforce'. *Human Resources Management Journal*, 10(1): 33–47.

Manning, A. (2005). *Monopsony in Motion: Imperfect Competition in Labor Markets*. Princeton, NJ: Princeton University Press.

Manning, A. and J. Swaffield (2008). 'The Gender Gap in Early-Career Wage Growth'. *Economic Journal*, 118(530), 983–1024.

Mantouvalou, V. (2011). *Study on Labour Inspection Sanctions and Remedies: The Case of the United Kingdom*. Geneva: International Labour Organization.

Marginson, P. (1991). 'Change and Continuity in the Employment Structure of Large Companies'. In A. Pollert (ed.), *Farewell to Flexibility?*, pp. 32–45. Oxford: Blackwell.

Mason, G., K. Mayhew, and M. Osborne (2008). 'Low-Paid Work in the United Kingdom: An Overview'. In C. Lloyd, G. Mason, and K. Mayhew (eds), *Low-Wage Work in the United Kingdom*, pp. 15–40. New York: Russell Sage Foundation.

Matthews, D. (2010). 'The Changing Face of Public Sector Employment 1999–2009'. *Economic and Labour Market Review*, 4(7): 28–35.

Meager, N. (1993). 'Self-Employment and Labour Market Policy in the European Community'. Discussion Paper FSI 93-901. Berlin: Wissenschaftszentrum für Sozialforschung.

Meager, N. (1996). 'Self-Employment as an Alternative to Dependent Employment for the Unemployed'. In G. Schmid, J. O'Reilly, and K. Schömann (eds), *International Handbook of Labour Market Policy and Evaluation*. Aldershot: Edward Elgar.

Meager, N. (2008). 'Self-Employment Dynamics and "Transitional Labour Markets": Some More UK Evidence'. In J. Muffels (ed.), *Flexibility and Employment Security in Europe*, pp. 195–222. Cheltenham: Edward Elgar.

Meager, N. and P. Bates (2001). 'The Self-Employed and Lifetime Incomes: Some UK Evidence'. *International Journal of Sociology*, 31(1): 27–58.

Meager, N. and P. Bates (2004). 'Self-Employment in the United Kingdom during the 1980s and 1990s'. In R. Arum and W. Müller (eds), *The Re-Emergence of Self-Employment*. Princeton, NJ: Princeton University Press.

Meager N., M. Kaiser, and H. Dietrich (1992). *Self-Employment in the United Kingdom and Germany*. London and Bonn: Anglo-German Foundation for the Study of Industrial Society.

Meager, N., P. Bates, and M. Cowling (2003). 'An Evaluation of Business Start-Up Support for Young People'. *National Institute Economic Review*, 186(1): 59–72.

Meager, N., R. Martin, and E. Carta (2011). *Skills for Self-Employment*. Evidence Report 31. London: UK Commission for Employment and Skills.

Metcalf, D. (1989). 'Water Notes Dry Up: The Impact of the Donovan Reform Proposals and Thatcherism at Work on Labour Productivity in British Manufacturing Industry'. *British Journal of Industrial Relations*, 27(1): 1–31.

Millán, J., J. Hessels, R. Thurik, and R. Aguado (2013). 'Determinants of Job Satisfaction: A European Comparison of Self-Employed and Paid Employees'. *Small Business Economics*, 40(3): 651–70.

Millward, N., A. Bryson, and J. Forth (2000). *All Change at Work? British Employment Relations 1980–1998, as Portrayed by the Workplace Industrial Relations Survey Series*. London: Routledge.

Mincer, J. and S. Polacheck (1974). 'Family Investment in Human Capital: Earnings of Women'. *Journal of Political Economy*, 82(2): 76–108.

Ministry of Employment and the Economy (2012). *National Working Life Development Strategy to 2020*. Helsinki: Ministry of Employment and the Economy.

Moncada, S., M. Utzet, E. Molinero, C. Llorens, N. Moreno, A. Galtés, and A. Navarro (2014). 'The Copenhagen Psychosocial Questionnaire II (COPSOQ II) in Spain: A Tool for Psychosocial Risk Assessment at the Workplace'. *American Journal of Industrial Medicine*, 57: 97–107.

Morgan, P. and N. Allington (2002). 'Has the Public Sector Retained Its "Model Employer" Status?' *Public Money and Management*, 22(1): 35–42.

Muñoz de Bustillo, R., E. Fernández-Macías, J.-I. Antón, and F. Esteve (2011). 'E pluribus unum? A Critical Survey of Job Quality Indicators'. *Socio-Economic Review*, 9: 447–75.

Muriel, A. and L. Sibieta (2009). 'Living Standards during Previous Recessions'. *IFS Briefing Note*, BN85. London: Institute for Fiscal Studies.

Murphy, P., D. Blackaby, N. O'Leary, and A. Staneva (2014). 'What Has Been Happening to the Public–Private Sector Differential in the UK? An Analysis Based on Counterfactual Wage Distributions'. Department of Economics Discussion Paper Series, Swansea University.

Mustard, C. (2004). 'Work-Related Stress in the UK: A New, "Management Standards" Approach'. *Work and Stress*, 18(2): 140–1.

NHS Pay Review Body (2012). *Market-Facing Pay: How Agenda for Change Pay Can Be Made More Appropriate to Local Labour Markets*. Cm 8501. London: Office of Manpower Economics.

NHS Pay Review Body (2014). *NHS Pay Review Body 28th Report: 2014*. Cm 8831. London: Office of Manpower Economics.

Nickell, S. and G. Quintini (2002). 'The Consequences of the Decline in Public Sector Pay in Britain: A Little Bit of Evidence'. *Economic Journal*, 112(477): F107–18.

Niedhammer, I., H. Sultan-Taïeb, J.-F. Chastang, G. Vermeylen, and A. Parent-Thirion (2014). 'Fractions of Cardiovascular Diseases and Mental Disorders Attributable to Psychosocial Work Factors in 31 Countries in Europe'. *International Archives of Occupational and Environmental Health*, 87(4): 403–11.

Nolan, B. and C. Whelan (2014). 'The Social Impact of Income Inequality: Poverty, Deprivation, and Social Cohesion'. In W. Salverda, B. Nolan, D. Checchi, I. Marx, A. McKnight, I. G. Tóth, and H. van de Werfhorst (eds), *Changing Inequalities in Rich Countries*, pp. 146–68. Oxford: Oxford University Press.

Nolan, J. P., I. C. Wichert, and B. J. Burchell (2000). 'Job Insecurity, Psychological Well-Being and Family Life'. In E. Heery and J. Salmon (eds), *The Insecure Workforce*, pp. 181–209. London: Routledge.

O'Donnell, G., A. Deaton, M. Durand, D. Halpern, and R. Layard (2014). *Wellbeing and Policy*. London: Legaturn Institute.

OECD (2010). *Gender Brief*. Social Policy Division, March. Available online at: <http://www.oecd.org/els/family/44720649.pdf>.

OECD (2011). *Divided We Stand: Why Inequality Keeps Rising*. Paris: Organisation for Economic Co-operation and Development.

OECD (2013a). *OECD Skills Outlook 2013: First Results from the Survey of Adult Skills*. Paris: OECD Publishing. Available online at: <http://dx.doi.org/10.1787/9789264204256-en>.

OECD (2013b). 'Protecting Jobs, Enhancing Flexibility: A New Look at Employment Protection Legislation'. In *OECD Employment Outlook 2013*. Paris: OECD Publishing.

OECD (2013c). *Employment Protection in the OECD and Selected Non-OECD Countries in 2013*. Paris: OECD Publishing.

OECD (2014a). 'How Good Is Your Job? A Framework for Measuring and Assessing Job Quality'. In *OECD Employment Outlook 2014*. Paris: OECD Publishing.

OECD (2014b). 'Non-Regular Employment Contracts, Job Security and Labour Market Divide'. In *OECD Outlook Employment 2014*. Paris: OECD Publishing.

Oesch, D. (2013). *Occupational Change in Europe: How Technology and Education Transform the Job Structure*. Oxford: Oxford University Press.

Office of Government Commerce (2008). *An Introduction to Public Procurement.* London: Office of Government Commerce.

Olsen, K. M., A. L. Kalleberg, and T. Nesheim (2010). 'Perceived Job Quality in the United States, Great Britain, Norway and West Germany, 1989–2005'. *European Journal of Industrial Relations*, 16(3): 221–40.

Olsen, W. and J. Morgan (2005). 'A Critical Epistemology of Analytical Statistics: Addressing the Sceptical Realist'. *Journal for the Theory of Social Behaviour*, 35(3): 255–84.

ONS (2012a). 'Estimating Differences in Public and Private Sector Pay at the National and Regional Level.' Newport: office of National Statistics, downloaded from http://www.ons.gov.uk/ons/dcp171776_288081.pdf, 22 November 2012.

ONS (2012b). 'Underemployed Workers in the UK, 2012'. Available online at: <http://www.ons.gov.uk/ons/rel/lmac/underemployed-workers-in-the-uk/2012/index.html>.

Parent-Thirion, A., E. Fernández Macías, J. Hurley, and G. Vermeylen (2007). *Self-Employed Workers: Industrial Relations and Working Conditions.* Dublin: European Foundation for the Improvement of Living and Working Conditions.

Parker, M. and J. Slaughter (1988). *Choosing Sides: Unions and the Team Concept.* Detroit, MI: Labor Notes.

Penn, R., M. Rose, and J. Rubery (eds) (1994). *Skill and Occupational Change.* Oxford: Oxford University Press.

Pfeffer, J. (1998). *The Human Equation: Building Profits by Putting People First.* Boston, MA: Harvard University Press.

Phelps, E. (1972). 'The Statistical Theory of Racism and Sexism'. *American Economic Review*, 62(4): 659–61.

Piore, M. J. and C. F. Sabel (1984). *The Second Industrial Divide: Possibilities for Prosperity.* New York: Basic Books.

Pollert, A. (1988). 'The "Flexible Firm": Fixation or Fact'. *Work, Employment and Society*, 2: 281–316.

Pollert, A. (1991). 'The Orthodoxy of Flexibility'. In A. Pollert (ed.), *Farewell to Flexibility?* Oxford: Basil Blackwell.

Powdthavee, N. (2011). 'Anticipation, Free Rider Problem, and Adaptation to Trade Union: Re-Examining the Curious Case of Dissatisfied Union Members'. *Industrial and Labor Relations Review*, 64(5): 1000–19.

Prag, P., M. das Dores Guerreiro, J. Nätti, M. Brookes, and L. den Dulk (2011). 'Quality of Work and Quality of Life of Service Sector Workers: Cross-National Variations in Eight European Countries'. In M. Bäck-Wiklund, T. van de Lippe, L. den Dulk, and A. Doorne-Huiskes (eds), *Quality of Life and Work in Europe: Theory, Practice and Policy*, pp. 77–94. Houndmills: Palgrave Macmillan.

Priestley, R. (1955). *Royal Commission on the Civil Service.* Cmnd 9613. London: HMSO.

Proctor, I. and M. Padfield (1999). 'Work Orientations and Women's Work: A Critique of Hakim's Theory of the Heterogeneity of Women'. *Gender, Work and Organisation*, 6(3): 152–62.

Purcell, K., T. Hogarth, and C. Simm (1999). *Whose Flexibility? The Costs and Benefits of 'Non-Standard' Working Arrangements and Contractual Relations.* York: Joseph Rowntree Foundation.

Ramsay, H., D. Scholarios, and B. Harley (2000). 'Employees and High-Performance Work Systems: Testing inside the Black Box'. *British Journal of Industrial Relations*, 38(4): 501–55.

Robinson, P. (2000). 'Insecurity and Flexible Workforce: Measuring the Ill-Defines'. In E. Heery and J. Salmon (eds), *The Insecure Workforce*, pp. 25–38. London: Routledge.

Roper, I., P. James and P. Higgins (2005). 'Workplace Partnership and Public Service Provision: The Case of "Best Value" Performance Regime in British Local Government'. *Work, Employment and Society*, 19(3): 639–49.

Rose, D. and D. J. Pevalin (2003). *A Researcher's Guide to the National Statistics Socio-Economic Classification*. London: Sage.

Rosenberg, S. (1989). 'From Segmentation to Flexibility'. *Labour and Society*, 14.

Rubery, J., J. Earnshaw, and B. Burchell (1993). *New Forms and Patterns of Employment: The Role of Self-Employment in Britain*. Baden-Baden: Nomos Verlagsgesellschaft.

Schnabel, C. (2013). 'Union Membership and Density: Some (Not So) Stylized Facts and Challenges'. *European Journal of Industrial Relations*, 19(3): 255–72.

Scott, J. and S. Dex (2009). 'Paid and Unpaid Work: Can Policy Improve Gender Inequalities?' In J. Miles and R. Probert (eds), *Sharing Lives, Dividing Assets: An Interdisciplinary Study*, pp. 41–60. Oxford: Hart.

Scraggs, E., C. van Stolk, B. Janta, C. Celia, S. Goshev, D. van Welsum, S. Patil, and L. Villalba-van-Dijk (2013). 'Encouraging Employers to Use Human Capital Reporting: A Literature Review and Implementation Options'. *UKCES Briefing Paper*. Wath-upon-Dearne: UK Commission for Employment and Skills.

Sennett, R. (1998). *The Corrosion of Character*. London: Norton.

Shane, S. (2009). 'Why Encouraging More People to Become Entrepreneurs Is Bad Public Policy'. *Small Business Economics*, 33: 141–9.

Smeaton, D. (2003). 'Self-Employed Workers: Calling the Shots or Hesitant Independents? A Consideration of the Trends'. *Work, Employment and Society*, 17: 379.

Smith, A. (1976). 'An Inquiry into the Nature and Causes of the Wealth of Nations'. In R. H. Campbell (ed.), *The Works and Correspondence of Adam Smith*. Oxford: Oxford University Press.

Smithson, J., S. Lewis, C. Cooper, and J. Dyer (2004). 'Flexible Working and the Gender Pay Gap in the Accountancy Profession'. *Work, Employment and Society*, 18(1): 115–35.

Soskice, D. (1999). 'Divergent Production Regimes: Coordinated and Uncoordinated Market Economies in the 1980s and 1990s'. In H. Kitschelt, P. Lange, G. Marks, and J. D. Stephens (eds), *Continuity and Change in Contemporary Capitalism*. Cambridge: Cambridge University Press.

Standing, G. (2011). *The Precariat: The New Dangerous Class*. London: Bloomsbury.

Stephens, Jr., M. (2004). 'Job Loss Expectations, Realizations and Household Consumption Behaviour'. *Review of Economics and Statistics*, 86(1): 253–69.

Storey, D. (1994). *Understanding the Small Business Sector*. London: Routledge.

Sutherland, J. (2013). 'Employment Status and Job Satisfaction'. *Evidence-Based HRM: A Global Forum for Empirical Scholarship*, 1(2): 187–216.

Sweeney, E. (2014). *Making Work Better: An Agenda for Government*. London: Smith Institute.

Tahlin, M. (2013). 'Distribution in the Downturn'. In D. Gallie (ed.), *Economic Crisis, Quality of Work, and Social Integration*, pp. 30–57. Oxford: Oxford University Press.

Tam, M. (1997). *Part-Time Employment: A Bridge or a Trap?* Aldershot: Avebury.

Taylor, P., I. Cunningham, K. Newsome, and D. Scholarios (2010). '"Too Scared to Go Sick": Reformulating the Research Agenda on Sickness Absence'. *Industrial Relations Journal*, 41(4): 270–88.

Taylor, R. (2002). *Diversity in Britain's Labour Market*. Swindon: ESRC.

Terry, M. and J. Smith (2003). 'Evaluation of the Partnership at Work Fund'. *DTI Employment Relations Series No 17*. London: Department of Trade and Industry.

Thompson, P. (2003). 'Disconnected Capitalism: Or Why Employers Can't Keep Their Side of the Bargain'. *Work, Employment, and Society*, 17(2): 359–78.

Thornley, C. (2007). 'Working Part-Time for the State: Gender, Class and the Public Sector Pay Gap'. *Gender, Work and Organisation*, 14(5): 454–75.

Tilly, C. (1996). *Half a Job: Bad and Good Part-Time Jobs in a Changing Labor Market*. Philadelphia, PA: Temple University Press.

Tomlinson, J. (2006). 'Routes to Part-Time Management in Service Sector Organizations: Implications for Women's Skills, Flexibility and Progression'. *Gender, Work and Organization*, 13(6): 585–605.

Tomlinson, J., W. Olsen, and K. Purdam (2009). 'Women Returners and Potential Returners: Employment Profiles and Labour Market Opportunities – A Case Study of the UK'. *European Sociological Review*, 24(2): 1–15.

Totterdill, P. (2009). *Workplace Innovation Policies in European Countries: Report to KOWIN*. Nottingham: UK Work and Organisation Network.

Totterdill, P. (2013). *The Future We Want? Work and Organisations in 2020*. Nottingham: UK Work and Organisation Network.

Tregaskis, O. (1997). 'The "Non-permanent" Reality!' *Employee Relations*, 19(6): 535–54.

UKCES (2010). 'High Performance Working: A Policy Review'. *UKCES Evidence Report No 18*. Wath-upon-Dearne: UK Commission for Employment and Skills.

van Wanrooy, B., H. Bewley, A. Bryson, J. Forth, S. Freeth, L. Stokes, and S. Wood (2013). *Employment Relations in the Shadow of Recession: Findings from the 2011 Workplace Employment Relations Study*. London: Palgrave Macmillan.

Vandenberg, R., H. Richardson, and L. Eastman (1999). 'The Impact of High Involvement Work Processes on Organisational Effectiveness: A Second Order Latent Variable Approach'. *Group Organization Management*, 24(3), 300–39.

Wallis, E., M. Stuart, and I. Greenwood (2005). 'Learners of the Workplace Unite! An Empirical Examination of the UK Trade Union Learning Representative Initiative'. *Work, Employment and Society*, 19(2): 283–304.

Walters, D., E. Wadsworth, H. Sampson and P. James (2012). *The Limits of Influence: The Role of Supply Chains in Influencing Health and Safety Management in Two Sectors*. Leicester: Institution of Occupational Health and Safety.

Walters, S. (2005). 'Making the Best of a Bad Job? Female Part-Timers' Orientations and Attitudes to Work'. *Gender, Work and Organization*, 12(3): 193–216.

Walton, R. E. (1985). 'From Control to Commitment in the Workplace'. *Harvard Business Review*, 85: 77–84.

Wanous, J. P., A. E. Reichers, and M. J. Hudy (1997). 'Overall Job Satisfaction: How Good Are Single-Item Measures?' *Journal of Applied Psychology*, 82(2): 247–53.

Ward, K., D. Grimshaw, J. Rubery, and H. Beynon (2001). 'Dilemmas in the Management of Temporary Work Agency Staff'. *Human Resource Management Journal*, 11(4), 3–21.

Warr, P. (1990). 'The Measurement of Well-Being and Other Aspects of Mental Health'. *Journal of Occupational Psychology*, 63(3): 193–210.

Warr. P. (2007). *Work, Happiness, and Unhappiness*. New York: Lawrence Erlbaum Associates.

Warren, T. (2001). 'Divergent Female Part-Time Employment in Britain and Denmark and the Implications for Gender Equality'. *Sociological Review*, 49(4): 548–67.

Warren, T. (2003). 'A Privileged Pole? Diversity in Women's Pay, Pensions and Wealth in Britain'. *Gender, Work and Organisation*, 10(5): 605–28.

Warren, T. (2004). 'Working Part-Time: Achieving a Successful "Work–Life" Balance?' *British Journal of Sociology*, 55(1): 99–122.

Warren, T. (2008). 'Universal Disadvantage? The Economic Well-Being of Female Part-Timers in Europe'. *European Societies*, 10(5), 737–62.

Warren, T. and P. Walters (1998). 'Appraising a Dichotomy: The Use of "Part-Time/Full-Time" in the Study of Women's Employment in Britain'. *Gender, Work and Organisation*, 5(2): 102–18.

Warren, T., G. Pascall, and E. Fox (2010). 'Gender Equality in Time: Low-Paid Mothers' Paid and Unpaid Work in the UK'. *Feminist Economics*, 16(3), 193–219.

Weiss, H. M. (2002). 'Deconstructing Job Satisfaction: Separating Evaluations, Beliefs and Affective Experiences'. *Human Resource Management Review*, 12: 174–94.

Westerholm, P. (2007). 'Closing the Swedish National Institute for Working Life'. *Occupational and Environmental Medicine*, 64: 787–8.

Westgaard, R. H. and J. Winkel (2011). 'Occupational Musculoskeletal and Mental Health: Significance of Rationalization and Opportunities to Create Sustainable Production Systems—A Systematic Review'. *Applied Ergonomics*, 42(2), 261–96.

White, M., S. Hill, P. McGovern, C. Mills, and D. Smeaton (2003). '"High-Performance" Management Practices, Work Hours and Work–Life Balance'. *British Journal of Industrial Relations*, 41(2): 175–95.

Wilkinson, R. G. and K. Pickett (2010). *The Spirit Level: Why Equality Is Better for Everyone* (Revised Edition). London: Penguin Books.

Williams, D. (2000). 'Consequences of Self-Employment for Women and Men in the United States'. *Labour Economics*, 7(5): 665–87.

Willman, P., R. Gomez, and A. Bryson (2009). 'Voice at the Workplace: Where Do We Find It, Why Is It There and Where Is It Going?' In W. Brown, A. Bryson, J. Forth, and K. Whitfield (eds), *The Evolution of the Modern Workplace*, pp. 97–119. Cambridge: Cambridge University Press.

Winch, G. (1998). 'The Growth of Self-Employment in Construction'. *Construction Management and Economics*, 16: 531–43.

Women and Work Commission (2006). *Shaping a Fairer Future*. Available online at: <http://www.equalities.gov.uk/what_we_do/women_and_work/women_and_work_commission.aspx>.

Wood, S. and A. Bryson (2009). 'High Involvement Management'. In W. Brown, A. Bryson, J. Forth, and K. Whitfield (eds), *The Evolution of the Modern Workplace*, pp. 151–75. Cambridge: Cambridge University Press.

Wood, S. J. and L. de Menezes (2011). 'High Involvement Management, High Performance Work Systems and Well-Being'. *International Journal of Human Resource Management*, 22(7): 1586–610.

Wood, S. J., M. Van Veldhoven, M. Croon, and L. de Menezes (2012). 'Enriched Job Design, High Involvement Management and Organizational Performance: The Mediating Roles of Job Satisfaction and Well-Being'. *Human Relations*, 65(4): 419–46.

Yandori, Y. and D. D. van Jaarsveld (2014). 'The Relationships of Informal High Performance Work Practices to Job Satisfaction and Workplace Profitability'. *Industrial Relations*, 53(3): 501–34.

Index